There is an art of reading
as well as an art of thinking
and an art of writing

ISAAC D'ISRAELI.

The Art of English

General Editor A. Dora Gough, B.A. (Hons.)

A Certificate Course for Secondary Schools

Keith Newson, M.A.

4

Illustrated by Tony Dyson
and Kenneth Hutchinson

SCHOFIELD AND SIMS LIMITED
HUDDERSFIELD

First Printed 1967
Reprinted 1968
Reprinted 1969
Reprinted 1970
Reprinted 1971
Revised and Reprinted 1972
Reprinted 1972
Reprinted Twice 1974
Reprinted 1975
Reprinted 1976
Revised and Reprinted 1977
Reprinted 1978
Reprinted 1979
Reprinted 1980

The Art of English is a series of ten books:

The Certificate Course
C1   7217 0003 9
C2   7217 0004 7
C3   7217 0005 5
C4   7217 0006 3
C5   7217 0007 1

The General Course
G1   7217 0008 X
G2   7217 0009 8
G3   7217 0010 1
G4   7217 0011 X
G5   7217 0012 8

Printed and bound in Great Britain by
Butler & Tanner Ltd
Frome and London

Contents

The passage in each chapter is followed by questions for *Appreciation and Discussion*. Where there is a poem, it is followed by a section *Discussing the Poem*. The *Techniques* exercises and composition subjects in *Topics for Written Work* are listed below. Each chapter also contains further sections of *Oral Work, Activities and Research*, and *Further Reading*.

Exercises marked * here, and in the text, can be omitted by pupils who are not studying clause analysis.

iii

ACKNOWLEDGMENTS

The author and publishers wish to thank the following for permission to include the copyright material listed below:

Routledge & Kegan Paul Ltd., for an extract from *Grandad with Snails* by Michael Baldwin.

The Literary Executors of the Dylan Thomas Estate, and J. M. Dent & Sons Ltd., for the poem *Schoolmaster* from *Quite Early One Morning* by Dylan Thomas, and an extract from *Portrait of the Artist as a Young Dog* by Dylan Thomas.

The Guardian, for an extract from *The N.S.P.C.C. In Need* by Terry Coleman

David Higham Associates Ltd., for extracts from *The Day of the Triffids* by John Wyndham, and *There is a Happy Land* by Keith Waterhouse, Michael Joseph, and for the poems *This Excellent Machine* by John Lehmann from *Poetry of the Thirties*, Penguin Books, and *My Friend Maloney* by Charles Causley from *Johnny Hallelujah*, Rupert Hart-Davis.

Scorpion Press, for the poem *Bedtime Story* from *The Broken Places* by George MacBeth. (1963).

The Executors of H. G. Wells, for an extract from *The History of Mr. Polly* by H. G. Wells.

The Observer, London, for text and diagram material from *The Observer Weekend Review*.

The Hogarth Press Ltd., for an extract from *The Wall* from *Fireman Flower* by William Sansom.

Christopher Logue, c/o Peter Janson-Smith Ltd., for his poem *Good Taste*.

William Heinemann Ltd., for extracts from *The Long and the Short and the Tall* by Willis Hall, and *The Grapes of Wrath* by John Steinbeck.

Faber & Faber Ltd., for the poem *O What is That Sound* from *Collected Shorter Poems* by W. H. Auden, an extract from the play *A Resounding Tinkle* by N. F. Simpson, and the poem *Night Ride* from *Collected Poems* by Herbert Read.

Hamish Hamilton Ltd., for fables from *Vintage Thurber* by James Thurber, copyright (c) 1963.

Her Majesty's Stationery Office, for material from *Britain: An Official Handbook, 1977*, and *The Annual Abstract of Statistics No. 113, 1976*. Also for permission to reproduce *Poster P.E.5, Parliamentary Election—Directions for the Guidance of the Voters in Voting*.

Laurence Pollinger Ltd., for an extract from *Shot Actress—Full Story* from *Twenty Tales* by H. E. Bates, Jonathan Cape, and for the poem *Poets Hitchhiking on the Highway* from *The Happy Birthday of Death* by Gregory Corso, New Directions, Inc.

Jonathan Cape Ltd., for the poem *Headline History* from *Collected Poems* by William Plomer.

Hugh Cudlipp, for an extract from *Publish and Be Damned.*

Penguin Books Ltd., for extracts from *The Press* by Wickham Steed, *Crime in a Changing Society* by Howard Jones, *The English Penal System* by Winifred Elkin, and *Your Money's Worth* by Elizabeth Gundrey.

The Joint Industry Committee for National Readership Surveys (JICNARS) for material from their *1976 National Readership Survey*.

Miss E. A. Wolfe, for the poem *The British Journalist* from *The Uncelestial City* by Humbert Wolfe, published by Gollancz.

The National Union of Teachers, for a quotation from *Popular Culture and Personal Responsibility: A Study Outline.*

Harold Matson Company, Inc., for an extract from *The Prize of Peril* by Robert Sheckley, reprinted by permission. Copyright (c) 1958 by Mercury Press, Inc. Copyright assigned 1959 to Robert Sheckley.

Laurence Pollinger Ltd., William Heinemann Ltd., and the Estate of the late Mrs. Frieda Lawrence, for an extract from *Tickets Please* from *The Complete Short Stories of D. H. Lawrence*, and the poem *Things Men Have Made* from *The Complete Poems of D. H. Lawrence.*

City Lights Books, for the poem *Breakfast* by Jacques Prévert, translated by Lawrence Ferlinghetti, reprinted by permission. Copyright (c) 1947 by Les Editions du Point du Jour.

Miss Sonia Brownell and Secker & Warburg Ltd., for extracts from *Animal Farm*, and *The Road to Wigan Pier* by George Orwell.

W. H. Allen & Company, for an extract from *The Loneliness of the Long Distance Runner* by Alan Sillitoe.

Hutchinson & Co. (Publishers) Ltd., for an extract from *The Courage of His Convictions* by Tony Parker and Robert Allerton.

Wilfred De'Ath, for an extract from a BBC interview entitled *Just Me and Nobody Else*, printed in *The Listener.*

A. D. Peters & Co., for extracts from *The Pedestrian* from *The Golden Apples of the Sun* by Ray Bradbury, and *Journey Down a Rainbow* by J. B. Priestley and Jacquetta Hawkes.

The Essex Music Group, for the poem *Little Boxes* by Malvina Reynolds.

Longmans, Green & Co. Ltd., for extracts from *The Hidden Persuaders* by Vance Packard, and *Confessions of an Advertising Man* by David Ogilvy.

Macmillan & Co. Ltd. and The Macmillan Company of Canada Ltd., for the poem *Au Jardin des Plantes* from *Weep Before God* by John Wain.

And the following for permission to use copyright photographs:

Paul Popper Ltd. pp. 76, 163, 180, 204, 259, 271. The National Film Board of Canada and their production *Never a Backward Step*, p. 112.

AUTHOR'S NOTE

THE ART OF ENGLISH is a five-year English series for secondary schools, comprising two complete but closely integrated courses. *The Certificate Course* is suitable for those pupils in grammar, comprehensive and modern schools who aim at an Ordinary Level Certificate in English Language. *The General Course* is designed for the less academic pupils in comprehensive and modern schools. The two courses are planned on a common basis, with obvious similarities in topics and layout. Both courses cover work for the Certificate of Secondary Education, though the approaches naturally differ.

Although *The Certificate Course* meets the demands of the most rigorous Ordinary Level Certificate syllabuses, it was devised in the belief that examination success should be the natural outcome of a wide and stimulating range of experience; it is therefore more than an English language textbook. The choice of poems and extracts is intended to develop pupils' reading, their critical awareness of literature and their interest in drama and film. The chapter topics lead to much discussion and further activities, and are particularly chosen as a stimulus to composition of all kinds.

Together, *The Certificate* and *General Courses* form the basis for a complete English syllabus for secondary schools.

Book Four of *The Certificate Course* covers a number of topics of social concern that most English teachers would wish to include at this stage: the mass media that daily influence our use of English, and the challenges of contemporary life that are repeatedly reflected in modern literature. To teachers wishing to pursue some of these topics further, I would recommend "Understanding the Mass Media" by Nicholas Tucker, a book to which I am considerably indebted.

The pattern of chapters remains substantially the same as in previous books. Each takes a long extract from a good, suitable book which can be recommended to pupils to read themselves. The self-contained extracts and poems arouse interest and discussion, offer ample comprehension and appreciation work, and then become the basis of work on techniques, which includes a full introduction to writing summaries and practice in clear thinking and appropriate English usage. Each chapter topic leads to at least two different kinds of composition, and to oral work and further activities, which now include film-making as well as drama, debate, and various research projects. Each chapter ends with some recommended reading: books either by the author of the extract or pursuing that chapter's interests.

For pupils following an Ordinary Level syllabus requiring formal analytical grammar, clause analysis is continued and developed in sections marked with an asterisk, both in the chapters and in the Supplementary Exercises. These also include other revision work.

CHAPTER ONE

Story from Childhood

Michael, aged seven, lives in his grandparents' house, the back garden of which has a wall at the bottom leading to an alley.

One day I sat talking to myself in the garden. I had two armies, one in the pile of stones and one in the grass. I could see the army in the grass advancing, and my lips were booming the guns.

"Got any snails?" said a voice.

I looked up. A clean boy, with a jacket on, stood on top of the wall that was the edge of the town. He was very smart for the alley. Generally I did not answer people from there. But he looked all right. I was not supposed to speak to boys without jackets; nor to the family without shoes down the road.

"Snails?" I asked. Then, as he climbed over the wall, "Be careful of the rhubarb."

"Rhubarb! My father's got fifty cabbages!" He kicked round the plants. "Yes: I can see you've got plenty. Half a mo: I'll be back with my bucket." And he was gone again. I heard his footsteps slap down the alley.

I went back to my battle. There was smoke all over the garden.

"Where are they, then?"

I looked up, feeling cross. He was already climbing the wall, with a creaking bucket. He wore sandals. I had always wanted sandals.

"Haven't you got me any?"

I went on with my game.

After a time I grew intrigued to hear the bucket creaking round and round the garden. He kept on talking to himself too, saying things like: "Yes, I thought so . . . I thought so . . . there's another one . . . that's worth a pretty penny . . ." just like a grown-up.

I went and watched him. He had a pile of snails in the bucket. "That's stealing," I said.

"What—snails? People kill snails."

"That's what my dad does," I said. "And Boss, and Nan. And Aunt Rene!" And I killed one with a stone.

"Spoil sport," he said.

"Who's that, Michael?" asked my grandmother's voice from the back door.

The boy got ready to run.

"It's only Nan," I said. Fancy anyone being afraid of Nan. Everyone knew she was kind.

"Yeah!" he mocked.

"Only me, Nan," I called out. The garden was very quiet. It was my first big lie.

"Come on then," he said. "Let's go." And he went over the wall.

I caught at the big sharp flints and struggled after him. It was hard to get up; but the alley was near on the other side. Wully the cat was coming along with a dead bird in his mouth like a ripe plum. I always found myself seeing things. We ran down the alley.

The world was much larger, flint walls, and mud, and edges of grass, as we ran past all the back gardens in a row. We came out at the green-grocer's where Nan took me to buy vegetables. The boy ran across the road. "Come on," he called.

I had never crossed a road before, but I went, wondering which was the way home. He opened a gate by a shop and we ran down a path. "Here they are," he said.

There were two tea-chests in the garden, joined by pieces of wood. He lifted the lids of the tea-chests, and I saw them—hundreds of snails, hundreds, eyes on horns, eyes going into horns, bodies going into houses, shells of all sorts of colours, black, brown, grey, mottled ones and striped ones. They were sticking to the floor, the walls, the lid, and to one another, in great bunches like conkers. They were wonderful.

He put back the lids, and then took a snail from his pocket. It was snow-white. "Whitewash," he explained. Then he brought out a handful of pink ones. I gasped. "The house," he said. I saw the house was painted pink, and that there were ladders and pots by the wall, and I understood him.

"You and me," he said.

"When?" I asked.

"Always," he said. Then he picked up the bucket and called out "C'mon." We went carefully through his father's fifty cabbages, leaf by leaf. We turned wood by the wall; we kicked over bricks and stones. Everywhere we went there were snails. We talked to them, kissed their shells, and put them in the bucket.

"C'mon," he said again. And we went out of the gate.

Once more I crossed the road, and once more went up the alley, which was now full of people. They called their words, but we had things to do. Over the wall we went, and into the rhubarb. The garden was wet and smelled of elderberry and cat.

"Where've you been?" called Nan.

"Hiding," I lied.

She came out and hooded her eyes in the sun. It was too much for them and she went in. We were poachers and the great adventure of the snails went on.

It went on for weeks. We collected them and their babies by the bucketful. His father would kill them among the weeds, so they were our secret. We prowled around one another's houses with them in our hands and pushed them down the backs of chairs so they would be comfortable. Sometimes we put them in the salad for a laugh, so the women would scream, and we could eat all of the family's lettuce. Sometimes we put them in our pockets and sat on them; but we tried to treat them kindly, because we loved them.

One day we raced our snails on the table where his father sold trousers. I had watched through a door while his father stood with a measure round his neck and chalk in his hands, talking to men with creases; I had watched the blinds drawn up and the cloth folded, and his father go in to tea. Then we pulled the table from the shop into the yard, and started our races. The table was leathery green and the snails moved along it unrolling silver slime. We raced them in twos and fours. A face stood at my shoulder.

Then another, breathing over my head.

Then another.

The *boys* had got in!

One put his hand on a snail and pulled it, plop, from the table. It was Beauty!

He held it high in the air while my partner grabbed at it. Then he bent down and scooped its shell in some sand. Beauty bubbled through the sand and the sand wriggled. We grabbed again. He held us off, and the shell snapped between his thumb and finger. He wiped it off on my partner's coat.

We started to cry.

They did not run in a hurry: they jeered until they heard

footsteps. Then they walked through the gate and slammed it shut.

His mother stood beside us.

We went on crying—but all she saw was the table covered with lines and the box of snails.

I knew it was the end, even if his father did not find out. She had told us off before, about him wrapping snails in his handkerchief and spoiling the wash. Last night he had taken some to bed with him and rolled on them. It was our last chance.

He went on crying.

He was doing well. His mother was holding his head; and I was wiping the table. Then his dad came out.

She was on our side, but his dad told us off about pockets, and cabbages, and spoiling the garden. It was no use her winking. She did not stop him, even when he said "At once!"

"Get rid of them, *at once*," he said. And they both went in.

My partner stopped crying the minute they went. He kicked at the table. Then he kicked a flowerpot smash against a wall.

"Upstairs," he said.

I looked at him, trying to know what he meant. With his red face I never knew. I did what he said because he seemed to know, to have done things before like my family had.

We picked up the smallest box and took it up through the shop, up the wooden stairs where his father kept shoes, with leather for laces, and bottles, and coloured ties.

Up in the attic we tipped them on to the dusty floor. The sticky ones we stuck on the walls.

"I'll know they're here," he said. He kissed one and wrapped it up in some cloth that had the white lines men wear for trousers.

We went downstairs for the other box.

His father's fifty cabbages stood like trees for a battle. We dropped all the snails into the slots of the cabbages and thought of them living there. We had one or two left.

"These are no good," he said.

So we killed them. . . .

When I went home I sat listening to stories, and wanted to say about the snails. But I couldn't. I wanted to do my own story, so I could nod, and hum, and look in the air, and cough by the fire, until they asked what my story was.

Then I should tell them.

(from *Grandad with Snails* by Michael Baldwin)

Appreciation and Discussion

NOTE: In Books Four and Five there will be no division into comprehension questions for discussion and those for written answers. More specific questions will generally be given first, and a selection of these could be used for written practice. These written answers should be *brief*, but usually *in complete sentences* and as far as possible *in your own words*.

1. What sort of people frequented the alley?
2. Why was Michael not supposed to speak to some of the neighbours?
3. How far had Michael already explored for himself?
4. What do the phrases "the wall that was the end of the town" and "the world was much larger" imply?
5. How big was Michael's "first big lie", and why *did* he lie about his friend?
6. How did some of the snails come to be coloured white and pink?
7. What things about the snail collector annoyed Michael and what did Michael find attractive about him? Does the passage imply that he was older than Michael?
8. What did the snail collector's father do for his living?
9. What kind of "boys" came in to spoil their snail races? What about their actions suggests that they were older?
10. Why was Michael's friend "doing well" when he went on crying in front of his mother? Why did she "wink"?
11. "We tried to treat them kindly because we loved them." Were the boys genuinely concerned for the snails? How do you think they felt about them? In what ways were they kind and unkind to them?
12. Why couldn't Michael tell his family about the snails? Why did he want to do so?
13. Does Michael seem to be an imaginative child? Find examples of his vivid or unusual fantasies or memories.
14. Discuss the author's choice of words or comparisons in the following:
    my lips were booming the guns; his footsteps slap down the alley; a bird in his mouth like a ripe plum; talking to men with creases; snails moved along it unrolling silver slime; a face stood at my shoulder; Beauty bubbled through the sand and the sand wriggled; cloth that had the white

lines men wear for trousers; fifty cabbages stood like trees for a battle; the slots of the cabbages.

15. Do you consider this rather jerky and pointed style effective? Does it suggest a child's-eye-view in any way?

16. Is this story a typical one of young children and the kind of games they play and the reactions of adults? Can you think of similar incidents in your own childhood?

Schoolmaster

Oh yes, I remember him well, the boy you are searching for:
he looked like most boys, no better, brighter, or more respectful;
he cribbed, mitched, spilt ink, rattled his desk and
garbled his lessons with the worst of them;
he could smudge, hedge, smirk, wriggle, wince,
whimper, blarney, badger, blush, deceive, be
devious, stammer, improvise, assume
offended dignity or righteous indignation as though to the
        manner born;
sullenly and reluctantly he drilled, for some small
crime, under Sergeant Bird, so wittily nicknamed
Oiseau, on Wednesday half-holidays,
appeared regularly in detention classes,
hid in the cloakroom during algebra,
was, when a newcomer, thrown into the bushes of the
Lower Playground by bigger boys,
and threw newcomers into the bushes of the Lower
Playground when *he* was a bigger boy;
he scuffled at prayers,
he interpolated, smugly, the time-honoured wrong
irreverent words into the morning hymns,
he helped to damage the headmaster's rhubarb,
was thirty-third in trigonometry,
and, as might be expected, edited the School Magazine.

 DYLAN THOMAS

Discussing the Poem

1. Have schoolboys changed much since this boy was at school? Discuss any references or words that now seem at all puzzling.
2. Dylan Thomas wrote this piece as part of a radio programme, "Return Journey", in which he imagined himself revisiting his home town after fourteen years away, and questioning people who might remember him as a child or young man, even if they did not recognise him now. Whose reply could this poem be? Why should he add "and, as might be expected, edited the School Magazine"?
3. Comment on the choice and variety of the words Dylan Thomas uses. Where is there *alliteration* in the poem? Pick out some examples of alliteration used to help link the end of one line with the beginning of the next.

Techniques

Exercise 1. How would you define or describe an "alley"? In the sense in which Michael Baldwin used the word, it is some kind of path or road. Words like "alley, lane, street, avenue" are all kinds of roads, but not exact synonyms; each has a separate DEFINITION. A definition of the meaning of a word (such as one might find in a dictionary) should be definite in two ways. It has to *include* everything that can bear that particular name, and yet not be narrow enough to *exclude* other, similar things. Thus, to define an "alley" as "a narrow footpath" is wrong because some alleys are not only for pedestrians; and to define it as "a road with buildings or high fences on each side" is wrong because almost every city street would be an "alley" by that definition.

Study the following definitions: do they seem satisfactory?

road—broad track with artificial hard surface for travelling on;

avenue—road (or approach to a house) bordered by regular rows of trees;

lane—narrow road bordered by hedges, etc.;

motorway—road specially built for fast motor traffic;

street—metalled road with houses on one or both sides.

(a) Try to write similar definitions for these four other kinds of roads:

by-pass; crescent; highway; promenade.

(b) How would you define the word "house"?

Without using a dictionary, write definitions for these eight kinds of houses:

castle; cottage; croft; hotel;
hovel; igloo; mansion; wigwam.

(c) Again without dictionary help, write short definitions for these eight kinds of rooms:

bedroom; cabin; dormitory; nursery;
pantry; refectory; studio; study.

(d) Write short definitions of the following ten vessels (containers for liquids):

barrel; basin; bottle; bucket; jug;
kettle; phial; tankard; tumbler; vase.

Exercise 2. Study carefully the following extract from an article published in *The Guardian* in 1966 about the National Society for the Prevention of Cruelty to Children, and then answer the questions given below.

Last year, the N.S.P.C.C. helped 120,805 children. It is a voluntary organisation and it is desperately short of money. It badly wants to open a new research department—last year it had to move from its old headquarters in Leicester Square to new offices—and now it has an overdraft at the bank. So it is launching an appeal for £250,000 to put it on its feet.

The pity is that most of the society's work is unknown. Only the atrocious cases . . . get in the papers. One reads about Patrick who was kept for five years in a hen coop, who when he was found at the age of seven could only jump about like a frog and imitate hen noises; about the girl whose body was so infested with sores that she had to be anaesthetised before she could be moved from her filthy bed; and about the 18-month-old child who was tied naked to a chair in a freezing cold room.

But the greater part of the society's work is not with such outright inhumanity. In a way the word cruelty in the title is misleading, and so is the traditional picture of the "cruelty man" rescuing maimed children from end-of-the-century slums. Children are still rescued, but of the 120,000 children helped last year only 9,632 had been assaulted. The rest had just been neglected. . . .

The public cannot be said to be entirely ignorant of this work, or altogether apathetic, but animals seem to attract more sympathy. In the last year for which there are figures the N.S.P.C.C. received £317,967 in legacies, a sum which is not quite half the £684,667 bequeathed in the same time to the R.S.P.C.A.

The R.S.P.C.A. are a bit unhappy when anyone makes this comparison, but it is no reflection on them that people prefer to leave their money to cats and dogs. Probably all it means is that most people think child cruelty is the State's business.

Relations between the two societies have always been friendly. Indeed, the beginnings of the N.S.P.C.C. owe something to a legal fiction accepted by a New York court that a child was a young animal.

It happened like this. In the 1870s a missionary in New York came across a child called Mary Ellen who was cruelly beaten by her father. Police told her they could do nothing, that animals but not children were protected by the law.

So she went to the New York Society for the Prevention of Cruelty to Animals, whose inspectors rescued the child and carried her, wrapped in a horse blanket, before a judge, who jailed her parents.

A New York S.P.C.C. was formed, and in 1882, the first English S.P.C.C. was started in Liverpool, based on the American model.

Today there is no need to resort to legal fictions. But every now and again an N.S.P.C.C. inspector finds a child in distress, wraps it in a blanket, and takes it off to hospital. Child welfare may be the State's business, but it is also the business of anyone else who will help. There are some families who can never have too much help.

TERRY COLEMAN

(a) Answer the following questions briefly, but in complete sentences and as far as possible in your own words:

(i) Give three reasons why the N.S.P.C.C. was short of money when this passage was written.

(ii) Why do the public get the impression that the Society's work is mainly dealing with cruelty? How far is this a true impression?

(iii) Who was known as "the cruelty man"?

(iv) Why, probably, do more people leave money to the R.S.P.C.A. than to the N.S.P.C.C.?

(v) Explain briefly, in *not more than 70 of your own words*, how the New York S.P.C.C. came to be founded.

(b) Each of the following statements about this extract is true or false or unknown (i.e. one cannot deduce it for certain from this passage). The first two answers are given as examples; of the remaining statements, 5 are true, 5 are false and 2 are unknown.

   (i) At the time of writing, the N.S.P.C.C. had not opened its new research department.—TRUE.
  (ii) The new offices of the Society are not in Leicester Square. —UNKNOWN.
 (iii) The word "cruelty" in the Society's title is misleading because there are no cases of cruelty any more.
 (iv) Less than 12% of children helped by the N.S.P.C.C. in 1965 had been assaulted.
  (v) Other children helped (not those assaulted) were all cases of neglect.
 (vi) The R.S.P.C.A. was left (in people's wills) half as much again as the N.S.P.C.C. in the last year for which figures were available.
 (vii) The writer was certain that the majority of people assumed the State should do something about cruelty to children.
(viii) The writer thought it likely that most people assumed that cruelty to animals was not the State's business.
 (ix) In the 1870s in New York, the law protected animals from cruelty, but not children.
  (x) The first society for preventing cruelty to children was started in New York.
 (xi) The first English society for the prevention of cruelty to children was not started for ten years after the New York society.
 (xii) A "legal fiction" (as used in this passage) is a story book that the law permits to be published.
(xiii) In Britain (at the time of writing), the government and local authorities undertake child welfare.
(xiv) The writer believed that State help meant there was no further need for the N.S.P.C.C.

(c) The words and phrases given below on the left appear in that order in the passage. The meanings given on the right are in an incorrect order. Pair off each with its appropriate meaning:
    e.g. voluntary—not compulsory, not set up by law.

voluntary	left by people's wills
research	something assumed to be true for convenience
launching	showing indifference, not caring
atrocious	made unconscious or unable to feel
imitate	use as a means or help to an end
infested	brutality
anaesthetised	beginning, opening
inhumanity	copy or mimic
maimed	overrun, plagued
apathetic	savagely cruel
bequeathed	crippled or mutilated
legal fiction	scholarly investigation
resort to	not compulsory, not set up by law

Exercise 3. Michael Baldwin has a large number of short, simple statements in the extract at the beginning of this chapter, where he might perhaps have combined them into longer and more complicated sentences. What effect did they have? Would it be true to say that using a large number of short sentences, or combining them simply with "and" and "then" sounds more child-like? For example, discuss the following pairs of alternatives:

(i) Generally I did not answer people from there. But he looked all right.

(ii) Although I generally did not answer people from there, he looked all right.

(i) He put back the lids, and then took a snail from his pocket.

(ii) When he had put back the lids, he took a snail from his pocket.

(a) Combine each of the following pairs of short statements into one, using the conjunction (or relative pronoun) suggested in brackets.

1. One day a boy appeared on the top of the wall. The wall was the edge of the town for Michael. (which)

2. Michael had never crossed the main road before. But he went with the boy, wondering about the way home. (although)

3. Michael met the young snail-collector. And he was never quite the same again. (after)

4. He was playing in the garden one day. The boy appeared over the wall. (as)

5. He heard Michael's grandmother's voice. He got ready to run. (when)
6. The boys jeered at them. Then the boys heard adult footsteps. (until)
7. Michael and his friend tried to treat the snails well. And they loved them. (because)
8. His parents were very angry. And they told him to get rid of all the snails. (so . . . that)
9. They dropped the snails into the cabbages. The snails could eat all the leaves. (so that)
10. Michael now had a story of his own to tell. But he had to listen to his grandmother's stories. (who)

*(b) Either *analyse* the sentences you have constructed in (a), using the column method explained in Book Three, or write out the subordinate clause you have introduced in each sentence, and state its function.

e.g. Although I generally did not answer people from there. . . .
Adverb clause of concession, modifying the verb "looked" in the main clause.

Topics for Written Work

1. "The memories of childhood have no order, and no end" wrote Dylan Thomas (Chapter 7 of this book contains an extract from his own memories of a visit to Grandpa's.) Try to delve into your own memories of early childhood and recall one incident, one day, one pastime or one particular friend round which you can build some vivid details. Enlarge on memory with imagination if you wish, but aim at a "child's-eye-view" of your subject.

Although the memory may be confused, try to give your account of it some order and shape. Work it out in paragraphs, and search for an interesting opening and conclusion. Try to fit your style to the subject, as Michael Baldwin has done, using also vivid descriptive words and comparisons to give a tangible sense of reality and first-hand experience.

2. Write a letter to a newspaper putting a strong case, briefly but intelligently, on one of the following topics:
(a) the amount of money given to child welfare and animal welfare organisations respectively;
(b) the way some children are neglected because both parents are out at work;
(c) parents who do not discipline their children enough;

(d) parents who do not try to understand their children as they grow up;

(e) child cruelty to pets, and animals generally;

(f) the poor example adults set young people today;

(g) the lack of adequate playgrounds, recreation grounds and other facilities for children and young people in a particular area;

(h) anything to do with parents and children that you may feel strongly about.

Letters for publication in a newspaper should be set out as business letters, with your address and the date in full, and addressed to the Editor, so-and-so newspaper. They should begin "Dear Sir," or "Sir," and be signed "Yours faithfully".

Even the least slick and popular newspapers are reluctant to print long and rambling letters in full. If yours is to be chosen for publication, it must be brief and to the point. Select your theme and your evidence with care and try to write in strong terms, but with due consideration to the opposite point of view. Mere sweeping invective is not sufficient.

Oral Work

1. Prepare a short talk on an organisation or institution that helps children in need, in which you will be trying to give a picture of the work the organisation does and appeal for financial or other help for it. Prepare some facts and figures and "case histories" to use as evidence. Articles or advertisements in the press and entries in reference books should help provide information, or you could write a short business letter to the secretary at the head office of your chosen organisation, asking for suitable facts and figures. Here are some possible subjects for your talk:

The N.S.P.C.C.; Dr. Barnardo's Homes; U.N.I.C.E.F.; Save the Children Fund; The Church of England Children's Society; The Children's Aid Society; The Shaftesbury Homes.

2. Girls in the class should prepare a short demonstration of baby care. Take a normal operation such as undressing, bathing and dressing a small baby, and prepare to show the rest of the class how to set about this, either miming the actions or using a large doll and the necessary clothes and other equipment. Most important of all, work out a clear and complete spoken commentary on what you are doing, explaining carefully how each task should be performed, and (where appropriate) why you choose to do it in this way. Be prepared to answer questions and criticisms from the rest of the class.

Boys could prepare a similar demonstration of the methods for making some simple toys for a baby brother or organising some games or entertainment for slightly older children.

Activities and Research

1. Using reference books such as *Who's Who*, the *Dictionary of National Biography*, the *Great Lives* volume of the *Oxford Junior Encyclopaedia*, and more limited biographical reference books or individual biographies, find out about the childhood and education of one or more well-known men or women, past or present. When a number of such studies have been made by members of the class, compare and contrast them, noting, for instance, how many showed early promise, as compared with those who gave no sign of their later talent.

After the main study is complete, imagine that you yourself are destined to fame, and make up a brief biographical note on your own childhood and education, such as might appear in one of these reference books when you become one of the great.

2. Study the "Letters to the Editor" in successive issues of a newspaper or magazine, and choose one example of a theme which aroused several correspondents to write, preferably one in answer to another, in subsequent issues. Then write your own contribution to the discussion. If you really feel strongly about it, and believe you have written a good letter, send it.

Further Reading

Grandad With Snails by MICHAEL BALDWIN (Hutchinson) (Fiction)
This autobiographical story of childhood covers Michael's colourful career between the years of seven and nine. While living in Grandad's house he takes part in many delinquent escapades—he gathers snails, forms his own gang, ties up the neighbours' door-knockers, and so on. Then he is suddenly evacuated to the country, where "Silky" initiates him into the delights of poaching, catching bad-tempered goats, and growing whiskers. Then, after Michael's return home, Grandad dies, and the boy realises with a shock that he has grown up.

Cider with Rosie by LAURIE LEE (Hogarth; Chatto & Windus; Penguin) (920 LEE)
The author of this autobiographical novel is a poet and novelist, like Michael Baldwin, but his rural childhood in Gloucestershire forty years ago makes an interesting contrast. He writes with great sympathy and humour about his family and their neighbours, and describes what it was like to grow up in a world very different from that of young people today.

There is a Happy Land by KEITH WATERHOUSE (Michael Joseph; Penguin) (Fiction)
This book captures the essence of childhood, in a way that very few others have managed to do. The narrator is a small boy from the backstreets of a grey Northern town (probably Leeds, where Keith Waterhouse grew up). Jingles, games, fantasies, nightmares, conversation in a secret language, fights, bouts of misbehaviour, the sinister Uncle Mad—all are presented in such a vivid, realistic way that the reader cannot help but recall the events and characters of his own childhood.

The Egg and I by BETTY MACDONALD (Mayflower)
A humorous autobiography by an American who gives an account of her life on a lonely chicken farm.

CHAPTER TWO

If . . . . .

A sudden disaster has blinded almost the entire population of the world.
One night Bill Masen and Josella Playton, two survivors in London,
see a light on top of the University Tower. The following morning, on
going to investigate, they find outside the gates a large crowd of blind
people whose sighted leader is shouting to a man inside.

He spat with contempt, and raised a long, oratorical arm.

"Out there," he said, waving his hand towards London at
large, "—out there there are thousands of poor devils only
wanting someone to show them how to get the food that's there
for the taking.—And you could do it. All you've got to do is
show them. But do you? Do you? No. What you do is shut
yourselves in here and let them bloody well starve when each
of you could keep hundreds alive by doing no more than coming out and *showing* the poor devils where to get the grub. God
almighty, aren't you people human?"

The man's voice was violent. He had a case to put, and he
was putting it passionately. I felt Josella's hand unconsciously
clutching my arm, and I put my hand over hers. The man on
the far side of the gate said something that was inaudible
where we stood.

"How long?" shouted the man on our side. "How in hell
would I know how long the food's going to last? What I do
know is that if bastards like you don't muck in and help, there
ain't going to be many left alive by the time they come to clear
this bloody mess up." He stood glaring for a moment. "Fact of
it is, you're scared—scared to show 'em where the food is.
And why? Because the more these poor devils get to eat, the
less there's going to be for your lot. That's the way of it, isn't
it? That's the truth—if you had the guts to admit it."

Again we failed to hear the answer of the other man, but,
whatever it was, it did nothing to mollify the speaker. He
stared back grimly through the bars for a moment. Then he
said:

"All right—if that's the way you want it!"

He made a lightning snatch between the bars, and caught the other's arm. In one swift movement he dragged it through, and twisted it. He grabbed the hand of a blind man standing beside him, and clamped it on the arm.

"Hang on there, mate," he said, and jumped towards the main fastening of the gates.

The man inside recovered from his first surprise. He struck wildly through the bars behind him with his other hand. A chance swipe took the blind man in the face. It made him give a yell, and tighten his grip. The leader of the crowd was wrenching at the gate fastening. At that moment a rifle cracked. The bullet pinged against the railings, and whirred off on a ricochet. The leader checked suddenly, undecided. Behind him there was an outbreak of curses, and a scream or two. The crowd swayed back and forth as though uncertain whether to run or to charge the gates. The decision was made for them by those in the courtyard. I saw a youngish-looking man tuck something under his arm, and I dropped down, pulling Josella with me as the clatter of a sub-machine gun began.

It was obvious that the shooting was deliberately high; nevertheless, the rattle of it and the whizz of glancing bullets was alarming. One short burst was enough to settle the matter. When we raised our heads the crowd had lost entity and its components were groping their ways to safer parts in all three possible directions. The leader paused only to shout something unintelligible, then he turned away, too. He made his way northwards up Malet Street, doing his best to rally his following behind him.

I sat where we were, and looked at Josella. She looked thoughtfully back at me, and then down at the ground before her. It was some minutes before either of us spoke.

"Well?" I asked, at last.

She raised her head to look across the road, and then at the last stragglers from the crowd pathetically fumbling their ways.

"He was right," she said. "You know he was right, don't you?"

I nodded.

"Yes, he was right. . . . And yet he was quite wrong, too. You see, there is no 'they' to come to clear up this mess—I'm quite sure of that now. It won't be cleared up. We could do as he says. We *could* show some, though only some, of these people where there is food. We could do that for a few days, maybe for a few weeks, but after that—what?"

"It seems so awful, so callous. . . ."

"If we face it squarely, there's a simple choice," I said. "Either we can set out to save what can be saved from the wreck—and that has to include ourselves: or we can devote ourselves to stretching the lives of these people a little longer, That is the most objective view I can take." . . .

She nodded slowly.

"Put like that, there doesn't seem to be much choice, does there? And even if we could save a few, which are we going to choose?—and who are *we* to choose?—and how long could we do it, anyway?"

"There's nothing easy about this," I said. "I've no idea what proportion of semi-disabled persons it may be possible for us to support when we come to the end of handy supplies, but I don't imagine it could be very high."

"You've made up your mind," she said, glancing at me. There might or might not have been a tinge of disapproval in her voice.

"My dear," I said. "I don't like this any more than you do. I've put the alternatives baldly before you. Do we help those who have survived the catastrophe to rebuild some kind of life?—or do we make a moral gesture which, on the face of it, can scarcely be more than a gesture? The people across the road there evidently intend to survive."

(from *The Day of the Triffids* by John Wyndham)

26

Appreciation and Discussion

1. What were the main arguments on either side in this dispute?
2. What was the main weakness or false assumption in the argument of the leader of the blind men (Coker)?
3. Is it true that the people inside the university building were simply "scared", in case they should starve?
4. Who would you imagine the "they" to be, who might "come to clear up this mess"? What reasons could Bill (the narrator) have for thinking no-one would come?
5. Josella began by thinking Coker (leader of the blind mob) was right; did she still think so after Bill had talked to her?
6. How would you have felt if you were one of the blind crowd (a) when the sighted people refused to help, and (b) when they began shooting?
7. Was Coker justified in using force to make those in the University help his party?
8. Was the group in the university justified in using force to defend itself? Is it significant that they were shooting high? Would they have been justified in shooting to wound or kill, if the blind mob had continued to attack?
9. Josella and Bill have to decide whether to join the sighted people in the university, or to look after themselves alone, or to join Coker in leading and helping blind people. Which would you have chosen, and why?
10. Many people, finding themselves and nearly everybody else suddenly deprived of sight, committed suicide. Would you have done so?
11. If the few sighted people were able to save and protect only a few of the blinded people, how should they choose them, in your opinion?
12. In this book, the dangers to the blinded population are increased by the existence of plant-like animals with lethal stings (the "triffids"), which have been developed by the 21st century. Can you imagine what aspects of life *today* would become dangerous to us if we all lost our sense of (a) sight, (b) hearing, (c) smell, (d) touch or (e) taste?
13. To survive, the sighted people had to form some sort of self-contained community; what kind of community would you think this should be? Would it need different rules of marriage or property, different arrangements for education or division of labour, from those in our society now?

Bedtime Story

Long long ago when the world was a wild place
Planted with bushes and peopled by apes, our
Mission Brigade was at work in the jungle.
   Hard by the Congo

Once, when a foraging detail was active
Scouting for green-fly, it came on a grey man, the
Last living man, in the branch of a baobab
   Stalking a monkey.

Earlier men had disposed of, for pleasure,
Creatures whose names we scarcely remember—
Zebra, rhinoceros, elephants, wart-hog,
   Lion, rats, deer. But

After the wars had extinguished the cities
Only the wild ones were left, half-naked
Near the Equator: and here was the last one,
   Starved for a monkey.

By then the Mission Brigade had encountered
Hundreds of such men: and their procedure,
History tells us, was only to feed them:
   Find them and feed them;

Those were the orders. And this was the last one.
Nobody knew that he was, but he was. Mud
caked on his flat grey flanks. He was crouched, half-
   Armed with a shaved spear

Glinting beneath broad leaves. When their jaws cut
Swathes through the bark and he saw fine teeth shine,
Round eyes roll round and forked arms waver
   Huge as the rough trunks

Over his head, he was frightened. Our workers
Marched through the Congo before he was born, but
This was the first time perhaps that he'd seen one.
   Staring in hot still

Silence, he crouched there: then jumped. With a long swing
Down from his branch, he had angled his spear too
Quickly, before they could hold him, and hurled it
　　Hard at the soldier

Leading the detail. How could he know Queen's
Orders were only to help him? The soldier
Winced when the tipped spear pricked him. Unsheathing his
　　Sting was a reflex.

Later the Queen was informed. There were no more
Men. An impetuous soldier had killed off,
Purely by chance, the penultimate primate.
　　When she was certain,

Squadrons of workers were fanned through the Congo
Detailed to bring back the man's picked bones to be
Sealed in the archives in amber. I'm quite sure
　　Nobody found them

After the most industrious search, though.
Where had the bones gone? Over the earth, dear,
Ground by the teeth of the termites, blown by the
　　Wind, like the dodo's.

GEORGE MACBETH

Discussing the Poem

1. A giant ant is telling this bedtime story to one of its children at some time in the distant future. What kind of creatures do these ants, on their "mission" in the Congo, seem to be? In what ways are they ant-like (notice the words "scouting for green-fly" and "Unsheathing his sting"), and in what ways do they seem to be thinking creatures?
2. What had apparently happened to men, by this time, and to the jungle creatures that we would find in the Congo today? Is there some suggestion that men *deserved* to be overtaken by new creatures in the process of "evolution"?
3. The last living man is referred to as "the penultimate primate": why? (Note that he was hunting a monkey when they found him.) What then happened to his body? What would the ants have preferred to do with it?
4. If mankind is ever to be overtaken by some "higher" creature who will dominate the world, as men do today, what do *you* think such a creature will be like?

Techniques

Exercise 1. Constructions using "both . . . and", "either . . .or" and "neither . . . nor" are a common source of confusion in English and serve as a reminder of the importance of word order, or of a word's position in a sentence, in determining meaning in English. Discuss the following variations in the use of "both" (with or without "and") in one basic sentence:

Both Josella and Bill had difficult decisions to face and make.

Josella and Bill both had difficult decisions to face and make.

Josella and Bill had difficult decisions both to face and to make.

Josella and Bill had difficult decisions to both face and make.

Josella and Bill had difficult decisions to face, and had to make both.

a) Explain the difference in meaning between the following four sentences using "neither . . . nor":

(i) Neither Josella nor Bill wants the blind people to starve or kill themselves in despair.

(ii) Josella and Bill neither want the blind people to starve nor kill themselves in despair.

(iii) Josella and Bill want the blind people neither to starve nor to kill themselves in despair.

(iv) Josella and Bill want neither to kill themselves in despair, nor the blind people to starve.

Now see if you can construct, and explain, three or four variations on the following pattern, by altering the position of "either . . . or" and making other small changes in punctuation or pronouns.

Either the sighted people must help the blind people or they must look after themselves.

(b) In these double constructions, it is important that both parts of the construction (e.g. the one after "both" and the second after "and") should be strictly parallelled, and grammatically the same kind of phrase or clause. The following is therefore incorrect:

The men inside the yard were determined both to frighten the crowd by shooting at them and that none of them should in fact be hurt.

Here "both" is followed by a phrase, and "and" is followed by a clause. How could this be corrected?

Similarly, if one half of the double construction is preceded by a preposition, so should the other half be. The following is therefore incorrect:

The bed was too hard for either comfort or for convenience.

Here we must either move the first "for", or omit the second one. What two correct sentences would we then have?

Rewrite all the following sentences, correcting mistakes of this kind:

(i) Josella and Bill had both difficult decisions to face and to make.

(ii) Josella and Bill neither want the blind people to starve nor to kill themselves in despair.

(iii) The sighted people must either help the blind people or they must look after themselves.

(iv) Several men inside the courtyard were both firing rifles and machine guns.

(v) The crowd seemed uncertain whether they should run or to charge the gates.

(vi) We set out either to save something from this wreck, or we try to help everyone.

(vii) We can neither hope for rescue any more nor can we hope to save everyone.

(viii) We cannot both help all the blinded people and also ourselves.

(ix) The decision was neither easy to make nor did we find it pleasant to have to make up our minds.

(x) The man's voice sounded both violent and passionate and uncontrolled, as if he was prepared neither for refusal nor for delay.

Exercise 2. Throughout Book Four we shall be including a number of exercises to offer practice with summarising or PRÉCIS writing. The main aim of any summary is to reproduce clearly and briefly the most important ideas of a given passage, without altering or distorting the writer's views or the thread of his argument, even if you disagree with them! Thus, while the original writer (or speaker) may have made very effective use of *repetition* in emphasising his points, the summary must cut this down to the basic essentials of what he wanted to say.

Study Bill's remarks in the passage, beginning: "Yes, he was right..." and ending: "...but after that, what?" (72 words) Would the following be an adequate summary of his argument?

He was partly right, partly wrong. I am now sure there is no one to come to clear this mess. We could show a few of these people where there is food for a few days or weeks, but what then? (40 words)

The use of "to clear up" where "to clear" would do is often called *redundancy*. Flagrant examples, like:

"He was killed in a fatal accident."

(what is wrong with this?) are faults of style. What does the word "redundancy" mean in industry? Has it a similar meaning when applied to the use of words?

The following passage is absurdly full of repetition and redundancy. It now contains about 130 words. You should be able to rewrite it in about 45 words simply by omitting unnecessary words and phrases. State (in brackets) at the end of your version exactly how many words you required.

They all agreed and unanimously decided to go on a cycling tour by bicycle from their homes in Manchester to the Lake District, all round the Lake District and then back home to Manchester, where they lived. But, on the other hand, they argued and strongly disagreed about the question of their itinerary, and particularly what route they should take through Lancashire, and whether they should take fast roads and cycle as fast as possible, seeing little except the tarmac and the behinds of the boys in front, or whether they should follow the country lanes and byways, and travel slowly and in a leisurely way, appreciating the countryside and the beauties of the scenery at their leisure, rather than hurrying to the Lake District.

Précis Rule 1. REDUNDANCY AND REPETITION:
All unnecessary words and phrases must be cut out, and nothing should be said more than once.

Exercise 3. In Book Three we considered conditional tenses. These use the auxiliary verbs *should* or *would*, and always imply some condition or a hypothetical wish or statement:

How would I know how long the food is going to last?

In the passage, the verbs *could* and *might* are used in a similar way:

And you could do it.

And even if we could save a few, which are we going to choose?

There might or might not have been a tinge of disapproval in her voice.

Conditional tenses can often be used to create conditional clauses without the conjunction "if", e.g.

Should they attack, then we shall have to use force to repel them.

which means:

If they should attack, then. . . .

This construction already sounds old-fashioned, and it is a relic of the SUBJUNCTIVE MOOD in English, which survives as a separate verb form of the verb "to be" and in a few familiar phrases:

Were I to be suddenly blinded, I should not know what to do.

Far be it from us to criticise the people in the university.

Long live the King.

God's will be done.

In each case the verb is not what one would expect in the normal INDICATIVE MOOD (I was; it is; the King lives; God's will will be done).

(a) Rewrite the following quotations from the Authorised Version of *The Bible* in more modern English. Each contains a verb in the subjunctive mood. For instance, St. John 9, verse 25, in the A.V. included the words:

Whether he be a sinner or no, I know not.

The Revised Standard Version of 1946 translated this:

Whether he is a sinner, I do not know.

or we might perhaps write:

I do not know whether he is a sinner or not.

(i) Though he were dead, yet shall he live.

(ii) For if the trumpet give an uncertain sound, who shall prepare himself to the battle?

(iii) If he sleep, he shall do well.

(iv) But thanks be to God, which giveth us the victory.

(v) But though I be rude in speech, yet not in knowledge.

(vi) For whether there be prophecies, they shall fail.

(vii) Therefore if any man be in Christ, he is a new creature.

(viii) Except the Lord build the house, they labour in vain that build it.

*(b) We can now see that adverb clauses of condition may be introduced by "if" or by no conjunction at all:

If I were to survive such a catastrophe, I should be utterly helpless.

Were I to survive such a catastrophe, I should be utterly helpless.

They can also be introduced by "provided (that)", "providing", and "unless":

Unless they found food, the blind people would die.

Provided (that) they found food, they would survive.

Pick out the adverb clause of condition in each of the following sentences. There is *one* adverb clause of concession amongst them.

(i) That is the truth, if you could admit it.

(ii) If we face it squarely, there is a simple choice.

34

(iii) Even if we could save a few, which are we going to choose?
(iv) Were he to argue all night, he would not convince me.
(v) Unless they opened fire, they could not disperse that mob.
(vi) It was all right to shoot, provided that they shot deliberately high.
(vii) If only there had been some help from outside, Coker would have been right.
(viii) Providing they could see, all were welcome in the university.
(ix) He would use force only if he had no alternative.
(x) Should such a catastrophe come, would it really be like this?

Topics for Written Work

1. Science fiction is largely concerned with the way human beings might react to a future that may bring new dangers, and when technical progress may force men to adjust themselves and human society to quite new conditions, in this world or elsewhere in space. Trying to imagine what would happen if we were faced with unprecedented events forces us to think again about human nature and the way of life we are used to. How far *do* we depend on a complicated system of trade and law and order for our food and comfort, for entertainment and protection? Could you look after yourself in a disaster? Would a threat to the human race force us all to be selfish and unscrupulous, or would it make us draw closer together in co-operation?

Imagine a national or international disaster sufficiently serious to cause a breakdown in normal law and order and put an end to supplies of food, power and so on. If everyone went blind. . . . If there were a few survivors from a nuclear war. . . . If the normal pattern of the seasons broke down. . . . If floods or earthquakes or volcanic eruptions obliterated vast areas of the earth. . . . If some terrible plant disease destroyed nearly all crops or some new virus swept away nearly all the world's population. . . . If electronic machines or some intelligence from outer space were about to take over. . . . If the temperature became unbearably hot or cold over nearly all the earth. . . .

Write either a short story on these lines or a description of what you would do in such circumstances. Do not try to cover too much ground: plan your work before you begin, and make sure that you can discuss the conditions necessary for survival, as well as telling the story of the disaster. For instance, ask yourself what supplies you would collect, where you would go, how many companions you would want and how you would choose them, in terms of age, sex, their skills and personal qualities, etc.

2. Shortly after the incident described in the extract, Josella and Bill found themselves at a discussion among the sighted people who had come to the university building, about their plans for survival. Imagine you are present, and write a short speech advocating one line of action as strongly and convincingly as you can. You could take Coker's point of view (although he was, of course, not actually present); you could advocate a policy of stock-piling vast supplies for a small community; you could recommend a democratic system of organisation or absolute obedience to one leader; you could advise the group to leave London and set up a remote and well-protected community, or even advise splitting into smaller groups.

Oral Work

1. The conversation in the extract raises a question that is already relevant, without any future catastrophe to bring it into prominence—is it merely a useless "moral gesture" to keep people alive when they are utterly disabled, mentally defective, or incurably ill? A few people advocate *euthanasia* or "mercy killing", at least for those in such misery that they want to commit suicide. Then there is the question of new-born or unborn children that are known to be defective or deformed. On the other hand, consider the question of who should decide in all these cases, and the fact that such decisions would be irrevocable, and one could never know later whether the victims might have lived useful and happy lives after all. This whole question should be a good topic for debate or serious discussion.

2. Prepare a short talk to the class in which you tell them what you think might (or should) happen in one of the following cases:

If all the world's seas rose thirty metres.

If we could be kept alive for ever, although old and infirm.

If we could all be kept permanently young.

If we learnt to communicate telepathically.

If machines could be organised to do all our work for us.

If we discover that an accessible planet, though uninhabited, will support human life.

If the world becomes seriously overpopulated.

If all the world's cereal crops and grass mysteriously died.

If a madman dropped nuclear weapons on Moscow, Peking and Washington.

If everyone in the world became suddenly deaf.

If the whole world fell into the power of one dictator.

If we found ourselves rapidly entering another ice-age.

Activities and Research

1. Find out as much as you can about "the foreseeable future" and what scientists believe are the likely developments in the next seventy years—your life-time. Aim at a good general picture, covering the main issues of population, food and housing, transport, industry and mechanisation, health and leisure. Then, if you wish, explore any particular line of development that you find especially interesting (such as space exploration, or automation), or consider the human problems, political or personal, that are likely to become the serious challenges to your generation. In all your research, however, keep the *likely* developments, that have a factual basis in the present, distinct from wilder or more personal speculation.

2. Modern science fiction writers are often concerned with the questions of what society *might* be like, under new circumstances or in remote space or time. A number of older works of literature have explored the same idea. Find out about Sir Thomas More's *Utopia,* Jonathan Swift's *Gulliver's Travels* (not only the voyage to Lilliput), and Samuel Butler's *Erewhon.* Books like the *Oxford Companion to English Literature* will give you quite a lot of useful information. Decide whether books like *Robinson Crusoe* or even *The Swiss Family Robinson* really come into the same category.

Prepare a short talk on this subject, with your own comment on some of the different ideas in these books and perhaps also the main features of your personal picture of an ideal society.

The Day of the Triffids by JOHN WYNDHAM (Hutchinson; Michael Joseph; Penguin)

Although always exciting, John Wyndham's science fiction novels are much more than straightforward adventure stories, for they also analyse attitudes and customs to be found in society today. The normal situation is in some way disturbed— in this case, by a disaster which blinds all but a few people, and by the presence of the triffids, dangerous walking plants. And we are then shown how well conventional values stand up to the stresses imposed by the new situation.

The Kraken Wakes by JOHN WYNDHAM (Longman; Michael Joseph; Penguin)

This is a story of conflict between Mankind and an alien form of life living in the deepest parts of the world's oceans. The almost imperceptible beginnings of the conflict, and the terrifying consequences demonstrate how easily misunderstanding and fear can lead to extreme violence. Although you may find parts of the story, which is told by a script writer, a little slow, the detail is always convincing.

The Midwich Cuckoos and *The Chrysalids* by JOHN WYNDHAM (both Michael Joseph; Penguin)

In these novels, the author imagines mankind faced with new species of human beings—are they a threat to human survival? Can we tolerate beings different from ourselves in our society? In Midwich, a number of children are born with intelligence, will-power and telepathic powers of communication that are quite superhuman. In *The Chrysalids*, a very puritanical community have survived a nuclear war, but they are fiercely against any people who show signs of mutation, and are born different from the narrowly defined "normal".

The Death of Grass (Pergamon) and *The World in Winter* (Eyre & Spottiswoode) by JOHN CHRISTOPHER

Two vivid stories of what *might* happen, if our prosperous and comfortable civilization were disturbed by major natural disasters. In the first all the grass and cereal crops begin to die, and governments are forced to take such drastic measures that law and order break down completely. In the second, a new Ice Age brings anarchy, horror and racial hatred to Europe and Africa.

38

CHAPTER THREE

A Curious Contest

After making a failure of his respectable married life, Mr. Polly had taken to the road and found himself a pleasant job as hired man at the Potwell Inn. The landlady, however, was terrorised by visits from her violent nephew, Uncle Jim, who was determined to evict Mr. Polly.

The private war between Mr. Polly and Uncle Jim for the possession of the Potwell Inn fell naturally into three chief campaigns. There was, first of all, the great campaign which ended in the triumphant eviction of Uncle Jim from the inn premises. . . .

He went to the crinkly paned window and peered out. Uncle Jim was coming down the garden path towards the house, his hands in his pockets, and singing hoarsely. Mr. Polly remembered afterwards, with pride and amazement, that he felt neither faint nor rigid. He glanced round him, seized a bottle of beer by the neck as an improvised club, and went out by the garden door. Uncle Jim stopped, amazed. His brain did not instantly rise to the new posture of things. "You!" he cried, and stopped for a moment. "You—*scoot!*"

"*Your* job," said Mr. Polly, and advanced some paces.

Uncle Jim stood swaying with wrathful astonishment, and then darted forward with clutching hands. Mr. Polly felt that if his antagonist closed, he was lost, and smote with all his force at the ugly head before him. Smash went the bottle and Uncle Jim staggered, half stunned by the blow, and blinded with beer.

The lapses and leaps of the human mind are for ever mysterious. Mr. Polly had never expected that bottle to break. In an instant he felt disarmed and helpless. Before him was Uncle Jim, infuriated and evidently still coming on, and for defence was nothing but the neck of a bottle.

For a time our Mr. Polly has figured heroic. Now comes the fall again; he sounded abject terror; he dropped that ineffectual scrap of glass and turned and fled round the corner of the house.

"Bolls!" came the thick voice of the enemy behind him, as

one who accepts a challenge, and bleeding but indomitable, Uncle Jim entered the house.

"Bolls!" he said, surveying the bar. "Fightin' with bolls. I'll show 'im fightin' with bolls!"

Uncle Jim had learnt all about fighting with bottles in the Reformatory Home. Regardless of his terror-stricken aunt, he ranged among the bottled beer and succeeded, after one or two failures, in preparing two bottles to his satisfaction by knocking off the bottom, and gripping them dagger-wise, by the necks. So prepared, he went forth again to destroy Mr. Polly. . . .

A careless observer, watching him sprint round and round the inn in front of the lumbering and reproachful pursuit of Uncle Jim, might have formed an altogether erroneous estimate of the issue of the campaign. Certain compensating qualities of the very greatest military value were appearing in Mr. Polly, even as he ran; if Uncle Jim had strength and brute courage, and the rich toughening experience a Reformatory Home affords, Mr. Polly was nevertheless sober, more mobile, and with a mind now stimulated to an almost incredible nimbleness. So that he not only gained on Uncle Jim but thought what use he might make of this advantage. The word "strategious" flamed red across the tumult of his mind. As he came round the house for the third time, he darted suddenly into the yard, swung the door to behind himself, and bolted it, seized the pig's zinc pail and stood by the entrance to the kitchen, and had it neatly and resonantly over Uncle Jim's head, as he came belatedly in round the outhouse on the other side. One of the splintered bottles jabbed Mr. Polly's ear—at the time it seemed of no importance—and then Uncle Jim was down and writhing dangerously and noisily upon the yard tiles with his head still in the pig pail, and his bottle gone to splinters, and Mr. Polly was fastening the kitchen door against him.

"Can't go on like this for ever," said Mr. Polly, whooping for breath, and selecting a weapon from among the brooms that stood behind the kitchen door. Uncle Jim was losing his head. He was up and kicking the door, and bellowing unamiable proposals and invitations, so that a strategist emerging silently by the tap door could locate him without difficulty, steal upon him unawares, and—!

But before that felling blow could be delivered, Uncle Jim's ear had caught a footfall, and he turned. Mr. Polly quailed, and lowered his broom—a fatal hesitation.

"*Now* I got you!" cried Uncle Jim, dancing forward in a disconcerting zigzag.

He rushed to close, and Mr. Polly stopped him neatly, as it were a miracle with the head of the broom across his chest.

Uncle Jim seized the broom with both hands. "Lea go," he said, and tugged. Mr. Polly shook his head, tugged, and showed pale, compressed lips. Both tugged. Then Uncle Jim tried to get round the end of the broom; Mr. Polly circled away. They began to circle about one another, both tugging hard, both intensely watchful of the slightest initiative on the part of the other. Mr. Polly wished brooms were longer—twelve or thirteen feet, for example; Uncle Jim was clearly for shortness in brooms. He wasted breath in saying what was to happen shortly— sanguinary, oriental, soul-blenching things—when the broom no longer separated them. Mr. Polly thought he had never seen an uglier person. Suddenly Uncle Jim flashed into violent activity, but alcohol slows movement, and Mr. Polly was equal to him. Then Uncle Jim tried jerks, and, for a terrible instant, he seemed to have the broom out of Mr. Polly's hands. But Mr. Polly recovered it with the clutch of a drowning man. Then Uncle Jim drove suddenly at Mr. Polly's midriff; but again Mr. Polly was ready, and swept him round in a circle. Then suddenly a wild hope filled Mr. Polly. He saw the river was very near, the post to which the punt was tied not three yards away. With a wild yell he sent the broom home under his antagonist's ribs. "Woosh!" he cried, as the resistance gave.

"Oh! *Gaw!*" said Uncle Jim, going backward helplessly, and Mr. Polly thrust hard, and abandoned the broom to the enemy's despairing clutch.

Splash! Uncle Jim was in the water, and Mr. Polly had leapt like a cat aboard the ferry punt, and grasped the pole. . . .

It was stupendous! Mr. Polly had discovered the heel of Achilles. Uncle Jim had no stomach for cold water. The broom floated away, pitching gently on the swell. Mr. Polly, infuriated by victory, thrust Uncle Jim under again, and drove the punt round on its chain in such a manner, that when Uncle Jim came up for the fourth time—and now he was nearly out of his depth, too buoyed up to walk, and apparently nearly helpless —Mr. Polly, fortunately for them both, could not reach him. . . .

The spirit was out of Uncle Jim for the time, and he turned away to struggle through the osiers towards the mill, leaving a shining trail of water among the green-grey stems. . . .

So it was the first campaign ended in an insecure victory.

(from *The History of Mr. Polly* by H. G. Wells)

Appreciation and Discussion

1. What might have made Mr. Polly feel either "faint" or "rigid" (see the second paragraph)?
2. What do the words "with pride and amazement" (in the second paragraph) suggest about Mr. Polly?
3. Did Uncle Jim expect Mr. Polly to be there? Why was he slow to take the situation in?
4. If the unexpected breaking of the bottle over Uncle Jim's head was a "lapse" in Mr. Polly's plans, what later thoughts or decisions might qualify as "leaps of the human mind"?
5. How did Uncle Jim propose to use bottles as weapons? Would his method in fact be nastier and more vicious than Mr. Polly's?
6. Where, apparently, was the landlady, Uncle Jim's aunt?
7. When they were grappling with the broom, which of Uncle Jim's tactics came nearest to success?
8. Why did Mr. Polly "abandon the broom to the enemy's despairing clutch" when Uncle Jim was falling into the river? What did Mr. Polly use as his weapon then?
9. Why was it "fortunate for them both" that Mr. Polly could not reach Uncle Jim again with the pole?
10. Why do you think this victory is called "insecure"?
11. What were Mr. Polly's advantages over Uncle Jim? Did they make victory simple? Was his victory due mainly to superior brain-power?
12. Discuss what you understand by the following words or phrases, and how effective they are in this passage:
    the lapses and leaps of the human mind; sounded abject terror; the lumbering and reproachful pursuit; neatly and resonantly over Uncle Jim's head; whooping for breath; bellowing unamiable proposals; sanguinary, oriental, soul-blenching things; the heel of Achilles.
13. In what ways is this brawl treated as if it were a more serious or more dignified contest or battle? Is it a form of humour to talk of "certain qualities of the very greatest military value (which were) appearing in Mr. Polly" when referring to a fight with bottles, pails and broomsticks? Are there other examples of this "mock heroic" treatment that you can quote?

Exercise 1. Of Mr. Polly, H. G. Wells writes:

New words had terror and fascination for him; he did not acquire them, he could not avoid them, and so he plunged into them. . . . He avoided every recognised phrase in the language, and mispronounced everything in order that he shouldn't be suspected of ignorance but whim.

"Sesquippledan," he would say. "Sesquippledan verboojuice."

Presumably that was Mr. Polly's version of "sesquipedalian verbiage or verbosity"—what does that mean? There is another example of his highly individual treatment of the language in the passage at the head of this chapter: what did Mr. Polly mean there? Elsewhere Mr. Polly apologises for being "intrudacious", tells us he was "just sitting there in melancholic retrospectatiousness", and describes an argument in which a shop assistant came to blows with his employer as a "heated altaclation".

Literature, like life, presents us with several examples of characters who muddled words in a comic way. Look for instance at what Dogberry, a self-important village official in charge of keeping the peace, has to say in Shakespeare's *Much Ado About Nothing*, Act III, scene 3, and Act IV, scene 2. But perhaps the best known example is Mrs. Malaprop in Sheridan's play, *The Rivals*. She has given her name to a particular kind of confusion in vocabulary, the MALAPROPISM, where a word is confused with another resembling it in pronunciation, but comically contrasted in meaning. Thus she confuses "obliterate" with "illiterate" when she tells her niece:

"to forget this fellow—to illiterate him, I say, quite from your memory."

and "extricate" with "extirpate" in:

"Now don't attempt to extirpate yourself from the matter."

(a) Study Mrs. Malaprop's speeches in Act I, scene 2 and again in Act III, scene 3 of *The Rivals* and try to find as many of her malapropisms as you can—in each case write down both the word she uses and the word she intended to use, if possible with a definition of each.

(b) Write down the twenty misused words in the following sentences, together with the correct word that was intended, making sure that you understand the meaning of both.

(i) The hydrogen bomb is considered a useful detergent.

(ii) Many firms have a telepathic address.

(iii) A parabola is a short story with a hidden morale.

(iv) We could pass the centuries on duty with impurity.

(v) Albert, the Prince Concert, was very much concerned with the Great Expedition of 1851.

(vi) He was writing with an inedible pencil, but the result was quite ineligible.

(vii) Trespassers in these plantations of valuable carnivorous trees will be persecuted.

(viii) The septic was not at all convicted by the parson who came with bull, hook, and handle to exercise the ghost who was supposed to vaunt the ancient aesophagus.

(c) Make up your own sentences containing amusing malapropisms—wherever possible, your sentence should still make some sort of sense with the incorrect words in it. Here are some possible pairs of confused words to use if you wish:

angel–angle	eliminate–illuminate
anthropology–anthology	epistle–apostle
asterisk–asteroid	evasion–invasion
bibulous–bilious	hysterical–historical
cannonball–cannibal	illusion–allusion
capsule–caption	infest–invest
caricature–character	monotonous–monogamous
condensation–condescension	nationalise–naturalise
conscious–conscientious	pelmet–pelvis
elegy–allergy	vacillation–vaccination

Exercise 2. VERBOSITY is a general term for the use of too many words; it includes *redundancy* and pointless repetition, as well as the use of *circumlocution* (roundabout descriptions of what could be plainly stated) and many *clichés* that complicate simple ideas by clothing them in well-worn metaphors. Verbose statements may be composed for humorous effect; in the passage:

Certain compensating qualities of the very greatest military value were appearing in Mr. Polly.

really means:

Mr. Polly was developing a useful strategy.

Make up similar simplified and shortened versions of the following two examples:

An observer . . . might have formed an altogether erroneous estimate of the issue of the campaign.

With a mind now stimulated to an almost incredible nimbleness.

45

(a) In *David Copperfield,* Charles Dickens has created in Mr. Micawber a pompous character who delights in verbosity. When Dickens writes:

"It was at Canterbury where we last met. Within the shadow, I may figuratively say, of that religious edifice, immortalised by Chaucer, which was anciently the resort of pilgrims from the remotest corners of—in short," said Mr. Micawber, "in the immediate neighbourhood of the cathedral."

He might have made Mr. Micawber say:

"We last met near the Cathedral in Canterbury."

Make up shorter, simpler versions of the following two further examples of Mr. Micawber's style of conversation and letter-writing, remembering that Mr. Micawber was frequently in serious debt.

(i) "I am at present, my dear Copperfield, engaged in the sale of corn upon commission. It is not an avocation of a remunerative description—in other words, it does *not* pay—and some temporary embarrassments of a pecuniary nature have been the consequence."

(ii) "The present communication is penned within the personal range (I cannot call it the society) of an individual, in a state closely bordering on intoxication, employed by a broker. That individual is in legal possession of the premises, under a distress for rent. His inventory includes, not only the chattels and effects of every description belonging to the undersigned, as yearly tenant of this habitation, but also those appertaining to Mr. Thomas Traddles, lodger, a member of the Honourable Society of the Inner Temple."

(b) It can be amusing and instructive to take a piece of plain and bold writing from the past and modernise it into the worst kind of modern verbosity. The following is such a paraphrase of two verses in the Authorised Version of the *Old Testament*:

It is not to be doubted that for every particular process there is a particular time of year that is appropriate, and that certain times are better suited to various activities, in the course of events here on the terrestrial globe, than are others. There is, for example, a suitable gestation period culminating in parturition, and timely decease should occur in the ripeness of senility. Moreover, there are certain suitable seasons for the germination of fertile seed, and one should make a clear distinction between these and the appropriate times of year for reaping the benefits of agricultural skills.

Before turning to Ecclesiastes, I, verses 1–2, make up your own shortened and simplified version of this passage.

Try writing your own verbose versions of some familiar verses from the Authorised Version of *The Bible*.

Exercise 3. We have already seen in Books Two and Three that certain parts of verbs, especially *present participles,* can in fact act as adjectives. *Present* and *past participles* are often called NON-FINITE parts of the verb, because a *finite verb* is one defined or limited by a particular subject, and therefore it is in the first or second or third person, singular or plural, and past, present, future or conditional tense. Non-finite parts of the verb are not so limited. When Uncle Jim "darted forward with *clutching* hands", it makes no difference whether the hands are clutching or will be clutching—"clutching" is not acting as a verb, but as an adjective, describing hands. Yet it remains a verb in so far as it can be modified by an adverb (or adverb phrase) and take an object:

   . . . with hands grimly clutching an ugly bottle.

Present participles always end in *-ing*; past participles usually end in *-ed* or *-t,* and are the parts of verbs used with "have" in forming perfect tenses:

   e.g. "improvised" in:

   He seized a bottle . . . as an improvised club.

In the following examples from the passage, state which word is a non-finite part of the verb, whether it is a present or past participle, what noun (or pronoun) it is describing, and note any adverb or objects that may still be attached to the non-finite part of the verb.

(a) Uncle Jim stopped, amazed.

(b) Uncle Jim stood swaying with wrathful astonishment.

(c) Uncle Jim staggered, half stunned by the blow, and blinded with beer. (2)

(d) Before him was Uncle Jim, infuriated and evidently still coming on. (2)

(e) Bleeding but indomitable, Uncle Jim entered the house.

(f) "Bolls!" he said, surveying the bar.

(g) He ranged among the bottled beer.

(h) So prepared, he went forth again to destroy Mr. Polly.

(i) A careless observer, watching him spring round and round the inn in front of the lumbering and reproachful pursuit of Uncle Jim, might have formed an altogether erroneous estimate. . . . (2)

Topics for Written Work

1. Choose a fight or struggle, on a limited scale, that you can describe in a detached and possibly humorous (mock heroic) way. Avoid any incident in which you were personally involved, or one that you have very strong feelings (of anger or shame or satisfaction) about. Describe two children fighting or a drunken brawl, or a public quarrel between husband and wife or between neighbours that are inveterate enemies. Alternatively, turn to the animal world and record a contest between any two creatures struggling for supremacy, or where one is hunting down another.

If you decide to use a mock heroic style with exaggerated language, then some verbosity will be appropriate, but when writing seriously you should aim to use plain words, lively comparisons, and an interesting variety of sentence constructions.

One possible subject for description could be the next encounter between Mr. Polly and Uncle Jim—the second of the "three chief campaigns". If you have not already read the book, study the characters and behaviour of the two contestants and imagine what might have been the course of their next battle.

2. According to two psychologists, Dr. Peter Watson and Dr. Sheila Jones, who have done research in the matter, English

48

does not lend itself to explaining complex regulations, even without redundancy, circumlocution and verbose vocabulary. They give the following example from regulations about retirement pensions for married women—which do you find easier to understand, (a) or (b)?

(a) "The earliest age at which a woman can draw a retirement pension is sixty. On her own insurance she can get a pension when she reaches that age, if she has then retired from regular employment. Otherwise she has to wait until she retires or reaches age sixty-five. At age sixty-five pension can be paid irrespective of retirement. On her husband's insurance, however, she cannot get a pension, even though she is over sixty, until he has reached the age sixty-five and retired from regular employment, or until he is seventy if he does not retire before reaching that age."

(b)

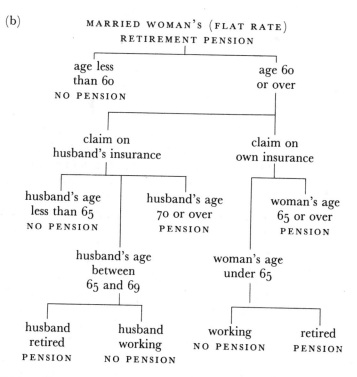

MARRIED WOMAN'S (FLAT RATE)
RETIREMENT PENSION

age less than 60
NO PENSION

age 60 or over

claim on husband's insurance

claim on own insurance

husband's age less than 65
NO PENSION

husband's age 70 or over
PENSION

woman's age 65 or over
PENSION

husband's age between 65 and 69

woman's age under 65

husband retired
PENSION

husband working
NO PENSION

working
NO PENSION

retired
PENSION

Either: Try to rewrite (a) so that the information in (b) is given clearly and simply and so that it can be understood without the help of the diagram,

Or: put the instructions given in the following diagram into the form of continuous writing. Try to make them clear without using headings or numbering points:

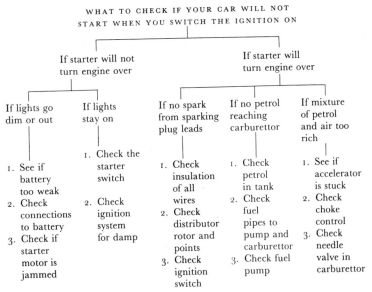

WHAT TO CHECK IF YOUR CAR WILL NOT
START WHEN YOU SWITCH THE IGNITION ON

If starter will not turn engine over		If starter will turn engine over		
If lights go dim or out	If lights stay on	If no spark from sparking plug leads	If no petrol reaching carburettor	If mixture of petrol and air too rich
1. See if battery too weak 2. Check connections to battery 3. Check if starter motor is jammed	1. Check the starter switch 2. Check ignition system for damp	1. Check insulation of all wires 2. Check distributor rotor and points 3. Check ignition switch	1. Check petrol in tank 2. Check fuel pipes to pump and carburettor 3. Check fuel pump	1. See if accelerator is stuck 2. Check choke control 3. Check needle valve in carburettor

Oral Work

1. Imagine you are a radio reporter arriving at the Potwell Inn just after the incident described in this extract from *The History of Mr. Polly*. Three volunteers act the parts of Mr. Polly, Uncle Jim and his aunt, the landlady, and you interview them about what happened, and the rights and wrongs of the case. This will be even more interesting if a tape-recording can in fact be made, and subsequently played back for class comment. It may also help to find out a little more about the three characters from the novel, although there is in fact a lot of information either stated or implied in the extract.

2. A similar series of radio interviews could be made using the conflict in the previous extract, from *The Day of the Triffids*, where the spokesman for Coker and his blind followers and for the sighted people at the University could be asked to justify themselves, and comment on the situation.

Tape-recorded interviews of this kind might suggest an interesting field of study of the techniques used by radio and television interviewers in probing and prompting in order to obtain lively and controversial comments on events.

Activities and Research

1. The life, work, ideas and novels of H. G. Wells would make excellent material for research. What kind of man was he? What was his philosophy of life? How many of his ideas have already been proved prophetic? What accounts for his continued popularity as a writer of science-fiction, and of other novels?

2. Find out something about the basic language and technique of simple film-making, and try to work out how you would film the story of Mr. Polly's encounter with Uncle Jim, shot by shot. Reckon a shot to be any continuous period with your cine-camera running, whether you are moving it to take in different views, or not. Ignore the further alterations and refinements that you could introduce in later editing and write down what you will do with the camera for each shot. Take into account these possible variables:

Distance: The camera can take close-ups, and medium, long, or distance shots.
Position: You can take a front or side view, etc.
Angle: You can shoot from above, below, etc.
Movement: In one shot you can "pan" from side to side, tilt up and down, and track (or zoom) in closer, or out.

Try to decide how many shots you need to tell the story effectively, and how much the actors and the camera-man will do during each shot. Assume it is to be a silent film.

You might start like this:

(1) General long shot of Potwell Inn from outside, with sign and front garden.
(2) Close up of sign: "POTWELL INN, teas with Hovis".
(3) Pan-shot round interior of bar-parlour: the landlady (fat and jolly) knitting in chair by windows, Mr. Polly drying glasses by bar, frosted glass in front door window.
(4) Medium shot of Uncle Jim (big, ill-kempt, hands in pockets, whistling) approaching front door down garden path.
(5) Rear medium shot of Mr. Polly peering through frosted glass (beer-glass and cloth in hand), from inside parlour. Uncle Jim as silhouette through glass.

Discuss the resulting "scenarios" when different members (or groups) of the class have completed their suggestions.

The History of Mr. Polly by H. G. WELLS (Collins; Longmans; Pan)

Mr Polly drifted through life from one mistake to another. He was ill-suited to become a draper's assistant and ill-equipped to resist the attractive dream of married life with his cousin Miriam and a shop of his own. Faced with bankruptcy, a nagging wife and permanent indigestion, he finally learns that, if you do not like your life, it is never too late to change it.

Tono-Bungay and *Kipps* by H. G. WELLS (Collins; Longmans)

George Ponderevo and Arthur Kipps also begin life as un-educated young men with no prospects. George, however, leaves the fashionable country house where his mother is in service to be apprenticed to his chemist uncle, who is marketing a patent medicine called "Tono-Bungay", worthless but skil-fully advertised. Kipps unexpectedly inherits £1,200 a year and finds that it brings more problems than comforts to live in a style for which you have not been educated.

Selected Short Stories by H. G. WELLS (Penguin)

This collection includes some of the author's best science fiction, such as *The Time Machine* and *The New Accelerator*, in which Professor Gibberne accidentally discovers a super stimulant that increases the speed of life so greatly that the users become invisible to ordinary people. It also includes imaginary travellers' tales like *The Country of the Blind*, in which a lost wanderer stumbles on a remote valley where everyone has been blind for many generations, and he finds his own sight is not an advantage after all. All the stories reflect the author's skill and command of detail, and many his sense of humour too.

CHAPTER FOUR

Time Stood Still

This story reflects very clearly the author's experiences in the Fire Service during the London blitzes.

It was our third job that night.

Until this thing happened, work had been without incident. There had been shrapnel, a few enquiring bombs, and some huge fires; but these were unremarkable and have since merged without identity into the neutral maze of fire and noise and water and night, without date and without hour, with neither time nor form, that lowers mistily at the back of my mind as a picture of the air-raid season.

I suppose we were worn down and shivering. Three a.m. is a mean-spirited hour. I suppose we were drenched, with the cold hose water trickling in at our collars and settling down at the tails of our shirts. Without doubt the heavy brass couplings felt moulded from metal-ice. Probably the open roar of the pumps drowned the petulant buzz of the raiders above, and certainly the ubiquitous fire-glow made an orange stage-set of the streets. Black water would have puddled the City alleys and I suppose our hands and our faces were black as the water. Black with hacking about among the burnt up rafters. These things were an every-night nonentity. They happened and they were not forgotten because they were never even remembered.

But I do remember it was our third job. And there we were —Len, Lofty, Verno and myself, playing a fifty-foot jet up the face of a tall city warehouse and thinking of nothing at all. You don't think of anything after the first few hours. You just watch the white pole of water lose itself in the fire and you think of nothing. Sometimes you move the jet over to another window. Sometimes the orange dims to black—but you only ease your grip on the ice-cold nozzle and continue pouring careless gallons through the window. You know the fire will fester for hours yet. However, that night the blank, indefinite hours of waiting were sharply interrupted—by an unusual sound. Very suddenly a long rattling crack of bursting brick and mortar perforated the moment. And then the upper half of that five-storey building heaved over towards us. It hung there, poised for a timeless second before rumbling down at us. I was thinking of nothing at all and then I was thinking of everything in the world.

In that simple second my brain digested every detail of the scene. New eyes opened at the sides of my head so that, from within, I photographed a hemispherical panorama bounded by the huge length of the building in front of me and the narrow lane on either side.

Blocking us on the left was the squat trailer pump, roaring and quivering with effort. Water throbbed from its overflow valves and from leakages in the hose and couplings. A ceaseless stream spewed down its grey sides into the gutter. But nevertheless a fat iron exhaust pipe glowed red-hot in the middle of the wet engine. I had to look past Lofty's face. Lofty was staring at the controls, hands tucked into his armpits for warmth. Lofty was thinking of nothing. He had a black diamond of soot over one eye, like the White-eyed Kaffir in negative.

To the other side of me was a free run up the alley. Overhead swung a sign—"Catto and Henley". I wondered what in hell they sold. Old stamps? The alley was quite free. A couple of lengths of dead, deflated hose wound over the darkly glistening pavement. Charred flotsam dammed up one of the gutters. A needle of water fountained from a hole in a live hoselength. Beneath a blue shelter light lay a shattered coping stone. The next shop along was a tobacconist's, windowless, with fake display cartons torn open for anybody to see. The alley was quite free.

Behind me, Len and Verno shared the weight of the hose. They heaved up against the strong backward drag of water-pressure. All I had to do was yell "Drop it"—and then run. We could risk the live hosing snaking up at us. We could run to the right down the free alley—Len, Verno and me. But I never moved. I never said "Drop it" or anything else. That long second held me hypnotised, rubber boots cemented to the pavement. Ton upon ton of red-hot brick hovering in the air above us numbed all initiative. I could only think. I couldn't move.

Six yards in front stood the blazing building. A minute before I would never have distinguished it from any other drab

54

Victorian atrocity happily on fire. Now I was immediately
certain of every minute detail. The building was five storeys
high. The top four storeys were fiercely alight. The rooms inside
were alive with red fire. The black outside walls remained
untouched. And thus, like the lighted carriages of a night

express, there appeared alternating rectangles of black and red that emphasised vividly the extreme symmetry of the window spacing: each oblong window shape posed as a vermilion panel set in perfect order upon the dark face of the wall. . . .

Three of the storeys, thirty blazing windows and their huge frame of black brick, a hundred solid tons of hard, deep Victorian wall, pivoted over towards us and hung flatly over the alley. Whether the descending wall actually paused in its fall I can never know. Probably it never did. Probably it only seemed to hang there. Probably my eyes digested its action at an early period of momentum, so that I saw it "off true" but before it had gathered speed. . . .

The second was timeless. I had leisure to remark many things. For instance, that an iron derrick, slightly to the left, would not hit me. This derrick stuck out from the building and I could feel its sharpness and hardness as clearly as if I had run my body intimately over its contour. I had time to notice that it carried a footlong hook, a chain with three-inch rings, two girder supports, and a wheel more than twice as large as my head.

A wall will fall in many ways. It may sway over to the one side or the other. It may crumble at the very beginning of its fall. It may remain intact and fall flat. This wall fell as flat as a pancake. It clung to its shape through ninety degrees to the horizontal. Then it detached itself from the pivot and slammed down on top of us.

The last resistance of bricks and mortar at the pivot point cracked off like automatic gun fire. The violent sound both deafened us and brought us to our senses. We dropped the hose and crouched. Afterwards Verno said that I knelt slowly on one knee with bowed head, like a man about to be knighted. Well, I got my knighting. There was an incredible noise—a thunderclap condensed into the space of an eardrum—and then the bricks and the mortar came tearing and burning into the flesh of my face.

Lofty, away by the pump, was killed. Len, Verno and myself they dug out. There was very little brick on top of us. We had been lucky. We had been framed by one of those symmetrical, oblong window spaces.

(from *The Wall* from *Fireman Flower* by William Sansom)

Appreciation and Discussion

1. Pick out the words and phrases that suggest this was a war-time air-raid fire, rather than a peace-time one.
2. Is there any indication here of which city this happened in?
3. How many men formed this team of fire-men and what was the job of each?
4. What state of mind was the author in before the wall began to fall?
5. Describe the area they were working in, as far as you can from this passage. What was to the right and left of them? What kind of building was on fire?
6. What effect did the falling wall have on the author (a) physically, and (b) mentally?
7. What dangers would there have been for the author and his companions if they had run for it?
8. What finally made the men react to their danger?
9. What prevented the author and two of his companions from being killed? Were they entirely unscathed?
10. How much does the author emphasise the clear alley to one side, and why?
11. Discuss and explain the meaning and effectiveness of:
    shrapnel; enquiring bombs; the neutral maze; lowers mistily; the petulant buzz of the raiders; a mean-spirited hour; the ubiquitous fire-glow; an every-night nonentity; the white-eyed kaffir in negative; deflated hose; charred flotsam; numbed all initiative; drab Victorian atrocity; extreme symmetry.
12. Try to explain what the author means by "Probably my eyes digested its actions at an early period of momentum, so that I saw it 'off true' but before it had gathered speed."
13. Why does the author begin several sentences in the second paragraph with "I suppose . . ." and "Probably . . ."?
14. Apart from particular dangers from falling or burning debris, what discomforts or strains did the firemen normally suffer when fire-fighting at night, according to this passage?
15. Discuss the author's choice of interesting or figurative verbs: e.g. black water would have puddled the City alleys; the orange dims to black; the fire will fester for hours; heaved over towards us; poised for a timeless second; water throbbed; a ceaseless stream spewed; etc.
    List others that seem vivid or unusual.

Good Taste

Travelling, a man met a tiger, so . . .
He ran. The tiger ran after him
Thinking: How fast I run . . . But

The road thought: How long I am . . . Then,
They came to a cliff, yes. The man
Grabbed at an ash root and swung down

Over its edge. Above his knuckles, the tiger.
At the foot of the cliff, its mate. Two mice,
One black, one white, began to gnaw the root.

And by the traveller's head grew one
Juicy strawberry, so . . . hugging the root
The man reached out and plucked the fruit.

How sweet it tasted!

CHRISTOPHER LOGUE

Discussing the Poem

1. What qualities and details in this poem remind you of a fable, or a fairy story?
2. How would the poem be altered, in meaning or effect, if it were not arranged in these lines, but simply followed the punctuation and was printed like prose? Read it aloud by lines and then by the punctuation only. What words and phrases carry extra emphasis in the verse lines?
3. *Are* pleasures snatched in the face of disaster or tragedy sweeter? Compare this idea with William Sansom's experience of heightened sensibility (in the prose extract): is there a connection?
4. If this poem is rather like a fable, then has it some sort of "moral" or message? Does "good taste" have anything to do with appreciating life and beauty even in a world overshadowed by the threat of death?

Techniques

Exercise 1. What is the difference between *simile, metaphor* and *personification?* Find an example of each in the passage.

To create interesting and striking comparisons, we need to use unlike objects, and show how they are comparable in particular respects. For instance, how is a helicopter like a dragon-fly? Clearly they are very different in many ways, but they are very similar in shape, if not size. Both hover and move in a similar way; the position and speed of the helicopter's blades are similar to those of a dragon-fly's wings; and the wheels or skids of the helicopter are comparable with the insect's legs.

(a) Explain the following possible comparisons:
  (i) Why is a torpedo like a porpoise?
  (ii) How can clouds be like mountains?
  (iii) When is the moon like a ship?
  (iv) Why is a ship like a bird?
  (v) Why is a fountain like a willow tree?
  (vi) How are pylons like giants?
  (vii) Why are wintry woods like a ruined church?
  (viii) How is a blast furnace like hell?
  (ix) Why is a gossip like a hen?
  (x) How is a cathedral like a cave?

(b) Take the following comparisons from the passage and find as many points of comparison as you can. Begin by stating whether each is a metaphor or a simile:

 e.g. The ubiquitous fire-glow made an orange stage-set of the streets.

  In this metaphor the effect of light from the fire is compared with that of orange stage-lights on scenery. The comparison suggests that the nearby buildings seemed unreal, like painted scenery, and that the glow was complete, like overall stage-lighting.

 (i) You just watch the white pole of water lose itself in the fire.

 (ii) A long rattling crack of bursting brick and mortar perforated the moment.

 (iii) From within, I photographed a hemispherical panorama.

 (iv) A needle of water fountained from a hole in a live hose-length.

 (v) We could risk the live hosing snaking up at us.

 (vi) Thus, like the lighted carriages of a night express, there appeared alternating rectangles of black and red.

 (vii) The last resistance of bricks and mortar at the pivot point cracked off like automatic gunfire.

 (viii) A thunderclap condensed into the space of an eardrum.

Exercise 2. When we aim to save words and write concisely, clauses can often be reduced to phrases, and phrases can often be reduced to single words of equivalent meaning:

 Cold water *which was blown back from the hose* was trickling into our collars.

 Cold water *from the hose* was trickling into our collars.

 Cold *hose* water was trickling into our collars.

(a) Make shorter versions of the following sentences, recasting them so as to save words, and then compare them with the sentences in the second paragraph of the passage on which they are based:

 (i) There is no doubt at all that the couplings, which were made of brass and were very heavy, felt to us as if they had been moulded out of metal that was as cold as ice.

 (ii) Water that looked unusually black would have been forming puddles in the narrow passage-ways of the City, and I would now suppose that both our hands and also our faces were as black as the water in the puddles looked.

 (iii) Things such as these were so unimportant as to be considered non-existent, and occurred every single night.

(b) By recasting sentences to save words, as well as cutting out repetition and redundancy, rewrite the following passage in about 75 words, instead of 180. Put in brackets at the end the exact number of words you have used.

In what was an experiment of considerable interest which was conducted by some psychologists, they gave a man a pair of spectacles which made everything appear to be inverted or upside down, and these the man wore for a period of fourteen days and nights. For the first part of the time, the man who was wearing the spectacles was not able to walk without someone to help him; and, when he tried at this stage to do some fencing, he would lift the weapon he was using up, when he should have been lowering it down, if he was going to defend himself. But, by slow and gradual degrees, his brain did learn slowly to see everything in the world around him the right way up. So the result was that, in the end, when the psychologists who were conducting the experiment removed the man's spectacles, for the first little while he had the feeling that the world was once more inverted, so that everything seemed to be upside down again, as it did when he first wore the spectacles.

Précis Rule 2. RECASTING SENTENCES:
Wherever possible, sentences must be simplified so that phrases do the work of clauses, and single words replace phrases.

Exercise 3. One of the difficulties about English spelling is the number of ways of spelling the same sound. Consider
> go, low, though, foe, sew, oh;
> crews, dues, boos, bruise, lose, fuse.

Similarly, the same letters may represent very different sounds, consider -gh in:
> trough, though, lough, ghoul, leghorn, thought.

Make other lists of examples like these.
(a) But to fix one spelling for one sound has its own problems. If you chose the sign -x for -cks, -cs, -ks and -x, then you would have
> clock—plural: clox
> antic—plural: antix
> mark—plural: marx

and: I pick, you pick, he pix.
Clearly there is some advantage in having a spelling related to the root word. All the words overleaf (which appear in the passage either in singular or in plural form) have the same sound to form their plural—how is this spelt in each case?

maze	warehouse	hose	express
alley	storey	atrocity	body
city	leakage	carriage	sense

(b) Each of the following words requires a plural ending, -es, -ies or -eys. Complete them correctly:

e.g. hors*es*, pon*ies*, donk*eys*.

marriag-	breez-	experienc-	anemon-
apolog-	apostroph-	appearanc-	gull-
spong-	merc-	emergenc-	pull-
antholog-	purs-	currenc-	gall-
strateg-	fanc-	parenthes-	bull-
berr-	attendanc-	tenanc-	monopol-
dais-	tendenc-	regenc-	
phras-	fallac-	enem-	

What spelling rules can be deduced from the formation of these plurals?

Topics for Written Work

1. Remember or imagine any moment of horror or tension when time seemed to "stand still". Make this, like William Sansom's piece, more a description of vivid details than a narrative of events leading up to or following the climax. The secret of this kind of writing is in the selection of detail and your choice of words and comparisons to describe them. Imagine the situation as clearly as you can and try to find exactly the right verb or adjective to convey this picture. Sometimes the details that stick in the memory are seemingly irrelevant (like the fake display cartons in the windowless tobacconist's in the alley)—but they form an important part of the picture you want to convey.

As an alternative to the moment of horror, you could take a period of quite careless happiness, when time seemed to stand still because you were so completely relaxed and unhurried and far away from pressing engagements or worries about the future.

2. Write a poem or a short vivid description about any kind of fire, from a large-scale forest or factory blaze to a few flames dancing in a domestic grate or a small camp fire. Flames and heat always transform the appearance of things in an interesting way; try in your poem to convey the unusual shapes, colours, sounds and smells, or to let your imagination carry you into a world of fire fantasy, seeing what exotic visions you can find in the flames.

1. Prepare an illustrated talk on the Great Fire of London and other large-scale blazes, including the London Blitz. Look particularly at *Pepys' Diary* for an eye-witness account of the Great Fire of 1666. The entries for September 2nd to 7th are particularly relevant, and another fire in Whitehall is mentioned under November 9th as well. Study also the entries for September 2nd to 7th, 1666, in John Evelyn's *Diary* (first published in 1918).

An alternative to a talk illustrated by readings would be an imaginary eye-witness radio commentary, perhaps with interviews with people involved or made homeless. This could be given straight to the class, or tape-recorded so that it could be carefully prepared in advance, perhaps with background sound effects.

Activities and Research

In Chapter Three we saw that a film "scenario" has to break down a story or incident into a series of single shots. Many simple stories can in fact be very effectively told by a series of *still* pictures. Discuss how the incident of the falling wall could be so told. Study the sequence of photographs on page 64. If members of the class can lend, or borrow from the school, some simple box cameras loaded with some black-and-white film, then a group or groups could go outside and demonstrate this very easily. Take a simple incident that might occur in any school playground—a quarrel, an accident in which something will be broken, a short chase or the scoring of a goal in any playground game, or something being lost and recovered. Think out in advance how many shots will be required to explain the situation and characters involved, and to develop the story to its climax and final solution. See if it is possible to keep the number of shots to those on one short reel of film, e.g. 12.

The resulting series of developed and printed photographs can be mounted in order, with a title and perhaps some very brief captions to accompany them. Alternatively, if a film camera is available, groups can try the further experiment of filming each still photograph for a second or two, in their logical order. The resulting cine-film may prove surprisingly effective. Watch for this device (filming of still photos or drawings) as used on television or in professionally made films.

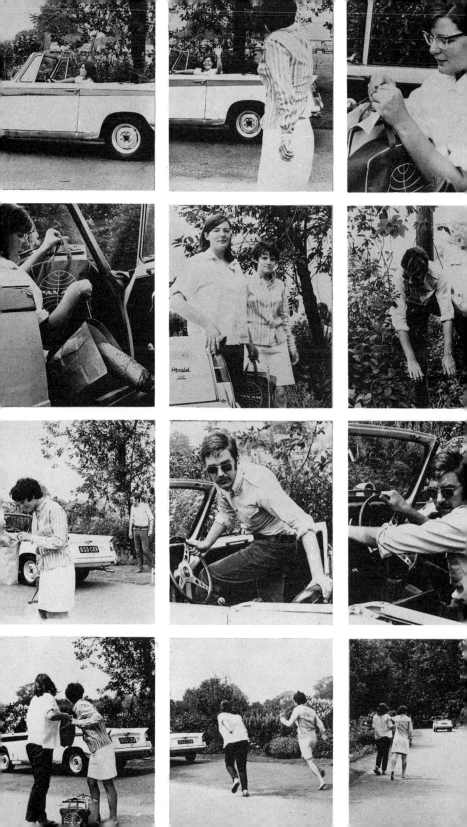

The Wall from *Fireman Flower* by WILLIAM SANSOM (Hogarth Press; Chatto & Windus)

The Wall is one of William Sansom's best known pieces and has been translated into several languages. During the Second World War, Sansom served as a London fireman, and he later insisted that "the Blitz taught me to write seriously. It impelled me to write down what I really thought rather than what I imagined people wanted." *Fireman Flower* was, in fact, the first of his books to be published; it contains "realistic" stories, such as the one printed in this chapter, modern fables, and pure fantasies.

The Stories of William Sansom (Hogarth Press)

For this collection William Sansom has drawn upon eight previous volumes of his stories and selected thirty-three of the best, including *The Wall*. Although you may find many of the stories rather difficult at this stage, there is a wide range to choose from—humour (*Three Dogs of Siena*, and *A Contest of Ladies*), terror (*How Claeys Died*), what Elizabeth Bowen in her introduction describes as "hallucination stories", (*A Saving Grace*), and, of course, a wealth of scenic description. Sansom is an outstanding short-story writer and it is certainly worthwhile searching through this collection for stories that appeal to you.

He has also written travel books, two children's stories, and a number of novels, one of the most recent of which is:

The Last Hours of Sandra Lee (Hogarth Press)

A light-hearted but searching comedy about office life and "the relationship of man and object".

The Small Back Room by NIGEL BALCHIN (Collins; Hutchinson)

This novel is also set on the "home front" of the Second World War. The hero is a clever young man hampered by physical deformity. His life at work with the "back room scientists", and at home with Susan, who he feels is too attractive to be completely his, is full of tension and difficulty. In a powerful climax to the story, he tries to prove himself by rendering a new and deadly kind of German booby-trap harmless, single handed.

CHAPTER FIVE

Conflict

The action of the play takes place in the Malayan jungle early in 1942. A British patrol, cut off by the Japanese advance on Singapore, has taken shelter in a deserted store-hut. Shortly after arriving there, they capture a Japanese soldier.

CAST :   *Sgt. Mitchem*   *Pte. Evans*
         Cpl. Johnstone   *Pte. Bamforth*
         L/Cpl. Macleish   *A Japanese Soldier*

(*Mitchem, Macleish, and Johnstone turn and look at the Prisoner.*)

EVANS (*crossing to join the group*) : What's the matter, Jock? What's happened?

MACLEISH : It's him. It's bright boy there. He's carrying a load of British issue fags.

EVANS : How did he get hold of them?

JOHNSTONE : How do you think? You can have three guesses. The thieving Nip!

MITCHEM (*drops the cigarette and grinds it beneath his heel*) : If there's one thing gets my hump it's knocking off—it's looting.

JOHNSTONE (*holding out the cigarette to Macleish*) : Well, come on, Jock, you'd better finish it. You're the one he gave it to. You reckon you're his mate.

MACLEISH (*snatching the cigarette*) : I'll ram it down his rotten throat! I'll make him eat the rotten thing! (*He hesitates—for a moment we feel that he is about to carry out the threat—he hurls the cigarette across the room.*)

JOHNSTONE : You don't want to waste it, Jock. Not now you've started it. You never know how much that fag has cost. He's happen stuck his bayonet end in some poor Herb for that.

EVANS : There's some of them would kill their mothers for a drag.

MITCHEM (*to Macleish*) : And you were telling me how they treat P.O.W.s.

EVANS : He wants a lesson, Sarge. He ought to have a lesson taught to him.

MACLEISH : I'll kill him!

MITCHEM: Will you! You swop sides quick. (*There is a pause as they turn to look at the Prisoner, who, uncertain of their attitude towards him, picks up the case, opens it, and offers a cigarette to Mitchem.*) Stick 'em! (*Mitchem strikes the case from the Prisoner's hand. The Prisoner raises his hands and places them on his head— on this occasion, however, the action is without humour.*) Thieving slob!

JOHNSTONE (*raising a fist*): Who goes in first?

MITCHEM: Hold it.

JOHNSTONE (*advancing threateningly on the Prisoner*): Who gets first crack?

MITCHEM: Hold it a sec.

(*Johnstone checks himself.*)

MACLEISH (*almost to himself*): My brother's just nineteen. He's only been out here a couple of months. I haven't seen him since he docked. They whipped him straight up country. He's only just nineteen. (*A loud appeal to the patrol—as if in the hope of receiving a denial.*) For all I know he's dead!

MITCHEM: John—see'f he's lugging anything else he's lifted from our lads.

MACLEISH (*moving to the Prisoner*): Get up! Get on your feet! (*The Prisoner cowers on the form and Macleish jerks him savagely to his feet.*) Do as you're told! (*Macleish goes through the Prisoner's pocket and removes the wallet.*) There's this.

JOHNSTONE (*taking the wallet*): I'll have a look at what's in this. You carry on.

MACLEISH (*as the Prisoner reacts slightly at the loss of the wallet*): Stand still!

(*Macleish goes through the Prisoner's trouser pockets and removes the usual miscellaneous assortment of articles: handkerchief, keys, loose change, etc. Macleish places these on the form. Johnstone, slowly and carefully, tears the photographs into pieces and drops these and the wallet on the floor. The Prisoner starts forward and Macleish rises and strikes him across the face. Bamforth, who has just re-entered from the veranda, notices this incident.*)

MACLEISH: I said, stand still!

BAMFORTH: What's up? What's he done to ask for that?

EVANS: He's been looting, Bammo. From our lads.

BAMFORTH (*crossing to join the group around the Prisoner*): He's been what?

MACLEISH: We caught him with a fag-case stuffed with British army smokes!

67

BAMFORTH: You Scotch nit! You dim Scotch nit! I gave him them!

MITCHEM: You did?

BAMFORTH: I'm telling you. I gave him half a dozen snouts!

EVANS: You gave them him?

(*Macleish edges away from the Prisoner and Bamforth positions himself between the Prisoner and the members of the patrol.*)

BAMFORTH: What's the matter, Taff? Are your ears bad? I slipped him half a dozen nubs!

MACLEISH: I didn't know. I thought . . . I thought he'd knocked them off.

JOHNSTONE (*to Bamforth*): And who gave you permission?

BAMFORTH: I've had this out with you before. You show where it says I have to grease up to an N.C.O. before I hand out fags. What's mine's my own. I decide what I do with it.

MACLEISH: How was I to know? I . . . I've told you, boy, I thought he'd knocked them off.

BAMFORTH: You know what thought did.

MACLEISH (*searching for words*): How was I to know? . . . I mean, he gave one of them to me . . . I'd lit it up . . . I was having a drag . . . I was halfway down the lousy thing before I realized, you know—I mean, before I knew it was a Blighty fag . . . So how was I to feel? . . . What would you have done? . . . You tell me, Bammo . . . I could have choked, you know . . . I've got a brother who's up country.

BAMFORTH: If he's dropped in with a gang of Nips who think like you, God help the kiddie. God help him!

MACLEISH: I thought he'd looted them!

BAMFORTH: And so you pull the big brave hero bull. The raving highlander. Aren't you the boy? So what you waiting for? Well, come on Jocko, finish off the job! (*Bamforth grabs the Prisoner, pinning his arms, and swings him round, holding him towards Macleish.*) Come on, come on! Come on, he's waiting for the hump. Let's see you slot him, Jock! Drop him one on! Let's see you do your stuff! Smash his face for him! Drop him one on!

MACLEISH: Lay off it, Bamforth.

MITCHEM: O.K., Bamforth, jack it in.

BAMFORTH: Haven't any of you got the guts to go the bundle? You were snapping at the leash when I walked in. What about you, Taff? You want to have a crack at him?

MITCHEM: I said drop it.

68

BAMFORTH (*loosing his hold on the Prisoner*): I didn't start it. (*The Prisoner sits on form and returns the articles to his trouser pockets.*)

EVANS: It was a mistake, Bammo.

BAMFORTH: You bet it was.

EVANS: We thought he'd whipped them.

BAMFORTH (*stoops and picks up the wallet and a piece of the torn photographs*): You bastards. You even had to rip his pictures up. You couldn't leave him them even!

EVANS: I'll give you a hand to pick them up.

BAMFORTH: You couldn't even leave him them!

EVANS (*bends down and collects the torn pieces of the photographs*): Happen he can stick them together again, Bammo. Here's a bit with a head on it. He could stick them together, easy enough, with a pot of paste and a brush. . . .

MACLEISH (*picks up the cigarette case from the floor and gives it to Bamforth*): He's better have this back too. He'll . . . Maybe he'll be feeling in need of a smoke.

BAMFORTH: Yeh . . . Thanks, Jock. (*He crosses to return the cigarette case.*)

JOHNSTONE: Bamforth! Just a minute, lad.

BAMFORTH: Yeh?

JOHNSTONE: I'd like a look at that before you hand it on to him.

BAMFORTH: Ask him. Not me. It's his.

JOHNSTONE: He'll get it back. I only want it for a minute.

BAMFORTH (*hesitates, then crosses and hands the case to Johnstone*): He'd better get it back.

JOHNSTONE: He will. (*He inspects the case, slowly turning it over in his hands, then tosses it to Bamforth. Bamforth crosses to return it to the Prisoner.*) Bamforth!

BAMFORTH (*turns*): You want something else?

JOHNSTONE: No, lad. Nothing. I was just wondering, that's all.

BAMFORTH: Well?

JOHNSTONE: Are you feeling in a generous mood today?

BAMFORTH: What's that supposed to signify?

JOHNSTONE: Did you give him the case as well?

BAMFORTH: I gave him half a dozen fags, that's all. I haven't got a case myself to give away. I gave him half a dozen snouts, I've told you half a dozen times. The case belongs to him.

JOHNSTONE: Does it?

BAMFORTH: The case is his.

69

JOHNSTONE: That's interesting. You'd better have another shufti at it, then.

(*Bamforth inspects the case and is about to return it to the Prisoner.*)

MITCHEM: Pass it over, Bamforth.

BAMFORTH: What for? It's his.

MITCHEM: I'd like to once it over for myself.

BAMFORTH (*tosses the case to Mitchem, who also examines it, then turns his glance upon the Prisoner*): All right! So it's a British case!

JOHNSTONE: Made in Birmingham.

BAMFORTH: So what? What's that supposed to prove?

MITCHEM: So tell us now how he got hold of it.

BAMFORTH: I don't know. Don't ask me.

JOHNSTONE: I bloody do! The way he got the snouts.

BAMFORTH: I gave him the fags.

JOHNSTONE: So you say.

BAMFORTH: I gave him the fags!

MITCHEM: And what about the case?

BAMFORTH: Look—I don't know. I've told you—I don't know.

EVANS: So he has been on the lifting lark? Half-inching from the boys up country.

MACLEISH: It begins to look that way.

(*Macleish and Evans move menacingly towards the Prisoner.*)

(from *The Long and the Short and the Tall* by Willis Hall)

Appreciation and Discussion

1. What nick-names are used in this extract for Macleish, Bamforth, Evans and the Japanese?

2. Can you guess why Macleish had been telling Mitchem how well the Japanese treated prisoners of war?

3. Explain why Macleish's feelings about his brother alter his attitude to the prisoner. Does this explain his friendliness as well as his hostility?

4. What does Johnstone's remark about the way the prisoner got the cigarette case indicate about his attitude to the prisoner and to all the arguments about him?

5. In the rest of this play Johnstone appears as the most vicious and violent of the British party. What actions and words of his in this extract contribute to that impression?

6. Much of the conflict in this play is between Bamforth and Johnstone. Judging from this extract, can you explain why their personalities might clash?

7. Sergeant Mitchem carries responsibility for the patrol and for their prisoner. Does his responsibility affect his words and actions in this extract?

8. Would either Johnstone or Macleish have been justified in killing (or in beating up) the prisoner if he *had* stolen the cigarettes?

9. Is there any argument Bamforth could *now* use to defend the prisoner, when he definitely does possess a British cigarette case?

10. Examine Bamforth's use of *sarcasm*: give examples and discuss whether they are effective.

11. What kind of character is Evans? Notice his attitude when he first hears the prisoner has British cigarettes and later when he picks up the pieces of the photographs.

12. The stage direction about the prisoner placing his hands on his head suggests some earlier comedy about this. Remembering that he spoke no English, can you guess what the comedy was?

13. Study the construction of this scene. Immediately before this there has been talk of whether the prisoner may have to be killed for the patrol's security, and this suggestion has horrified Macleish. Then Bamforth wakes up and goes outside, while Macleish smokes a cigarette given him by the prisoner. Notice how the tension now rises and falls again, how violence nearly breaks out, and how periods of calm or sympathy are contrasted with those of intense passion.

14. This incident includes several examples of hasty or irrational judgements. How justified were Macleish, Johnstone and Bamforth in their attitudes to the prisoner? Did they have other motives or excuses for their attitudes, apart from reasonable evidence?

15. Since the prisoner might endanger their lives, whether they took him back, or whether they left him behind, would they be justified in killing him? How *should* prisoners of war be treated? Is it ever justifiable to treat them as criminals?

O What is that Sound

O what is that sound which so thrills the ear
   Down in the valley drumming, drumming?
Only the scarlet soldiers, dear,
   The soldiers coming.

O what is that light I see flashing so clear
   Over the distance brightly, brightly?
Only the sun on their weapons, dear,
   As they step lightly.

O what are they doing with all that gear,
   What are they doing this morning, this morning?
Only their usual manoeuvres, dear,
   Or perhaps a warning.

O why have they left the road down there,
   Why are they suddenly wheeling, wheeling?
Perhaps a change in their orders, dear.
   Why are you kneeling?

O haven't they stopped for the doctor's care,
   Haven't they reined their horses, their horses?
Why, they are none of them wounded, dear,
   None of these forces.

O is it the parson they want, with white hair,
  Is it the parson, is it, is it?
No, they are passing his gateway, dear,
  Without a visit.

O it must be the farmer who lives so near.
  It must be the farmer so cunning, so cunning?
They have passed the farmyard already, dear,
  And now they are running.

O where are you going? Stay with me here!
  Were the vows you swore deceiving, deceiving?
No, I promised to love you, dear,
  But I must be leaving.

O it's broken the lock and splintered the door,
  O it's the gate where they're turning, turning
Their boots are heavy on the floor
  And their eyes are burning.

W. H. AUDEN

Discussing the Poem

1. In this poem, there are apparently two speakers. Examine each verse to decide which speaker says which lines. Is the pattern invariably a question in the first half of the verse and a reply in the second half?
2. Who are the characters involved in this incident? Is it mainly a man and a woman, and if so, which is the "quarry" that the scarlet soldiers are hunting? What scene do you imagine as the setting for this conversation?
3. How is the sense of fear and tension built up? Is the *repetition* playing an important part in this? Examine the *rhyme*: what is different about the rhymes in the last verse?
4. Sometimes this poem is given the alternative title *Ballad*. Compare it with examples of the traditional ballad. Do you notice any differences? Examine particularly the last line of each verse, as compared with the normal last lines of quatrains in traditional "ballad metre".

Exercise 1. The extract from the play is naturally full of *slang* *colloquialisms*, *idiomatic* phrases and even *jargon*. What do you understand by each of these terms? Here are some examples from the extract:

> *slang*—fags; Nip; knocking off;
> *colloquialism*—I'll make him eat the rotten thing;
> *colloquial dialect*—He's happen stuck his bayonet . . . ;
> *idiom*—he wants a lesson;
> *jargon*—sarge; P.O.W.s.

These terms overlap, but it should be possible to explain the difference and to find one more example (at least) of each in the extract.

Generally, these categories of English are undesirable in formal written English. Why is this so? What are the obvious exceptions to this principle? Much English slang, apart from being incomprehensible to many people, has unfortunately close associations with blasphemous or rude ideas that many find distasteful. Even such common words as "blimey" and "bloody" were originally curses ("may God blind me" and "By our Lady"), and the latter has all the unpleasant associations of bleeding as well. The frequent use of slang is also often a sign of poverty of vocabulary, although not perhaps in the case of men like Bamforth!

(a) Take the following slang words and phrases from the extract and state briefly what you think each means, e.g.

> fags—cigarettes, fag-ends.
> Nip—Japanese (originally Nipponese)
> knocking off—stealing (also: ceasing work)

(i) gets my hump	(ix) nubs
(ii) a drag	(x) to grease up to
(iii) stick 'em	(xi) Blighty
(iv) slob	(xii) pull the . . . bull
(v) lugging	(xiii) drop him one on
(vi) has lifted	(xiv) guts
(vii) nit	(xv) to go the bundle.
(viii) snouts	

(b) Make a list of all the printable current slang words in common use among your contemporaries—the vocabulary peculiar to your age-group or your particular school or area.

Give an accurate translation, and (if you know it) an idea of the origin of the word. For example, the words "hep", "hep cat" and "hipster", which were common among teenagers in the early 1960's, meant "in the know, having good taste", or a follower of current trends in fashion; and they derive from the cry "hep!" which North American horse-drivers called to their teams; hence "to get hep" meant "to liven up".

Exercise 2. (a) In addition to writing complete and well-written summaries, it is useful to be able to make quick outline *notes* of the main points covered by a particular passage. These notes can be in the form used in part (b) of this exercise, and certainly do not need to be in complete sentences or in your own words.

Make notes on the following passage:

Primitive and barbarous tribes had no idea of giving special treatment to prisoners of war. When prisoners were captured in the kind of battles that were fought in pre-Roman times, and for many centuries later among smaller tribes and primitive peoples, they were either summarily slaughtered or permanently enslaved, and little distinction would be made between the fighting men and any women, children or other civilians who might be captured.

The Roman idea of conquest was more concerned with imposing law and order on the civilian population, and in the Roman Empire it was possible for captured enemies to become freedmen in the course of time, as well as for members of subject races to become Roman citizens. The practice in Mediaeval Western Europe was also sometimes quite humane, because the widespread habit of paying ransom money for the release of captives often made prisoners quite valuable and therefore worth preserving.

The Treaty of Westphalia in 1648 is often taken as marking the beginning of modern thinking about prisoners, because it allowed for the release of prisoners without ransom. During the seventeenth and eighteenth centuries civilised nations generally came to accept that humane treatment of enemy prisoners was not only right but also expedient, since it might mean that their own soldiers would be better treated if captured by the enemy.

The Geneva Conventions of 1864, 1906, 1929 and 1949 sought to regulate the treatment of prisoners by international agreement, and laid down that prisoners, although confined, should be treated generally as well as one's own soldiers, and returned home immediately hostilities were ended.

(b) Expand the following notes into two paragraphs of continuous writing (in complete sentences):

1929 Geneva Convention–all military prisoners covered–principles of treatment: 1. full information on prisoners taken; 2. sanitary quarters away from military zone; 3. sufficient, wholesome food; 4. medical attention; 5. pay on agreed scales; 6. free passage for letters and parcels; 7. non-officers given reasonable work of non-military kind;–1949 Convention extended definition–included volunteers, resistance fighters, civilians accompanying army or resisting invasion–forbad: reprisals, physical violence or insult, extorting information (exc. for name, date of birth, service no., rank) – punishments and discipline on same principles as for captors themselves.

Exercise 3. The passage from *The Long and the Short and the Tall* contains a number of *noun clauses*, although several of them are made difficult to isolate by having no introductory conjunction:

You reckon you're his mate.

This means that you reckon, or assume, *something*, and this "something" (object of the verb "reckon") is represented by the clause "you are his mate"—it could have been introduced by the conjunction "that", but this is not in fact necessary. The word *that* is "understood".

Others are introduced by the relative adverb "how":

You never know how much that fag has cost.

Here, too, *what* you will never know is represented by a clause, a noun clause object of the verb "will . . . know".

(a) Write out the noun clauses in the following sentences; most of them are objects of verbs in the main clauses, but one is the subject. State in each case what verb the clause is subject or object of:

(i) We feel that he is about to carry out his threat.
(ii) You were telling me how they treat P.O.W.s.
(iii) I thought he had knocked them off.
(iv) What is mine is my own.
(v) I decide what I do with it.
(vi) I thought he had looted them.
(vii) We thought he'd whipped them.
(viii) I have told you I don't know.

(b) In addition to the words "what", "that", and "how", and no introductory word (or "that" understood), noun clauses can be introduced by "why", "if", "whether", "which", "who", "when" and "where". These constructions are particularly common when following various verbs of telling,

e.g. He explained where the patrol were.

This means that he explained the information about their position—the "where" clause does not tell us where he did the explaining, and is therefore *not* an adverb clause of place.

Complete each of the following to include a noun clause. Make sure that you insert only enough to make *one* clause, with one subject and one verb. Underline your noun clause and state (in brackets) whether it is subject or object of the main verb.

(i) Bamforth told them all that . . .
(ii) What the . . . changed their minds about the prisoner.
(iii) The prisoner could not understand why . . .
(iv) The members of the patrol could not agree whether . . .
(v) Who should . . . was the really difficult question.
(vi) Mitchem alone decided when . . .
(vii) Evans just could not be sure if the prisoner . . .
(viii) Johnstone knew for certain which of them . . .

77

Topics for Written Work

1. Write a short play, or a critical scene from a play, in which some kind of conflict or argument comes to a head. Willis Hall's handling of plot is exceptional, but much of the interest in *The Long and the Short and the Tall* lies not so much in the situation and the sequence of events, as in the convincing variety of personalities he has portrayed. Even in the short extract we have used, Johnstone's vicious cruelty and Bamforth's fluent and aggressive championship of the "underdog" are very clear, and there are hints of the personalities of Macleish, a rather humourless character, and of Evans, who is easily swayed by every argument and wave of feeling. In creating your own drama, begin by deciding very firmly what kind of person each of the participants is to be, and try to suit every word and every action to that pattern.

The situation could be a much more homely and familiar one than Willis Hall's. A domestic scene, at a meal or round the television, for instance, or an argument in the street, at the department store or in the local laundrette. Any situation where people may "rub one another up the wrong way", and set loose a flood of angry talk, should be good potential drama.

2. Using the information that you will find in *Exercise* 2, together with the entry under PRISONERS OF WAR in the *Encyclopaedia Britannica*, similar entries in other encyclopaedias, and your general knowledge, write a short essay on the subject of the treatment of prisoners in war-time, in theory and practice.

Oral Work

This chapter should provide a number of opportunities for classroom drama or play-reading.

1. Act out the scene reproduced in the extract, working out an appropriate layout for the stage and any further stage-directions, etc., not given in the text. In fact, although they say nothing in our extract, two other privates, Whitaker (a nervous and immature man) and Smith (an older, quieter man than the others) are both present, on watch by the windows of the hut. If none of the cast know the full play it might be interesting to continue beyond the extract here, improvising the development of the situation further.

2. Many of the scenes or short plays written by members of the class should be suitable for class-room acting, or for tape-recording with suitable sound-effects. For this a group should choose a particular script and rehearse this for performance.

3. If copies of *The Long and the Short and the Tall* are available, a play-reading of it or of a much longer extract, will certainly prove stimulating.

Activities and Research

1. Find out what you can about the history of censorship of plays, and the position as it stands at the moment. Who is responsible for licensing plays, and what kinds of plays are refused permission? What kinds of performances can be given of unlicensed plays? A useful summary of the current procedure will be found in the *Writers and Artists Year Book* which will be found in most public libraries.

Compare censorship of plays with the regulations covering film "censorship" and the limitations on the free publication of books, etc. If possible, find out something about restrictions in other countries.

The Long and the Short and the Tall by WILLIS HALL (Evans; Heinemann; Penguin) (822.91)
As you will have gathered from the extract, this gripping play is concerned with the predicament of the British patrol, who cannot decide what they should do with their Japanese prisoner, with whom they become friendly but who still remains a source of danger, and who, when one of the patrol shoots him in a fit of panic, is finally the indirect cause of their discovery.

Journey's End by R. C. SHERRIFF (Heinemann) (822.08)
This play makes an obvious and interesting contrast with *The Long and the Short and the Tall*. It is set in the First World War, in the trenches at the European front, and has a cast of officers, not other ranks. There are interesting contrasts of attitudes and motives, too, partly due to the different periods of history, but also because the two playwrights had such different purposes in writing.

A Town Like Alice by NEVIL SHUTE (Heinemann; Pan)
The earlier part of this novel is the moving story of a group of European prisoners who are sent from place to place across the jungles of Malaya because the Japanese officers are reluctant to take responsibility for them. From this endurance test, Jean Paget emerges as a heroic and resourceful leader, and her qualities are applied after the war when she settles in Australia to help develop a town like Alice Springs.

Billy Liar by KEITH WATERHOUSE (Michael Joseph; Penguin)
Keith Waterhouse and Willis Hall have done much of their writing for film and television together, and they co-operated on the film script for this story. It has also been made into a play. Billy "Liar" Fisher tries to make up for the frustrations of his rather inadequate family and job by escaping into a dream-world, but his lies and fantasies complicate all his relationships, including those with three girls, all of whom expect him to marry them!

CHAPTER SIX

Modern Fables

The fable is a short story, frequently illustrating a moral. Those of the best known fabulist, Aesop of Ancient Greece, were usually of an instructive and serious nature, and this is how the Fable has generally come to be regarded. But these absurd and witty pieces by James Thurber show that the fable form can be used in quite a different way.

THE LITTLE GIRL AND THE WOLF

One afternoon a big wolf waited in a dark forest for a little girl to come along carrying a basket of food to her grandmother. Finally a little girl did come along and she was carrying a basket of food. "Are you carrying that basket to your grandmother?" asked the wolf. The little girl said yes, she was. So the wolf asked her where her grandmother lived and the little girl told him and he disappeared into the wood.

When the little girl opened the door of her grandmother's house she saw that there was somebody in bed with a nightcap and nightgown on. She had approached no nearer than twenty-five feet from the bed when she saw that it was not her grandmother but the wolf, for even in a nightcap a wolf does not look any more like your grandmother than the Metro-Goldwyn lion looks like Calvin Coolidge. So the little girl took an automatic out of her basket and shot the wolf dead.

MORAL: *It is not so easy to fool little girls nowadays as it used to be.*

THE GLASS IN THE FIELD

A short time ago some builders, working on a studio in Connecticut, left a huge square of plate glass standing upright in a field one day. A goldfinch flying swiftly across the field struck the glass and was knocked cold. When he came to he hastened to his club, where an attendant bandaged his head and gave him a stiff drink. "What the hell happened?" asked a sea gull. "I was flying across a meadow when all of a sudden the air crystallized on me," said the goldfinch. The sea gull, and a hawk, and an eagle all laughed heartily. A swallow listened gravely. "For fifteen years, fledgling and bird, I've flown this country," said the eagle, "and I assure you there is no such thing as air crystallizing. Water, yes; air, no." "You were probably struck by a hailstone," the hawk told the goldfinch. "Or he may have had a stroke," said the sea gull. "What do you think, swallow?" "Why, I—I think maybe the air crystallized on him," said the swallow. The large birds laughed so loudly that the goldfinch became annoyed and bet them each a dozen worms that they couldn't follow the course he had flown across the field without encountering the hardened atmosphere. They all took his bet; the swallow went along to watch. The sea gull, the eagle, and the hawk decided to fly together over the route the goldfinch indicated. "You come, too," they said to the swallow. "I—I—well, no," said the swallow. "I don't think I will." So the three large birds took off together and they hit the glass together and they were all knocked cold.

MORAL: *He who hesitates is sometimes saved.*

THE SHRIKE AND THE CHIPMUNKS

Once upon a time there were two chipmunks, a male and a female. The male chipmunk thought that arranging nuts in artistic patterns was more fun than just piling them up to see how many you could pile up. The female was all for piling up as many as you could. She told her husband that if he gave up making designs with the nuts there would be room in their large cave for a great many more and he would soon become the wealthiest chipmunk in the woods. But he would not let her interfere with his designs, so she flew into a rage and left him. "The shrike will get you," she said, "because you are helpless and cannot look after yourself." To be sure, the female chipmunk had not been gone three nights before the male had to dress for a banquet and could not find his studs or shirt or suspenders. So he couldn't go to the banquet, but that was just as well, because all the chipmunks who did go were attacked and killed by a weasel.

The next day the shrike began hanging around outside the chipmunk's cave, waiting to catch him. The shrike couldn't get in because the doorway was clogged up with soiled laundry and dirty dishes. "He will come out for a walk after breakfast and I will get him then," thought the shrike. But the chipmunk slept all day and did not get up and have breakfast until after dark. Then he came out for a breath of air before beginning work on a new design. The shrike swooped down to snatch up the chipmunk, but could not see very well on account of the dark, so he batted his head against an alder branch and was killed.

A few days later the female chipmunk returned and saw the awful mess the house was in. She went to the bed and shook her husband. "What would you do without me?" she demanded. "Just go on living, I guess," he said. "You wouldn't last five days," she told him. She swept the house and did the dishes and sent out the laundry, and then she made the chipmunk get up and wash and dress. "You can't be healthy if you lie in bed all day and never get any exercise," she told him. So she took him for a walk in the bright sunlight and they were both caught and killed by the shrike's brother, a shrike named Stoop.

MORAL: *Early to rise and early to bed makes a male healthy and wealthy and dead.*

THE BEAR WHO LET IT ALONE

In the woods of the Far West there once lived a brown bear who could take it or let it alone. He would go into a bar where they sold mead, a fermented drink made of honey, and he would have just two drinks. Then he would put some money on the bar and say, "See what the bears in the back room will have," and he would go home. But finally he took to drinking by himself most of the day. He would reel home at night, kick over the umbrella stand, knock down the bridge lamps, and ram his elbows through the windows. Then he would collapse on the floor and lie there until he went to sleep. His wife was greatly distressed and his children were very frightened.

At length the bear saw the error of his ways and began to reform. In the end he became a famous teetotaller and a persistent temperance lecturer. He would tell everybody that came to his house about the awful effects of drink, and he would boast about how strong and well he had become since he gave up touching the stuff. To demonstrate this, he would stand on his head and on his hands and he would turn cartwheels in the house, kicking over the umbrella stand, knocking down the bridge lamps, and ramming his elbows through the windows. Then he would lie down on the floor, tired by his healthful exercise, and go to sleep. His wife was greatly distressed and his children were very frightened.

MORAL: *You might as well fall flat on your face as lean over too far backward.*

(from *Vintage Thurber* by James Thurber)

83

Appreciation and Discussion

1. What is a *fable*? Discuss this form with some conventional examples (some of *Aesop's* fables, for example). Why did Thurber call his *Fables for our Time?*

2. What do you understand by the term *parody*? In writing parodies of fables, one can make fun of a well-known "moral", one can make up quite pointless morals, or one can make up a new moral embodying some useful piece of wisdom. Which is Thurber doing in each of these Fables?

3. What folk tale is *The Little Girl and the Wolf* based upon? Does the first paragraph generally accept the conventions of the children's story? Where does Thurber's humorous version begin to diverge from the original story?

4. Who or what are the Metro-Goldwyn lion and Calvin Coolidge? Are they appropriate in the context of a traditional fairy story?

5. How are human and animal characteristics and points of view comically mixed in *The Glass in the Field*? What kinds of human beings do these birds stand for?

6. What proverb is being parodied in this fable? Are there other traditional proverbs that in fact already embody this moral?

7. Discuss what you know about chipmunks. Is Thurber's choice of animals in *The Shrike and the Chipmunks* deliberate and significant?

8. What two human attitudes to life do the male and female chipmunk stand for?

9. What is a shrike and what kind of danger in life does it stand for in this fable?

10. What proverb is Thurber parodying in this moral? Is there indeed some other "lesson" to be learnt from this fable?

11. What was it that the bear could "take or leave alone" in our fourth fable? What does this saying normally mean?

12. How far is this story of the brown bear treating the characters as bears, and how far as human beings? Do you think Thurber is making fun of stories like *The Three Bears*, where the bears are completely human in their habits?

13. Express the moral of this fourth fable in your own words.

14. What is made of repetition in this last story?

15. Discuss Thurber's style in all these fables:
    (a) In what ways does he imitate the style of fairy stories
        or folk tales? (Consider stock phrases like "Once upon
        a time . . .", repetition, simple sentence structure,
        etc.).
    (b) Is there some contrast of child-like style with adult
        subject matter?
    (c) What elements of incongruity and anti-climax are
        there?
16. Are traditional fables, or these comic modern imitations
    of them, useful for impressing a truth upon an audience
    unwilling to accept it? If so, why?

From: *A New Song of New Similes*

Pert as a pear-monger I'd be,
   If Molly were but kind;
Cool as a cucumber could see
   The rest of womankind.

Like a stuck pig I gaping stare,
   And eye her o'er and o'er;
Lean as a rake with sighs and care,
   Sleek as a mouse before.

Plump as a partridge was I known,
   And soft as silk my skin,
My cheeks as fat as butter grown;
   But as a groat now thin!

I, melancholy as a cat,
   And kept awake to weep;
But she, insensible of that,
   Sound as a top can sleep.

Hard is her heart as flint or stone,
   She laughs to see me pale;
And merry as a grig is grown,
   And brisk as bottled ale.

85

The God of Love at her approach
   Is busy as a bee;
Hearts, sound as any bell or roach,
   Are smit and sigh like me.

Ay me! as thick as hops or hail,
   The fine men crowd about her;
But soon as dead as a door nail
   Shall I be, if without her.

JOHN GAY (1685–1732)

Discussing the Poem

1. Was this poem meant to be taken seriously? Is the title ironic?
2. Check that you understand any words or phrases that are no longer familiar:

        e.g. pert, pear-monger, a stuck pig.

   If you look up "grig" you will find that this simile is still in use.
3. These verses are packed with well-worn similes that have become *clichés*: make two lists, one of those that are still familiar, and the other of those similes that have passed out of fashion since Gay's time.
4. Try making up a short poem full of current *clichés*, especially similes and proverbs.

Techniques

Exercise 1. In the "morals" of these Fables, and particularly in the two based on well-known proverbs, Thurber is making fun of proverbial wisdom. Certainly proverbs are often trite over-simplifications, and often contradictory:

     Look before you leap.

     but: He who hesitates is lost.

Can you think of other examples of proverbs contradicting one another?

Proverbs and sayings, like many popular idioms and figurative expressions, are also liable to become *clichés*— characters like Joxer Daly in Sean O'Casey's play *Juno and the Paycock* show narrowness rather than breadth of imagination by producing a proverb to suit every opinion or every new turn of events.

You bring your long-tailed shovel, an' I'll bring me navvy. We mighten' want them, an', then agen, we might: for want of a nail the shoe was lost, for want of a shoe, the horse was lost, an' for want of a horse the man was lost—aw, that's a darlin' proverb, a daarlin' . . ."

a) List all the proverbs you can remember, or look up, in which the words "better" or "best" occur.

    e.g. Half a loaf is better than no bread.

        Make the best of a bad bargain.

Make sure that you understand their meanings and can give clear explanation of each.

Try making up one or two similar "proverbs" of your own.

b) There are twenty well-known proverbs in the following passage. Write each one out in its usual form, and give a simple explanation of it in non-figurative language:

    e.g. To be "like a dog in a manger" means to harm others out of spite, when it is no advantage to oneself.

THE DOG IN THE·MANGER

There were once two dogs who worked for an ass. Now as you know, when the cat's away, the mice will play, so, when the ass left his stable and was out of sight and out of mind, the younger dog went to sleep in his master's manger. When the ass began to find that it never rains but it pours and that enough was as good as a feast, he thought there was no place like home and decided to return to his stable. Now absence makes the heart grow fonder, so in the darkest hour before the dawn he was making more haste and less speed down the long lane that has no turning to his stable. When the ass saw the dog he realised that he who hesitates is lost, and he decided to strike while the iron was hot and set a thief to catch a thief, for why should one keep a dog and bark oneself? So he called the older dog to him. But you cannot teach an old dog new tricks and there is honour among thieves, for birds of a feather flock together. The ass had to admit that he had been counting his chickens before they were hatched, for possession is nine-tenths of the law. Thus he had to let the sleeping dog lie in his manger, knowing that what must be, must be.

Exercise 2. In the Appreciation and Discussion section above, the term "anti-climax" was used. CLIMAX and ANTI-CLIMAX (or BATHOS, as it is often called) are familiar *figures of speech*. All orators are aware of the power of repetition to lead to an impressive climax. One of Sir Winston Churchill's war speeches includes this famous passage:

    . . . We shall defend our island, whatever the cost may be, we shall fight on the beaches, we shall fight on the landing grounds, we shall fight in the fields and in the streets, we shall fight in the hills; we shall never surrender.

Comic writers are particularly fond of anti-climax, where instead of the anticipated ending, we come upon something ludicrously unexpected.

Discuss the bathos in the following examples and say which, if any, seem amusing:

(a) The speaker placed his glass carefully on the table, wiped his lips on his napkin, rose solemnly to his feet, cleared his throat and held up his hand for silence, and then burst into a helpless fit of giggles.

(b) I can resist everything—except temptation.

(c) You can fool all the people some of the time and some of the people all the time, but to fool all the people all of the time requires an advertising agency.

(d) You could have knocked me down with a crowbar.

(e) By sheer courage and cool presence of mind he saved from the burning wreck of the house, his mother, all her precious savings, three valuable old paintings, and his safety razor.

(f) A thing worth doing is worth doing badly.

(g) There was an old woman who swallowed a fly, a spider, a bird, a cat, a dog, a cow, and a horse—she died, of course.

(h)
        This dog and man at first were friends;
            But when the pique began,
        The dog, to gain some private ends,
            Went mad and bit the man.

        Around from all the neighbouring streets,
            The wond'ring neighbours ran,
        And swore the dog had lost its wits,
            To bite so good a man.

        The wound it seemed both sore and sad
            To every Christian eye;
        And while they swore the dog was mad,
            They swore the man would die.

        But soon a wonder came to light,
            That showed the rogues they lied:
        The man recover'd of the bite,
            The dog it was that died.

OLIVER GOLDSMITH

Make up some examples of bathos of your own.

Exercise 3. Examples and illustrations add interest and explanation to any piece of writing, but when we come to make a summary of it, they are nearly always dispensable. Take Thurber's vivid sentence:

> Even in a nightcap a wolf does not look any more like your grandmother than the Metro-Goldwyn lion looks like Calvin Coolidge. (22 words)

This could be shortened (although, of course, impoverished) by omitting the illustration:

> Even in a nightcap a wolf does not resemble your grandmother. (11 words)

(a) Shorten each of the following by omitting all forms of illustration of the main points in the sentences; apply Précis Rules 1 and 2 where appropriate also.

  (i) In the end a little girl, no more than nine or ten years old, did come along carrying a basket of food, including apples, oranges, peaches and other fruit, some bread, a pie, and some cream cheese for her grandmother.

 (ii) A short time ago, perhaps two or three years back, some builders who were working on a studio for a rich artist who wanted to settle in Connecticut, left a huge square of plate glass, which was as big as any window you have ever seen, standing upright in a field one day.

(iii) A goldfinch, flying as swiftly as he could across this particular field with the glass in it, struck the glass very hard indeed, so hard that he was knocked out completely by the impact.

 (iv) The male chipmunk liked arranging all their nuts, their hazels, walnuts, almonds and beech-nuts, in all sorts of artistic shapes and patterns, including triangles and circles, ovals and oblongs, lines and zigzags, with different textures from their different shapes and sizes. He thought that this was much more amusing and satisfying than just to accumulate more and more nuts, piling them up in a great hoard to see how many nuts you could pile up compared with other chipmunks round about.

(b) By stating the main facts and arguments of the following passage, and omitting all the illustration, reduce it from about 240 words to about 50 words. Apply Précis Rules 1 and 2, and state at the end the exact number of words you use.

The ordinary British housewife of today, the typical Mrs. Smith or Mrs. Brown of the suburbs of our great cities, buys goods from all over the globe, from the Arctic to the Equator, from China to Peru, and carries home every day purchases that have been produced and transported by many workers throughout the world. She may buy fruit, such as apples from South Africa and oranges from Israel, dairy produce, including Australian butter or New Zealand cheese, or manufactured goods such as cheap toys for the children from Hong Kong. For the world seems a smaller place than it was in her grand-mother's day: communications have improved. Refrigerated ships, for instance, now bring meat from South America that is no dearer than English fresh meat, indeed quite the reverse; and it is now quite worthwhile even to fly foods into Britain, such as early vegetables from the Scillies or the Channel Islands, not just for a millionaire's table at a West End hotel, but for the ordinary public to buy in local markets like Brixton or North End Road. With this fast, cheap transport, countries have become interdependent, each one relying on many others for essential supplies, and this is a strong argument for teaching more geography and economics at schools, so that each of those Mrs. Smiths and Mrs. Browns learns something of the countries we buy from, and of the complexities of world trade.

Précis Rule 3. ILLUSTRATIONS:
Providing the main point is clearly stated, leave out all examples and illustrations of it.

Topics for Written Work

1. Try writing your own "fables for our time". Look again at the different possible methods. You can take an existing proverb and make fun of it, for example:
   A king may look at a cat.
   All work and no play makes Jack a millionaire.
   A rolling stone is worth two in a bush.
Or you can take an existing fable or folk tale and give it a new twist, for instance:
   Cinderella.
   The Fox and the Crow.
   How the Camel got the Hump.
Or you can make up a new short tale to illustrate some moral of your own. Here is an example by a pupil:

Walley Bee
Once upon a time there was a kangaroo named Walley Bee. He was a very agile kangaroo and could jump 100 feet in one pace; he could even jump across a whole valley in a few strides. But Walley was very careless and did not worry if he knocked down his neighbours' wheat fields or fences or even his neighbours themselves.

After a while Walley's neighbours decided that it was about time they had a talk to him about his irresponsibility.

90

Walley, after being told off and threatened by his neighbours, decided to be careful from then on. He looked before he jumped over a valley or a fence; and after doing this for a few days decided that it was quite the best thing to do in future.

One day Walley went up into the mountain. While he was hopping along, he came across a gaping hole in the ground and, doing as his neighbours had told him, he looked over the edge to see what was there before he jumped. But the sight of the great space of nothing below made him giddy and he fell headlong into the deep hole and he was killed.

MORAL: *Leap before you look.*

KEITH

2. Think carefully about the two boys and two girls in the picture below. Write *either* a description of each of them as you imagine their personalities, *or* a story involving all four and bringing out the kind of people you think they are.

Oral Work

Traditional fables, Thurber's satirical modern fables, and the class's own compositions may all be suitable for "dramatisation". This could take several different forms. In some cases, a narrator could re-tell the story while a number of actors mime the actions of the characters. In other cases the story could be completely told through the words and actions of the characters, or with a narrator playing a small part at the beginning and end.

Other fables (perhaps especially those containing animals who act more like animals than human beings) might best be dramatised in a sound recording, with animal "voices", sound effects and a linking narration, all tape-recorded. A number of fables on tape, linked by music, could form a pleasant "magazine programme".

Activities and Research

1. Look up FABLES in encyclopaedias (consult the Index volume first) and other reference books (such as the *Oxford Companion to English Literature*), and borrow a copy of *Fables of Aesop* (translated by S. A. Handford, Penguin, 1954). From your researches, prepare a short talk or written account on traditional fables. Include information on Aesop, La Fontaine and others who have used the fable form, describe the characteristics of typical fables, and illustrate all you have to say with your own choice of examples.

2. Thurber gets comedy from the incongruous "modernisation" of old tales or putting an inappropriate moral or proverb to a story. In a similar way, see what absurd or witty effects you can achieve by putting different newspaper headlines

together, putting new captions to photographs or advertisements, or superimposing parts of one picture upon another. Aim at an element of satire or an absurd kind of humour, using excerpts cut from newspapers and magazines and mounted on sheets of coloured paper, with your own material added.

Further Reading

Fables for our Time included in *The Thurber Carnival* (Hamish Hamilton; Penguin)
This selection of JAMES THURBER's work has been made from nine books. In addition to the *Fables*, the collection has "The Secret Life of Walter Mitty", some very funny stories from *My Life and Hard Times* and "The Pet Department" from *The Owl in the Attic*. These make a good introduction to Thurber's rather dry, wistful kind of humour, and to his equally personal style of drawing.

Further Fables for our Time (Hamish Hamilton) offers some more fables in the same witty, sophisticated and absurd mould as those printed in this chapter.

The White Deer by JAMES THURBER (Hamish Hamilton; Penguin)
This is a collection of "mad, beautiful fairy stories", illustrated by the author and intended for children, but perhaps enjoyed even more by adults.

The Catcher in the Rye by J. D. SALINGER (Hamish Hamilton; Penguin)
Holden Caulfield's adventures, feelings, reactions and cynical comments on the difficulties of growing up in New York have become a modern American classic, but this is still a very popular book, and not only because it is still extremely funny.

CHAPTER SEVEN

Dreams and Visions

In the middle of the night I woke from a dream full of whips and lariats as long as serpents, and runaway coaches on mountain passes, and wide, windy gallops over cactus fields, and I heard the old man in the next room crying, "Gee-up!" and "Whoa!" and trotting his tongue on the roof of his mouth.

It was the first time I had stayed in Grandpa's house. The floorboards had squeaked like mice as I climbed into bed, and the mice between the walls had creaked like wood as though another visitor was walking on them. It was a mild summer night, but curtains had flapped and branches beaten against the window. I had pulled the sheets over my head, and soon was roaring and riding in a book.

"Whoa there, my beauties!" cried Grandpa. His voice sounded very young and loud, and his tongue had powerful hooves, and he made his bedroom into a great meadow. I thought I would see if he was ill, or had set his bedclothes on fire, for my mother had said that he lit his pipe under the blankets, and had warned me to run to his help if I smelt smoke in the night. I went on tiptoe through the darkness to his bedroom door, brushing against the furniture and upsetting a candlestick with a thump. When I saw there was a light in the room I felt frightened, and as I opened the door I heard Grandpa shout, "Gee-up!" as loudly as a bull with a megaphone.

He was sitting straight up in bed and rocking from side to side as though the bed were on a rough road; the knotted edges of the counterpane were his reins; his invisible horses stood in a shadow beyond the bedside candle. Over a white flannel nightshirt he was wearing a red waistcoat with walnut-sized brass buttons. The over-filled bowl of his pipe smouldered among his whiskers like a little, burning hayrick on a stick. At the sight of me, his hands dropped from the reins and lay blue and quiet, the bed stopped still on a level road, he muffled his tongue into silence, and the horse drew softly up.

"Is there anything the matter, Grandpa?" I asked, though

e clothes were not on fire. His face in the candlelight looked
ke a ragged quilt pinned upright on the black air and patched
l over with goat-beards.

He stared at me mildly. Then he blew down his pipe,
attering the sparks and making a high, wet dog-whistle of
e stem, and shouted: "Ask no questions."

After a pause, he said slyly: "Do you ever have nightmares boy?"

I said: "No."

"Oh, yes, you do," he said.

I said I was woken by a voice that was shouting to horses

"What did I tell you?" he said. "You eat too much. Who ever heard of horses in a bedroom?"

He fumbled under his pillow, brought out a small, tinkling bag, and carefully untied its strings. He put a sovereign in my hand, and said: "Buy a cake." I thanked him and wished him good night. As I closed my bedroom door, I heard his voice crying loudly and gaily, "Gee-up! gee-up!" and the rocking of the travelling bed.

In the morning I woke from a dream of fiery horses on a plain that was littered with furniture, and of large, cloudy men who rode six horses at a time and whipped them with burning bed-clothes. Grandpa was at breakfast, dressed in deep black. After breakfast he said, "There was a terrible loud wind last night," and sat in his arm-chair by the hearth to make clay balls for the fire. Later in the morning he took me for a walk through Johnstown village and into the fields on the Llanstephan road. . . .

On the last day but one of my visit I was taken to Llanstephan in a governess cart pulled by a short weak pony. Grandpa might have been driving a bison, so tightly he held the reins, so ferociously cracked the long whip, so blasphemously shouted warning to boys who played in the road, so stoutly stood with his gaitered legs apart and cursed the demon strength and wilfulness of his tottering pony.

"Look out, boy!" he cried when we came to each corner, and pulled and tugged and jerked and sweated and waved his whip like a rubber sword. And when the pony had crept miserably round each corner, Grandpa turned to me with a sighing smile: "We weathered that one, boy."

When we came to Llanstephan village at the top of the hill he left the cart by the "Edwinsford Arms" and patted the pony's muzzle and gave it sugar, saying: "You're a weak little pony, Jim, to pull big men like us."

(from "*A Visit to Grandpa's*" from *Portrait of the Artist as a Young Dog* by DYLAN THOMAS)

96

1. What was the boy (i.e. the narrator, Dylan Thomas) dreaming about just before he woke in the night?

2. Is there some connection between his dream and what he was doing just before he went to sleep? (What part of the second paragraph gives a hint about this?)

3. Why did the boy feel frightened when he saw there was a light in Grandpa's room?

4. What was Grandpa doing in bed that night? Was he dreaming, or consciously playing out his fantasy? (Give some reasons for your answer.)

5. How ashamed was Grandpa of his midnight game? Why was he ashamed at all?

6. How did Grandpa try to explain his behaviour away (a) in the night, and (b) after breakfast next morning? (Was it in fact a windy night?)

7. Why did Grandpa give Dylan a sovereign? Would that in fact have been more than enough to "buy a cake"?

8. Was there a connection between this midnight experience and Dylan's later dreams?

9. What was ludicrous about the way Grandpa drove the pony and cart? Was it at all reminiscent of his midnight fantasy?

10. Do you consider Grandpa more childish than his grandson? How old do you imagine each was?

11. Might Grandpa have been deliberately "playing" to amuse his grandson? How close a bond do you feel there is between them?

12. This extract is rich in interesting or vivid use of words. Discuss each of the following and how effective it is:
The floorboards had squeaked like mice . . . and the mice between the walls had creaked like wood as though another visitor was walking on them.
. . . his tongue had powerful hooves, and he made his bedroom into a great meadow.
. . . his hands dropped from the reins and lay blue and quiet, the bed stopped still on a level road, he muffled his tongue into silence, and the horse drew softly up.
. . . pulled and tugged and jerked and sweated.
. . . with a sighing smile.

13. Discuss the following similes: are they original or unusual? What is being compared to what in each one, and in what respects are they comparable?

(a) Lariats as long as serpents;

(b) as loudly as a bull with a megaphone;

(c) rocking from side to side as though the bed were a rough road;

(d) The overfilled bowl of his pipe smouldered among his whiskers like a little, burning hayrick on a stick;

(e) His face . . . looked like a ragged quilt pinned upright on the black air and patched all over with goat-beards;

(f) Grandpa might have been driving a bison, so tightly he held the reins . . .;

(g) waved his whip like a rubber sword.

14. The title of this chapter is taken from *The Bible*: "Your sons and your daughters shall prophesy, and your young men shall see visions, and your old men shall dream dreams" (Acts 2, verse 17, and Joel 2, verse 28). Is vivid imagination something you associate both with childhood and with old people? Is there some distinction between seeing visions (imagining something you have no experience of) and dreaming dreams (perhaps with a greater element of memory)?

Techniques

Exercise 1. Dylan Thomas's comparisons, especially his metaphors, are often rich and complex: several comparisons are implied in:

". . . the bed stopped still on a level road, he muffled his tongue into silence, and the horses drew softly up."

Similarly Shakespeare is fond of piling comparison upon comparison in his richest writing. The famous "To be or not to be" speech from *Hamlet* fuses several metaphors together:

"Whether 'tis nobler in the mind to suffer
The slings and arrows of outrageous fortune,
Or to take up arms against a sea of troubles,
And by opposing, end them?"

This is *not* what is meant by MIXED METAPHOR. *Mixed metaphors* form a fault of style that arises from the uncritical use of ready-made or familiar comparisons, in such a way that they begin to clash, often ludicrously, in meaning or effect. The comparisons, in fact, are nearly always *clichés*.

e.g. In the last war, the British kept the home fires burning on a rather sticky wicket.

Such *clichés* or outworn metaphors can be as absurd when misapplied singly:

e.g. The planners now require a complete breakdown of
all the traffic using the High Street.

Try to see what the writers or speakers of the following *clichés*
and mixed metaphors wanted to say, and rewrite their statements in plain English, or with vivid and original metaphors
or comparisons:

(a) He poured the soothing oil of compassion on the burning
flames of desire.

(b) Put on the armour of conscience before you launch into
the race of life.

(c) The problem was a real Augean stable, and when it came
to cleaning it up, the lot fell on me.

(d) Oh, what a tangled web we lay up for ourselves when we
stray from the path of duty!

(e) Never fear, we have a fine helmsman at the wheel of our
national affairs, and as good a captain as any first eleven
might desire.

(f) In our noble struggle to preserve eternal values, time is
not even on our side.

(g) Owing to the extended bottleneck in the supply of flooring
materials, the architects have put a lower ceiling on the
number of square feet to be covered.

(h) It is no use crying over spilt milk when the birds have
flown.

(i) If you ask me, someone has been fishing in troubled waters
on the playing fields of Eton.

(j) We have simply shot past the target and have completely
exposed the opposition, and not left them a leg to stand on.

Exercise 2. The extract contains several sentences of *reported
speech* as well as a number of pieces of *direct speech* conversation.
Find in the passage the reported speech equivalents for these
sentences and compare them closely.

(i) "I will see if he is ill," I thought, "or has set his bedclothes
on fire."

(ii) For my mother had said: "He lights his pipe under the
blankets, and you must run to help if you smell smoke in
the night."

(iii) "I was woken by a voice that was shouting to horses," I
said.

(iv) "Thank you, Grandpa," I replied. "Good night."

Notice that thoughts, as well as spoken words, can be recorded as direct speech; and notice the indirect way in which thanks and greetings are reported.

(a) Re-write the following piece of reported speech in direct speech wherever appropriate. You will see that it is conversation from the passage: make your own version first, and then compare it with the original.

Then he blew down his pipe and shouted that I should not ask questions. After a pause, he asked me slyly whether I ever had nightmares. I replied that I did not, but he contradicted me. When I said I was woken by a voice that was shouting to horses, he exclaimed that that just proved what he had said. He told me I ate too much and asked sarcastically who had ever heard of horses in a bedroom . .

Then he put a sovereign in my hand and told me to buy a cake. I thanked him and wished him good night.

It is very likely that your direct speech version, even if correct may be different from the original. Discuss the possible differences. Notice also that we are now dealing with a reported speech version in the *first person*—strictly speaking this breaks the first rule for reported speech given in Book Three. Under what circumstances is this possible?

(b) Make an ordinary (third person) reported speech version of the following discussion about old people:

Your version should begin like this:

> The psychiatric worker opened the discussion by saying that there was . . .

"There is one basic difficulty about growing old," said the psychiatric worker, opening the discussion, "and this is one of adjustment. At a time of life when you feel too old to change, you will find that you have repeatedly to meet new situations. First, your children are growing up; they are leaving home, and quite possibly want to travel miles away to make their own lives. Then comes retirement, and you suddenly find yourself without the firm daily routine of work you have been used to."

"I quite agree," added the doctor, "and illness and death will now bring new problems. If one partner in a marriage dies, the other has to adjust to a lonely existence. In any case, many elderly people will be moving into a smaller house or flat, and this usually means making new friends in a new area. If I recommend an elderly patient to move in with his married children, this causes problems too: he has to fit in with the way of life of a young family. The children are probably noisy, and the young parents will almost certainly resent any advice or interference from the older relative if they feel he is criticising."

"Yes, all this is true," said the welfare worker, "but I believe it may be even worse for the old person who wants to remain independent. Isn't he growing slower and less confident, while the world around him changes bewilderingly? The traffic moves faster, buildings rise higher, machines become more complicated, and simple actions like shopping or filling in forms may be changed and modernised beyond recognition. Can we blame these old people who seem to retreat into a world of fantasy of their own?"

Exercise 3. In writing summaries we have to treat similes and elaborate metaphors in much the same way as illustrations and examples—the passage is bound to be impoverished without them, but they are not the briefest way of stating the main facts.

Although the extract from "A Visit to Grandpa's" is not the sort of writing that one would often wish to summarise, the second and third paragraphs are a good example of the kind of précis one can make by cutting out figurative language. Compare the following with the original paragraphs (which contained about 240 words):

Grandpa was shouting as if driving horses in his bedroom. I went to see if he was ill or had set his bed alight by smoking, which my mother had warned me about. I went quietly but clumsily to his door, and was frightened to see a light. Grandpa was sitting rocking the bed like a coach. He was wearing a coach-driver's jacket over his nightshirt, smoking his pipe, but he stopped pretending to drive horses when he saw me. (80 words)

By simplifying all the figurative language, and applying Précis Rules 1, 2 and 3, rewrite the following description in about 70 words. It now contains about 220. State at the end the exact number of words you have used.

The castle, which was grey and forbidding, stood in a commanding position on the cliff-top, like a sentinel on watch or a coast-guard peering through the mist and spray to where the sky merged with the sea. It was indeed almost impregnable, for the cliff was high and precipitous, almost as sheer as the damp stone walls of the battlements above, and the rocky coast was so treacherous that no captain in his right mind would have attempted a landing on that shore, not even when the sea was as calm as a mill-pond, which was rare enough on that wild and stormy coast. Inland, too, the ground fell away in a steady slope from the castle hill, miles of bare, lifeless heath, as desolate as the sea it flanked, where only a few stunted trees or bushes grew, all bent double by the prevailing wind, like crippled old beggars feeling their way down to the nearest human habitation, several miles away. There was therefore no opportunity for surprise attack from land any more than from the sea, and the castle rose grim and single, easily seen from every part of the heath, as if its first lords had wished to emphasise that here they had built the invincible, unchallenged master of both land and sea.

Précis Rule 4. FIGURATIVE LANGUAGE:
Similes should be omitted, and elaborate metaphors and other figures of speech simplified.

Topics for Written Work

1. Write a description of an old person in a typical setting. Select those features of his or her face, figure or limbs, or details of his clothes or habits, that seem typical of his age. Reflect in carefully chosen words and comparisons the way he moves about or talks, and his typical mannerisms; and use the background in which you imagine or remember him to harmonise or contrast with his aged features.

Here is Dickens' description of the grandfather in *The Old Curiosity Shop*. The narrator has been showing his little granddaughter her way home to the shop:

He was a little old man with long grey hair, whose face and figure, as he held the light above his head and looked before him as he approached, I could plainly see. Though he was much altered by age, I fancied I could recognise in his spare and slender form something of that delicate mould which I had noticed in the child. Their bright blue eyes were certainly alike, but his face was so deeply furrowed, and so very full of care, that here all resemblance ceased.

The place through which he made his way at leisure was one of those receptacles for old and curious things which seem to crouch in odd corners of this town, and to hide their musty treasures from the public eye in jealousy and distrust. There were suits of mail standing like ghosts in armour here and there; fantastic carvings brought from monkish cloisters; rusty weapons of various kinds; distorted figures in china, and wood, and iron, and ivory; tapestry, and strange furniture that might have been designed in dreams. The haggard aspect of the little old man was wonderfully suited to the place; he might have groped among old churches, and tombs, and deserted houses, and gathered all the spoils with his own hands. There was nothing in the whole collection but was in keeping with himself— nothing that looked older or more worn than he.

This description might serve to some extent as a model, but your own composition should be firmly based on real old people that you have seen or met or that you know well.

2. Describe any dream, day-dream, nightmare (or even vision) as richly and vividly as you can. Again, it is best to begin with a real experience in mind, even in a world of pure fantasy. Try to recapture the dream-like succession of inconsequential and bewildering events, and make as much use of figurative language and vivid vocabulary as you can.

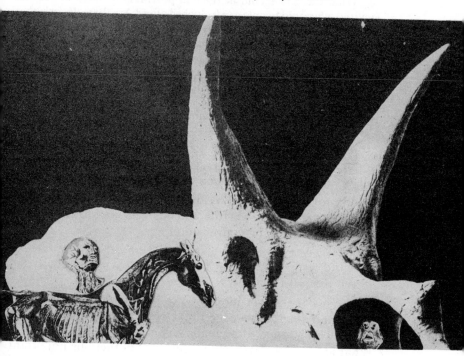

Oral Work

1. Spend a few moments trying to imagine what it is like to be old, retired, living on a pension, no longer very active, perhaps alone most of the time if your former wife or husband has already died, or feeling that you are a burden to younger people if you live with grown-up children.

Discuss some of the problems of elderly people:

(a) Why is this an increasing problem? Will it become even more acute in the future if medicine is improved, or if more work is done by machines?

(b) Where *do* people get money to live on after retirement? What are the basic pension rates at the moment, and what other sources of income might old people have?

(c) Is it desirable for old people to live independently as long as possible? What kind of housing would you recommend, and why? Why should rehousing old people so often prove difficult, or expensive?

(d) What problems do old people have if they live alone, that young and middle-aged people would not have?

(e) What can and should be done in providing homes and hospital facilities where old people can be looked after? Are there dangers that younger relatives will too readily push old people into these places?

(f) What are the special problems of adjustment for an old person living with grown-up children? Do we respect old people less than we used to, say a hundred years ago, or less than they are respected in France, or in other countries like India or Japan, or in primitive cultures?

(g) Suicide rates are very high among old people. Why? Should we feel ashamed of this?

2. If a series of good questions is carefully prepared, and some elderly people can be found who are really keen to co-operate, then tape-recorded interviews with old people in your district could prove very interesting. But the success of such a project depends very much on the interviewers and their skill in provoking interesting conversation.

Activities and Research

1. Discuss the implications of the information given in the graph and diagram on page 105. Does it seem likely that more people will survive to a greater age in Britain in the future? What about other parts of the world? Will there be important changes in the balance between numbers of old people, young people and those of working age, or in the balance between the sexes? You will find other useful, up-to-date figures in the *Annual Abstract of Statistics*, published by the Central Statistical Office, and available in good reference libraries.

2. Find out what opportunities there are in your district to go out and help old people at week-ends and in the evenings. Many schools and youth clubs have their own schemes. If yours has not, see if one could be started. The organisation called *Task Force* works in a number of London Boroughs, directing the volunteers from schools and youth organisations, and the Chief Welfare Officer at your local council offices can probably help you to help those whose need is greatest.

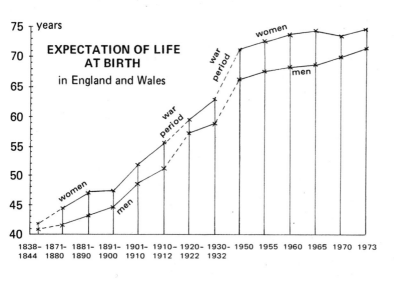

EXPECTATION OF LIFE AT BIRTH
in England and Wales

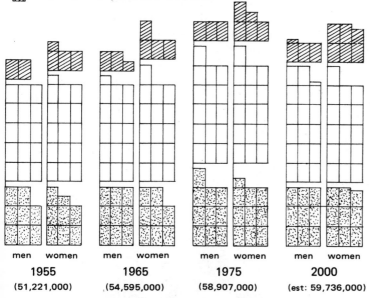

☐ = 1,000,000 persons under 20 years.

☐ = 1,000,000 persons aged 20 to 64 years.

▨ = 1,000,000 persons over 65 years.

men	women	men	women	men	women	men	women
1955		1965		1975		2000	
(51,221,000)		(54,595,000)		(58,907,000)		(est: 59,736,000)	

GROWTH AND DISTRIBUTION (by age and sex) OF POPULATION IN UNITED KINGDOM

A Visit to Grandpa's from *Portrait of the Artist as a Young Dog* by
DYLAN THOMAS (Dent)
Dylan Thomas first won fame as a poet, and his poetic talents
are evident in all his writings. His style may seem puzzling
at first but it is always full of rich and exciting images which
can often be enjoyed without being fully understood. *Portrait*
of the Artist, a "fictional autobiography", is probably the least
demanding of his prose works. If you enjoy it, try his other books,
but be prepared to find them more difficult.

A Prospect of the Sea by DYLAN THOMAS (Dent)
Stories of childhood, madmen, fantasy, and the subconscious,
plus a satirical essay entitled *How to be a Poet*, make up this
collection.

Quite Early One Morning by DYLAN THOMAS (Dent) (828)
This is a collection of Thomas's broadcast talks, and includes
"Return Journey", from which the piece "Schoolmaster"
(in Chapter I of this book) was taken. The title piece was in
fact an earlier version of Thomas's remarkable radio play:
Under Milk Wood by DYLAN THOMAS (Dent) (822)
In this play, which was not completed until ten years after his
radio talk, we hear first the dreams of the sleeping inhabitants,
then we follow the people as they get up and go about their
business, until night falls at the end of the Spring day.
As with most of Dylan Thomas's work, *Under Milk Wood* must
be heard to be fully appreciated. The complete play, with the
original radio cast, is available on two long-playing records,
issued by the Argo Record Company, who have also issued
Homage to Dylan Thomas, which includes *A Visit to Grandpa's*,
read by Emlyn Williams. Two records of Dylan Thomas
reading his own prose and poetry have been issued by Caedmon.

I Capture the Castle by DODIE SMITH (Heinemann; Penguin)
The story of an eccentric family who live in an old castle, told
in diary form by the sharp-witted younger daughter.

CHAPTER EIGHT

The Press

A retired actress, Miss Porteus, a reserved and lonely person who kept a milliner's shop, had been found dead by Mr. Sprake, the owner of the watchmaker and jeweller's shop next door. Miss Porteus, wearing a pink nightgown, was lying on her bathroom floor, shot in the chest. On the afternoon of her death, Mrs. Sprake had seen a middle-aged man in the backyard of the milliner's.

By afternoon the crowd was packed thick right across the street. They were pressed tight against my window. I put the shutters up. Just as I was finishing them, four men came up and said they were newspapermen and could I give them the facts about Miss Porteus.

Before I could speak they pushed into the shop. They shut the door. Then I saw that there were not four of them but twelve. I got behind the counter and they took out notebooks and rested them on my glass showcases and scribbled. I tried to tell them what I had told the local man, the truth, and nothing more or less than the truth, but they didn't want that. They hammered me with questions.

What was Miss Porteus like? Was her real name Porteus? What else besides Porteus? What colour was her hair? How long had she been there? Did it strike me as funny that an actress should run a milliner's shop? When had I last seen the lady? About the bathroom . . . about her hair . . .

I was flustered and I said something about her hair being a little reddish, and one of the newspapermen said:

"Now we're getting somewhere. Carrots," and they all laughed.

Then another said: "Everybody says this woman was an actress. But where did she act? London? What theatre? When?"

"I don't know," I said.

"You've lived next door all this time and don't know? Did you never hear anybody say if she'd been in any particular play?"

"No. I . . . Well, she was a bit strange."

"Strange?" They seized on that. "How? What Mysterious?"

"Well," I said, "she was the sort of woman who'd come ou in big heavy fox furs on a hot summer day. She was different."

"Crazy?"

"Oh, no!"

"Eccentric?"

"No. I wouldn't say that."

"About her acting," they said. "You must have heard something."

"No." Then I remembered something. At a rehearsal of the Choral Society, once, her name had come up and somebody had said something about her having been in *Othello*. I remember it because there was some argument about whether Othello was a pure black or just a half-caste.

"*Othello?*" The newspapermen wrote fast. "What was she? Desdemona?"

"Well," I said, "I don't think you ought to put that in. I don't know if it's strictly true or not. I can't vouch for it. I don't think—"

"And this man that was seen," they said. "When was it? When did you see him? What was he like?"

I said I didn't know, that I hadn't seen him, but that my wife had. So they had my wife in. They questioned her. They were nice to her. But they put down, as in my case, things she did not say. Yellow tie? Dark? How dark? Foreign looking? Actor. Every now and then one of them dashed out to the post office. They questioned us all that afternoon.

The next morning the placards of the morning newspapers were all over Claypole. "Shot Actress—Full Story." It was my story, but somehow, as it appeared in the papers, it was not true. I read all the papers. They had my picture, the picture of Miss Porteus's shop, looking somehow strange and forlorn with its drawn blind, and a picture of Miss Porteus herself, as she must have looked about 1920. All over these papers were black stabbing headlines: "Search for Shot Actress Assailant Goes On." "Police anxious to Interview Foreigner with Yellow Tie." "Real Life Desdemona: Jealousy Victim?" "Eccentric Actress Recluse Dead in Bathroom." "Mystery Life of Actress who wore Furs in Heat Wave." "Beautiful Red-Haired Actress who Spoke to Nobody." "Disappearance of Dark-looking Foreigner."

It was Saturday. That afternoon Claypole was besieged by hundreds of people who had never been there before. They moved past Miss Porteus's shop and mine in a great stream, in cars and on foot and pushing bicycles, staring at the dead actress's windows. . . .

Hundreds of people who had seen Miss Porteus's shop every day of their lives suddenly wanted to stare at it. . . .

There sprang up, gradually, a different story about Miss Porteus. It began to go all over Claypole that she was a woman of a certain reputation, that the milliner's shop was a blind. "Did you ever see anybody in there, or going in? No, nor did anybody else. Did anybody ever buy a hat there? No. But the back door was always undone." That rumour gave cause for others. "Sprake," people began to say, "told me himself that she lay on the floor naked. They put the nightgown on afterwards." Then she became not only a woman of light virtue and naked, but also pregnant. "That's why," people began to say, "she either shot herself or was shot. Take it which way you like. But I had it straight from Sprake."

As the story of Miss Porteus grew, the story of my own part in it grew. . . .

I used to belong, in Claypole, to a Temperance club, the Melrose; we had four full-sized billiard tables and in the evenings I went there to play billiards and cards, to have a smoke and a talk and so on. Next to the billiard room was a small cloakroom, and one evening, as I was hanging up my coat, I heard someone at the billiard table say:

"Old Sprake knows a thing or two. Ever struck you it was funny old Sprake knew the colour of that nightgown so well?"

I put on my coat again and went out of the club. I was trembling and horrified and sick. What I had heard seemed to be the crystallisation of all the rumours that perhaps were and perhaps were not going round Claypole. It may have been simply the crystallisation of my own fears. I don't know, I only know that I was suspected of things I had not done and had not said; that not only had she been murdered, but that I knew more than I would say about that murder. I was harassed by fears and counter-fears. I did not know what to do. . . .

Then something happened. It was important and it suddenly filled the front pages of the newspapers again with the mystery of Miss Porteus's death. The police found the man with the yellow tie. It was a sensation. . . .

That was the end. It was established, beyond doubt, that Miss Porteus had taken her life. And suddenly all the mystery and sensation and horror and fascination of Miss Porteus's death became nothing. The papers were not interested in her any longer and her name never appeared in the papers again.

I no longer live at Claypole. All those odd, unrealised rumours that went round were enough to drive me mad; but they were also enough to kill my wife. Like me, she could not sleep, and the shock of it all cracked her life right across, like a piece of bone. Rumour and shock and worry killed her, and she died just after the facts of Miss Porteus's death were established. A month later I gave up the business and I left the town. I could not go on. . . .

Poor Miss Porteus. She took her life because she was hard up, in a fit of despair. There is no more to it than that. But nobody in Claypole ever believed that and I suppose very few people ever will. In Claypole they like to think that she was murdered; they know, because the papers said so, that she was a strange and eccentric woman; they know that she acted in a play with a black man; they know, though nobody ever really said so, that she was a loose woman and that she was pregnant and that somebody shot her for that reason; they know that I found her naked in the bathroom and that I was a bit queer and that I knew more than I would ever say.

They know, in short, all that happened to Miss Porteus. They can never know how much has happened to me.

(from *Shot Actress—Full Story*, a short story by H. E. Bates)

Appreciation and Discussion

1. Who do you think "the local man" (in the second paragraph) was? How would he be connected with the crowds and the arrival of the journalists?
2. Sprake says, "I tried to tell them . . . the truth, and nothing more or less than the truth, but they didn't want that." Why didn't the reporters want the bare truth?
3. Judging from the reporters' questions and the details they seized upon, what kind of story *did* they want?
4. Was the resulting newspaper story really untrue, in your opinion?
5. Why did crowds of people want to see Miss Porteus's shop?
6. Why were the newspapers no longer interested in Miss Porteus when it was certain that she had committed suicide?
7. Why do you think nobody in Claypole would ever really believe the facts of her death? To what extent can the newspapers be blamed for that?

8. Examine the newspaper headlines: what emphasis do they give to the story? Are they really misleading?
9. Do you blame the newspapers for the rumours that sprang up? How far are the papers responsible and how far the ordinary people who passed them on?
10. How malicious were the people who made up and passed on these rumours? Are they to blame at all for Mrs. Sprake's death and for driving Mr. Sprake out of Claypole?
11. What do you think the newspapers and their reporters would say in their own defence in a case like this? Could they legitimately blame their readers for wanting this treatment of the news?
12. Recall and discuss any recent real-life examples of:
    (a) simple facts being altered or distorted by newspaper reports;
    (b) the public flocking to visit some place where something exciting or sordid has recently occurred, although there is nothing much to see; (Do you admit to having felt this kind of curiosity yourself?)
    (c) a person's reputation or peace of mind being damaged or disturbed by rumours and by unpleasant newspaper publicity.
13. Would it be fair to call the style in which the story is written rather weak? Could its colloquialisms (find examples) be attributed to the fact that it is supposed to be narrated by Sprake himself?

HEADLINE HISTORY

GRAVE CHARGES IN MAYFAIR BATHROOM CASE,
ROMAN REMAINS FOR MIDDLE WEST,
GOLFING BISHOP CALLS FOR PRAYERS,
HOW MURDERED BRIDE WAS DRESSED,

BOXER INSURES HIS JOIE-DE-VIVRE,
DUCHESS DENIES THAT VAMPS ARE VAIN,
DO WOMEN MAKE GOOD WIVES?
GIANT AIRSHIP OVER SPAIN,

SOPRANO SINGS FOR FORTY HOURS,
COCKTAIL BAR ON MOORING MAST,
"NOISE, MORE NOISE!" POET'S LAST WORDS,
COMPULSORY WIRELESS BILL IS PASSED,

ALLEGED LAST TRUMP BLOWN YESTERDAY,
TRAFFIC DROWNS CALL TO QUICK AND DEAD,
CUP TIE CROWD SEES HEAVENS OPE,
"NOT END OF WORLD," SAYS WELL-KNOWN RED.

WILLIAM PLOMER

Discussing the Poem

1. Look up "vamps" and "joie-de-vivre" and other words and
   references that puzzled you. The "cocktail bar" was in the
   cabin of an airship moored to the mast.
2. Each line is a separate and genuine headline. Discuss what
   each could have been about originally.
3. By the *juxtaposition* of the headlines and playing on possible
   secondary meanings, the poet has painted a picture of a
   decadent world rapidly nearing its end. Discuss the way he
   has done this.
4. Make up headlines (stating which national newspaper they
   might appear in) for some imaginary situations: the sudden
   disappearance of New York, the coming of the Day of
   Judgement, the arrival of beings from Outer Space, the
   marriage of the President of Communist China to a British
   Princess, Noah's Flood or Jonah's safe return from inside
   the whale, etc.
5. Make up a poem composed entirely of headlines, real or
   imaginary (not necessarily those made up for question 4).

Exercise 1. According to Hugh Cudlipp in his book *Publish and Be Damned,* the day in 1935 when the *Daily Mirror* was transformed into a mass circulation paper was heralded primarily in the paper's *headlines*:

"First eye-opener was the transformation of the news pages. Sledgehammer headlines appeared on the front page in black type one inch deep, a signal that all could see of the excitements to come. Human interest was at a premium, and that meant sex and crime. . . . The headline occasionally occupied twice as much space as the story itself, and there was no mistaking the strident appeal of the stories:
        'MARRIAGE AT 9 SHOCKS U.S. WOMEN'
        'UMBRELLA IN COFFIN MEMENTO OF ROMANCE'
        'GIRL FINDS MOTHER AFTER TWENTY YEARS IN STREET VIGIL'."

What is the point of a newspaper headline? Is it intended to be an informative summary of the news that follows? Collect examples of sensational headlines from newspapers and discuss the appeal they are making.

(a) What quite different stories could the following headlines introduce?
  (i) P.M. on Trial.
  (ii) Drug Charges.
  (iii) A Fortune in Tea Leaves.
  (iv) Million Pound Spree.
  (v) New Russian Threat.
  (vi) Squeeze Cost Him His Job.
  (vii) Killer Hunted.
  (viii) Married at Ten.
  (ix) Sex in Fashion.
  (x) Abandoned Girls in London.

(b) Because of their shorthand style, the ELLIPSIS or omission of words, headlines are frequently *ambiguous*. These double meanings can normally be explained in grammatical terms.
        e.g. Wore Fur Coat Out in Hot Sunshine
might mean (1) someone wore out a fur coat in the heat, where "out" is part of the phrasal verb, "to wear out"; or (2) someone went out wearing a fur coat in the heat, where "out" is an adverb ("outside"), modifying the verb "wore".

Explain the two (or more) meanings in each of the following headlines, using grammatical terms.
 (i) Dramatic Search for Actress Killer.
 (ii) Dark Foreigner Sought for Interview.
 (iii) Retiring Actress Found Shot in Chest.
 (iv) Murderer Shot into Actress's Bathroom.
 (v) Police Seek Killer with Guns.
 (vi) Mystery Jams up Claypole High Street.
 (vii) Peeping Tom Gives Murderer Clue.
(viii) Nosey Woman has Key to Case.
 (ix) Did She See Man Firing Through Bathroom Window?
 (x) Swift Reports from Claypole High Street.

Exercise 2. Study the following two extracts from newspapers before discussing or writing answers to the questions below. From the front page of the *Views of the World:*

SHOULD THESE MEN HANG?

Last week a policeman shot in Soho—this week a running battle in Battersea. Dangerous armed men are still loose. VIEWS OF THE WORLD asks its twelve million readers the vital question: Should we bring back hanging for killers of policemen and prison warders?

Can we deny any longer that Britain's underworld is trigger-mad? The time has come to ask ourselves: Were we wrong to abolish the death penalty?

Seven out of ten of your letters are in favour of hanging. The debate is now wide open. What do *you* say? The great British public's voice must be heard again.

Parliament abolished the death penalty for all offences in November, 1965. For eight years before that we had had the rope for all "capital" murders—and those included killing of police or prison officers and all second murders.

That year, the Gallup Poll showed that the "abolitionists" in Parliament were defying the will of the nation—that a three-to-one majority still supported hanging.

Now we face a new wave of ugly violence. Many responsible men believe we must think again. They argue that a man facing a life sentence for robbery with violence is not going to hesitate to shoot his way out when cornered.

The academics still cling to their statistics showing that hanging does not deter, but a number of M.P.s have already signed the motion calling for a change in the law. *It is time the people's views were heard.*

From the Editorial of the *National Independent*:

NO QUICK CURE

The Home Secretary is well aware that it would be quite wrong to make any major policy decision about capital punishment in the shadow of recent tragic incidents in Soho and Battersea. Successive holders of that office have quite correctly maintained that this is a matter to be discussed dispassionately in the light of the available crime figures for this country and for other advanced nations which have abolished the death penalty. The pressure of public opinion, swayed by the heartening wave of sympathy for the police victims of violence, does not alter the fact that there has still been no overall rise in the number of murders committed, and that increases in convictions for crimes of violence have remained constant since the total abolition of capital punishment in 1965.

The increase in violent crime is a world-wide problem, and there is no simple panacea for so complex a social evil. Present arrangements for the licensing and sale of firearms certainly require investigation. Nor should we diminish our efforts—by long-term analysis and research—to find the roots of crime and deepen our understanding of the criminal mentality. One thing is certain—we shall not solve this problem if the public is apathetic or the government reluctant to spend the taxpayer's money. If the mounting support for the police leads to a better paid, highly mobile and efficiently equipped constabulary, then we shall be building up a really effective deterrent to the criminal: the certainty that he will be caught.

1. What items of news, as far as you can tell from reading these comments, prompted these newspaper reactions?
2. Both these newspapers are imaginary, but their styles are typical. What kind of reader do you think each would be mainly aimed at?
3. Is there any element of self-advertisement in either or both of these newspapers' pieces?
4. Generally, one newspaper piece is in favour of restoring hanging and the other is against it. Why doesn't each editor state his position more definitely?
5. If the *Views of the World* printed, alongside this piece, a ballot-form on which readers could vote for or against restoring the death penalty, what would you expect the result of such a poll to be?
6. The terms "hanging", "death penalty", "the rope", and "capital punishment" all mean the same. In what ways are these terms *emotionally toned,* and how and why do the pieces differ in their use of the various terms?

7. Contrast the language of the two passages whenever either mentions criminals or violence.
8. What features of style (paragraphing, vocabulary, sentence structure) and lay-out (headlines, opening statements, different type) make the first piece easier to read than the second? Which is more thoughtful and more thought-provoking, in your opinion?
9. How does each piece indicate that the number of crimes of violence is increasing? To what extent is each of them misleading us about this?
10. Richard Hoggart wrote in *The Uses of Literacy*, quoting a very common view of class divisions: ". . . the world is divided into 'Them' and 'Us'. 'They' are 'the people at the top', 'the higher-ups', the people who give you your dole, call you up, tell you to go to war, fine you . . ." How does the *Views of the World* piece imply a similar contrast between a governing minority and the popular opinions of the majority? Whose side is the paper on, and how does it indicate its attitude to 'Us' and 'Them'?
11. Imagine you are the Home Secretary's personal assistant and have to prepare notes for him on what the papers are saying; how would you summarise the attitudes and advice of *these* two papers?
12. If you were the Home Secretary, how much, if at all, would you let either of these papers, or any result of an opinion poll conducted later by the *Views of the World*, influence you? Give some reasons.

Exercise 3. Examine these sentences with *noun clauses* printed in italics:
(i) The reporters put down *what she did not say*.
(ii) They reported *that Mrs. Sprake had seen a dark foreigner*.
In each case the noun clause is the object of the main verb—the clauses tell us what the reporters wrote, in the same way the word "story" is object of this sentence:
(iii) They put down the whole *story*.
   Now compare these two sentences containing adjective clauses:
(iv) The reporters put down words *that she did not in fact say*.
(v) They reported the story *that Mrs. Sprake had told them*.
   In these sentences the verb already has a noun as object ("words", "story"); the clause is there to describe that object noun further, and is not itself the object. Since the same introductory word "that" is used, these clauses are easily confused; a good test is to try substituting the word "which" (or "who") for the word "that": in examples (i) and (ii) "which" certainly would not fit, but in (iv) and

(v) "which" could take the place of "that".

In both types of construction, the word "that" is often omitted altogether.

(vi) They told me *they were newspaper men.*

(vii) They told me the facts *they had already learnt.*

Which of these examples (vi) and (vii) contains a noun clause, and which an adjective clause?

(a) Are the clauses in italics in each of the following sentences examples of a noun clause or an adjective clause? What verb is each the subject or object of, or what noun is it qualifying?

   (i) I told them *what I told the local man.*

   (ii) Those were the facts *that I knew for certain.*

   (iii) But I realised *that they were not satisfied with this.*

   (iv) They put down things *she did not say.*

   (v) *What I heard* seemed to be a crystallisation of all the rumours *that were perhaps going round Claypole.* (2)

   (vi) They know *how she was murdered by a foreigner who wore a yellow tie.* (2)

(b) Break each of the following sentences into two clauses. One should be a main clause and the other a subordinate noun clause or a subordinate adjective clause—state which verb each is subject or object of, or which noun (or pronoun) it qualifies.

   (i) Four men asked whether I could give them the facts about Miss Porteus.

   (ii) Everybody says this woman was an actress.

   (iii) Didn't anybody say if she had been in any particular play?

   (iv) She was the sort of woman that wore heavy furs in summer.

   (v) I felt I was suspected of knowing her too well.

   (vi) I was suspected of things I had not done.

   (vii) In Claypole they believe she was murdered.

   (viii) They also know she acted in a play called *Othello.*

   (ix) They know everything that happened to Miss Porteus.

   (x) They can never know how much has happened to me.

(c) The following headlines contain *elliptical* noun clauses, where several words (often the verb itself) have been omitted. Rewrite each as a complete sentence, and then show which part of that sentence is a noun clause.

   e.g. What Police Will Do Now Uncertain (2)

could mean (1) "What the police will now do is uncertain" (the noun clause subject of "is" has been underlined);

or it could mean (2) "What the Police will do is now uncertain." (the noun clause subject of "is" has been underlined).

   (i) Police Say Killer Is Armed.

   (ii) Stranger Explains Why He Was Scared.

   (iii) Stranger Explains: He Was Scared.

(iv) Sprake Alleges Rumours Killed Wife.
  (v) Inspector Sure Murderer Shot Three Times. (2)
  (vi) Reporters Believe Foreigner Shot First. (2)
 (vii) Witness Swears Corpse Walked On. (2)

Topics for Written Work

1. What do *you* think the ideal newspaper should be like? At
the end of his book *The Press*, Wickham Steed (a pre-war editor
of *The Times* and a well-known journalist) summed up his
ideals—is there much that is outdated about the following, or
much to add, so many years later?

"The newspaper I dream of would reflect the distractions of modern
life no less faithfully than existing papers reflect them, but it would
treat them as distractions, not as things that matter. It would search
out the truths behind these appearances and proclaim them . . .
calling cant and humbug by their names.

"It would be quite fearless. It would not 'hedge' in its treatment
of thorny subjects; and if, as would be inevitable, it made mistakes,
it would avow them. It would only accept such advertisements as it
thought honest . . .

"My newspaper would, of course, make every effort to get the
news, and would put its main news on the front page—where it
ought to be. It would not fear to print several consecutive columns of
one good 'story' . . . Nor would it cheat its readers by superabundant
headlines or by vain repetitions . . .

"My ideal newspaper would give 'all the news that's fit to print'
as vividly as possible, whether the news suited its 'policy' or not."

In writing your own account of the ideal newspaper, work
out what you believe is the correct balance between serious
news, entertainment and comment or background information.
What should be the standards of a newspaper in seeking stories
or uncovering scandals (is it right for them to pay criminals for
their memoirs, for instance?): and are there some kinds of
behaviour that should *not* be given publicity, since they
encourage imitators? (It is often claimed that publicity
encourages hooliganism, for instance.)

Consider, too, whether your paper is to be profit-making,
how far it will please the advertisers, and how it is to be "free"
from the influence of its owners, or the tastes of its readers, or
threats of prosecution.

2. Study carefully the table of figures overleaf, and discuss
the questions raised below:

ADULT READERSHIP OF NATIONAL DAILY AND SUNDAY NEWSPAPERS (1975–76)

NEWSPAPER	PERCENTAGE OF ADULT READERSHIP BY SOCIAL CLASS				
	TOTAL	A, B	c(1)	c(2)	D, E
Daily Mirror	30%	14%	24%	38%	62%
The Sun	29%	13%	22%	38%	58%
Daily Express	18%	40%	22%	17%	30%
Daily Mail	12%	30%	16%	10%	17%
Daily Telegraph	8%	67%	12%	4%	4%
Daily Record	5%	3%	3%	6%	13%
The Times	3%	30%	3%	1%	1%
The Guardian	3%	19%	4%	1%	2%
Financial Times	2%	19%	2%	1%	*
News of the World	32%	17%	23%	40%	75%
Sunday Mirror	29%	20%	27%	38%	51%
Sunday People	28%	16%	23%	34%	59%
Sunday Express	22%	76%	32%	17%	25%
Sunday Post	11%	10%	9%	11%	28%
Sunday Times	9%	71%	14%	5%	4%
Sunday Mail	6%	4%	4%	7%	12%
The Observer	5%	35%	8%	3%	3%
Sunday Telegraph	5%	35%	7%	3%	2%

Notes: The figures are quoted by kind permission of the JICNARS National Readership Survey (1976). All figures are percentages; the asterisk * represents less than 1%. The social grades A and B represent "upper middle" and "middle" class people in higher and intermediate managerial, administrative or professional occupations. C1 represents "lower middle" class people in supervisory or clerical or junior managerial, administrative or professional occupations. C2 are skilled working class manual workers. The D and E grades are working class and other people doing semi-skilled or unskilled work, casual and lowest grade workers, state pensioners, widows, etc.

(a) Which are the three most popular national daily newspapers (i) with the total adult population, (ii) with each social class group? Consider each class in turn.

(b) Which are the three most popular Sunday newspapers with the total population and with each social class in turn?

(c) Add up the total percentages of readers for (i) all dailies and (ii) all the Sunday newspapers. If either (or both) of these figures comes to more than 100%, explain this.

(d) The *Daily Record* and *The Observer* both have a readership of 5% of the total adult population, yet if you add the percentages for the four social classes together, one total is only 25% whereas the other is 49%. Explain this, if you can.

(e) Is there any evidence for saying (i) that Sunday papers generally are more popular than daily papers, or (ii) that the newspaper reading habit is more widespread in one social class than in another?

(f) *The Times* has 30 times as great a percentage of A, B class readers as of D, E class readers. Make the same kind of calculation for other newspapers. Which has the greatest and which the least difference in class of readership?

(g) Divide the newspapers into three categories: (i) those with mainly upper and middle class readers, (ii) those with mainly working class readers, and (iii) those with a mixed class readership.

(h) If you were responsible for advertising goods that would appeal (i) to a wealthy, exclusive market, (ii) to a cheap mass market, and (iii) to people of all classes and levels of income, which newspapers would you recommend most strongly in each case, to carry your advertisements?

When you have examined and discussed these figures, try to write a piece of comment to accompany them, such as might be suitable for a serious newspaper article. Assume that the figures will be published alongside your article, and so it is your task to call attention to interesting conclusions and trends, and not just to quote figures. Keep any speculation (for instance, if you think a particular newspaper is likely to close down soon) distinct from the facts you can prove from the figures.

Discuss all or some of the following "provocative remarks". One or two members of the class might undertake to prepare a full and well-documented defence of each point of view:

1. Now that we have radio and television to provide news and comment, newspapers are no more than marginal entertainment. '

2. You cannot believe what the newspapers say—they are full of lies and distortions—so I see no point in reading them.

3. No newspaper ever has the right to pry into anyone's private affairs. Personal lives, even of famous or notorious people, should not be the subject of public curiosity.

4. When millionaires like Lord Thompson (pictured on page 112) can own 148 newspapers and 153 magazines all over the world, running them for profit, while many newspapers are forced out of business, the idea of an independent press enjoying free competition seems ridiculous.

5.   "You cannot hope   But seeing what
       to bribe or twist,   the man will do
     Thank God! the   Unbribed, there's
       British journalist.   no occasion to."

(from *The British Journalist* by Humbert Wolfe)

6. There is no great difference between the so-called "quality" newspapers and the popular press. Both are packed full of sex, crime, sport and political scandal, all surrounded by adverts. It is just that the "top" papers dress it all up in long words and put the pin-ups into their colour supplements.

7. Only a newspaper without advertising could be really free: it would not need to please manufacturers or increase its circulation, so it could state the truth fearlessly. It would cost the reader three or four times as much, but it would be worth it!

8. "Of course you have got to give the public what it wants . . . You try and raise its standards as well . . . It is only the people who conduct newspapers and similar organisations who have any idea quite how indifferent, quite how stupid, quite how uninterested in education of any kind the great bulk of the British people are."—Cecil King (at a conference on *Popular Culture and Personal Responsibility*).

1. Make a table listing the main national daily and Sunday newspapers (perhaps including the two London evening papers), in which you give details of ownership, political policy and circulation. Find the most up-to-date information you can, in reference books like *Whitaker's Almanack* or *BRITAIN, an Official Handbook* (H.M.S.O.). The latter sets out information like this:

TITLE	CONTROLLED BY	CIRCULATION AVE. (JAN.–JUNE 1976)
Daily Mirror (1903)	Reed Publishing Holdings Ltd.	3,837,091

Try to find out what national newspapers have ceased publication, been amalgamated with larger ones, changed hands or been launched in the last twenty years. Has the tendency been towards greater or less competition? Is one political point of view losing more ground than the others?

2. Make a survey of the use of space in different newspapers. Collect as many copies as possible of the different national dailies for any one particular day. Decide upon the list of categories into which the contents of the papers can conveniently be divided: Advertisements, Home Political News, Foreign News, Sports News and Comment, Crime and "human interest" News, Editorial Comment and Leading Articles, Reviews and the Arts, Short Stories and Features, Readers' Letters and Special Sections for Women or Children, Cartoons and Crosswords and Puzzles, etc. How long a list you make must depend on the number of people doing the analysis and the time available for it. When the categories are agreed, different groups measure how many "column inches" particular papers devoted to each kind of material. It is useful to record in brackets how much of each figure was devoted to photographs and headlines. (If a photograph stretches over the width of three columns, then you measure its depth in inches, and multiply by three.) And the results can finally be given as proportions or percentages of the total area of the

paper (again measured in column inches).

The table of figures will form an excellent basis for com parisons and contrasts in the treatment of that day's news, an groups can then go on to contrast the styles in which differer papers handle similar news items, and the various ways i which their political bias or the differing interests of the readership have influenced their treatment of the day's new

A smaller project could take simply one type of news, or on big news story, and compare and contrast the treatment receives from all the main national newspapers.

Further Reading

Shot Actress—Full Story, taken from *Twenty Tales* by H. 1
BATES (Cape), also appears in *Short Stories of our Time* (ed
D. R. BARNES) (Harrap)
This selection of stories was chosen "because pupils enjo
reading them", and it includes Bill Naughton's "Late Nigh
on Watling Street", a very authentic tale of long-distanc
truck-drivers, and Doris Lessing's vivid "Through the Tunnel'

Stories of Flying Officer "X" by H. E. BATES (Cape)
During the Second World War, H. E. Bates served in the R.A.I
and, under the pseudonym of "Flying Officer X", wrote som
of the best stories about the war in the air.
Several of his other successful novels, such as *Fair Stood th
Wind for France* (Michael Joseph; Longman; Penguin) a stor
of escape from occupied France, *The Purple Plain* (Nelson; Per
guin) and *The Jacaranda Tree* (Longman; Penguin), also dea
with the war, in Europe and in Burma. Novels such as *My Unc
Silas* (Cape) and *The Darling Buds of May* (Michael Joseph
Penguin), on the other hand, are pure comedy.

Scoop by EVELYN WAUGH (Penguin)
This is an irreverent novel about pre-war Fleet Street, i
which an unassuming and innocent contributor to the "Dail
Beast", the author of the weekly country notes, is sent by mistak
to cover the crisis in Ishmaelia, an African republic. The resu
is hectic and highly amusing.

CHAPTER NINE

The Absurd

The sort of play written by N. F. Simpson is known as the "Drama of the Absurd", and the world it presents on the stage appears completely nonsensical and eccentric. In this extract, two comedians are putting on a short, "goonish" sketch, for no explicable reason, in a room adjoining the living room of a suburban house.

(*First Comedian is sitting at his improvised desk writing. He leans forward, presses a button, and says "Ping". The door from the living room opens to admit a man of no particular age between forty and sixty, whose nondescript appearance and defeated air contrast with the brisk ebullient manner the First Comedian has assumed. This is the Second Comedian. He approaches the desk and sits diffidently down. When after a few minutes the First Comedian disengages his attention from what he is writing, the Second Comedian leans forward.*)

SECOND COMEDIAN: It's my feet, Doctor.

FIRST COMEDIAN: What's the matter with your feet?

SECOND COMEDIAN: I was rather hoping you might be able to tell me that, Doctor.

FIRST COMEDIAN: Let me see them.

(*Second Comedian takes off shoes and socks.*)

SECOND COMEDIAN: They're all right now. It's when they suddenly swivel round they catch me.

(*Second Comedian holds out both legs quite straight in front of him. First Comedian stands over them.*)

FIRST COMEDIAN: What are these?

SECOND COMEDIAN: They're my kneecaps, Doctor.

FIRST COMEDIAN: They ought to be much higher up your legs than this.

SECOND COMEDIAN: I can't seem to keep them up, Doctor.

FIRST COMEDIAN: Take everything off except your trousers and lie down over there.

(*First Comedian goes to wash-basin where he begins washing his hands, while Second Comedian goes into the corner, where the desk conceals him, to undress.*)

FIRST COMEDIAN: Eardrums still getting overheated?

SECOND COMEDIAN: Only when I listen to anything, Doctor.

    (*Second Comedian comes out and lies down on the couch. Fir*
Comedian examines his chest.)

FIRST COMEDIAN: Breathe in deeply. Again. Yes—you're havin

trouble with your breathing. Breathe out. Do you notice any difference?

SECOND COMEDIAN: None at all, Doctor.

FIRST COMEDIAN: And do you know why? The reason you notice no difference is that there isn't any. All the time while you're breathing out, there's air forcing its way in. It's trying to push past. Breathe in again. (*He reflects for a moment.*) Do you ever feel as though the air you're getting is the wrong kind of air?

SECOND COMEDIAN: I just don't get the air, Doctor.

FIRST COMEDIAN: Somebody must have it if you don't.

SECOND COMEDIAN: It's my lungs, Doctor.

FIRST COMEDIAN: Nonsense. There's nothing wrong with your lungs. They're both perfectly fit.

SECOND COMEDIAN: I don't think they hit it off, Doctor. They're at daggers drawn practically the whole time. Over the air.

FIRST COMEDIAN: And your breathing's twisted to blazes as a result. Let me see your tongue. Open your mouth. (*He looks inside.*) You've had this jaw to pieces, haven't you?

SECOND COMEDIAN: It was some years ago, Doctor.

FIRST COMEDIAN: It doesn't matter how long ago it was. It's not a question of time. You laymen start dismantling these parts, but you've no idea how to put them together again. Here's a tooth which has been put back upside down. You're biting on the root.

(*First Comedian begins to use the stethoscope.*)

SECOND COMEDIAN: I've been told I can expect all my teeth to turn turtle eventually.

FIRST COMEDIAN: What are you doing about it?

SECOND COMEDIAN: Consulting you, Doctor.

FIRST COMEDIAN: I thought you'd come to me about your feet.

(*First Comedian grimaces as he continues to sound Second Comedian's chest.*)

FIRST COMEDIAN: What on earth are you carrying round in this blood stream of yours?

SECOND COMEDIAN: Only my blood, Doctor.

FIRST COMEDIAN: You've got a hell of a noisy circulation.

SECOND COMEDIAN: I have, Doctor. It keeps me awake.

FIRST COMEDIAN: I should think so. It sounds like a mobile iron foundry. You need a silencer for it. I'll give you a letter to take to the King's Cross Blood, Brain, and Bowel Hospital. You can have it under the National Health.

SECOND COMEDIAN: I'd like them to look at my arteries while I'm there as well, Doctor. They seem to have venous blood in them.

FIRST COMEDIAN: It's when you get arterial blood in the veins that you need to begin worrying. Turn over and let me look at your back.

(*Second Comedian turns painfully over and First Comedian stands looking for some moments in silence.*)

SECOND COMEDIAN: I've had it some time, Doctor.

FIRST COMEDIAN: I can see that. And we can write off these kidneys.

SECOND COMEDIAN: I hardly ever use them, Doctor.

FIRST COMEDIAN: How long have your ribs been like this?

SECOND COMEDIAN: As long as I can remember, Doctor.

FIRST COMEDIAN: And how long is that? Months? Years?

SECOND COMEDIAN: I can't altogether recall, Doctor.

(*First Comedian goes back to his desk where he takes up a pen and begins writing briskly.*)

FIRST COMEDIAN: You can get your clothes on.

(*While Second Comedian gets dressed, First Comedian goes on writing. When Second Comedian reappears, he puts down his pen.*)

FIRST COMEDIAN: Sit down, Mr. Avalanche.

(*Second Comedian sits down hesitantly and waits for First Comedian to begin.*)

FIRST COMEDIAN: I don't suppose there's much I can tell you that you don't know already. It's an obsolete body, of course, as you realize. And, I'm afraid you'll have to do the best you can with it. You must learn to co-operate with your organs.

SECOND COMEDIAN: The small of my back is too big, Doctor.

FIRST COMEDIAN: There's nothing to be gained by pretending it isn't. In fact I'll be quite frank with you, Mr. Avalanche —it's a great deal larger than it should be. Not only in your case, but with a surprisingly large number of people. But there's absolutely no need for you to have any misgivings about it. People go on—some of them with far less wrong with them than you have by a long way—they go on living active lives sometimes for years. There's no reason at all Mr. Avalanche, why given time you shouldn't have a good twenty or thirty years in front of you.

SECOND COMEDIAN: With a transparent pelvis, Doctor?

FIRST COMEDIAN: The main thing is to keep that blood circulat ing. Take precautions, but don't overdo it. Sleep whenever you can with your eyes closed. Keep off strong poisons of all kinds—and breathe. Breathe all the time. If it doesn't seem to be showing results, make sure it isn't because you're under water. Keep at it: the more you breathe the better you'll feel.

SECOND COMEDIAN: I've been having a lot of trouble with my slanting bowel since I became allergic to smells, Doctor.

FIRST COMEDIAN: You will for a time, but it's nothing to worry about. Take this letter to the Blood, Brain, and Bowel Hospital and they'll give you a thorough overhaul.

SECOND COMEDIAN: I shall feel a lot easier, Doctor.

FIRST COMEDIAN: And get those feet seen to. They'll be no good to you while they swivel. You should be seeing somebody about them. The feet should never swivel. Hand that letter in to the almoner and you can come back here when the specialist has seen you.

SECOND COMEDIAN: Thank you, Doctor. And I'll come in again as you say when I've been examined.

FIRST COMEDIAN: Next Thursday. I can't see you before then. And I'll give you something for those elbows, to see if we can't get them bending the right way.

SECOND COMEDIAN: Very good, Doctor.

(*Second Comedian goes listlessly out, switching off the lights as he does so.*)

(from *A Resounding Tinkle* by N. F. Simpson)

Appreciation and Discussion

1. Give the meaning of the following words and phrases *as used in this* extract: improvised; nondescript appearance; ebullient manner; assumed; diffidently; disengages his attention; grimaces; obsolete; to have misgivings; allergic to; the almoner; listlessly.

2. Give a more formal equivalent for these idiomatic or colloquial constructions:
(a) I don't think they hit it off.
(b) They're at daggers drawn.
(c) Your breathing's twisted to blazes.
(d) I can expect all my teeth to turn turtle.
(e) We can write off these kidneys.
(f) Don't overdo it.
(g) Keep off strong poisons.

(h) Keep at it.

(i) I shall feel a lot easier.

(j) Get those feet seen to.

3. Discuss the following kinds of joke, finding at least one example of each kind from the passage: (a) puns; (b) absurd impossibilities; (c) incongruities; (d) absurdly obvious ideas; (e) comic imitations (or parodies) of conventional language; (f) *non-sequitur* arguments, where the conclusions contradict the premises.

4. How many of the jokes in this passage depend on misconceiving one's body as a machine? What other comic ideas of the human body are used?

5. In what ways are the remarks of the doctor and the patient typical of doctors and patients? Is there an element of satire in this?

6. Why is the doctor-patient relationship good material for comedy? Are there other stock relationships that are frequently made fun of?.

7. How should the two parts (first comedian and second comedian) be played? Suggest appropriate dress, properties and mannerisms for the two characters.

8. Is this comedy of situation, comedy of character, slapstick comedy, satire or verbal repartee? Discuss these kinds of comedy, and whether the comedy of the absurd should be a distinct category of its own.

9. What is funny about absurdities? Would it be true to say that this world of comic fantasy is most effective on the stage when played absolutely "straight", and against a completely normal background?

Of course I tried to tell him
but he cranked his head
    without an excuse.
I told him the sky chases
    the sun
And he smiled and said:
    "What's the use"
I was feeling like a demon
    again
So I said: "But the ocean chases
    the fish."
This time he laughed
    and said: "Suppose the
        strawberry were
            pushed into a mountain,"
After that I knew the
    war was on—
So we fought:
He said: "The apple-cart like a
                broomstick angel
        snaps and splinters
                old dutch shoes."
I said: "Lightning will strike the old oak
        and free the fumes!"
He said: "Mad street with no name."
I said: "Bald killer! Bald killer! Bald killer!"
He said, getting real mad,
        "Firestoves! Gas! Couch!"
I said, only smiling,
        "I know God would turn back his head
        if I sat quietly and thought."
We ended by melting away,
    hating the air!

                                GREGORY CORSO

Discussing the Poem

1. Would you classify this as a nonsense poem in a similar
category to the nonsense verse of Edward Lear or Lewis Carroll?
Compare it with poems like "The Jumblies" and others in
Lear's *Nonsense Songs*, and with "Jabberwocky", "The Walrus

and the Carpenter" and "The Hunting of the Snark" among Lewis Carroll's poems.

2. Is it at all significant that the two characters in this poem are both poets? Do they compete with words or images? Can you see any significance in the rest of the title (". . . Hitchhiking on the Highway")?

3. How should the poem be read aloud? Does one speaker become more angry and noisy than the other? Practise reading it dramatically, with two or three different readers taking parts.

4. Try writing a nonsense poem of your own. Remember that the best nonsense verse has always played with words or sounds, or else made fun of accepted ideas and conventions.

Techniques

Exercise 1. Ambiguities often take the form of *puns*; these can be of two kinds, those that depend on two distinct words that happen to sound alike (technically known as *homonyms*) and those words that happen to have two (or more) distinct meanings (sometimes known as *homographs*). "Peer, pier; see, sea; sweet, suite" are pairs of homonyms; "mine" is an example of a homograph. A dictionary entry might be set out as follows:

mine, 1. *pron.* The one(s) belonging to me.

adj. (pred. only) Belonging to me. (O.E.)

mine, 2. *n.* Deep excavation from which minerals are extracted; explosive charge detonated in a container, hole containing this charge.

v.t. & i. Dig for minerals, extract or search for minerals from the earth; burrow under, lay explosive charges underground or in water. (O.F.)

miner, *n.* Worker in a mine, esp. a coal-mine.

Examine this carefully: how many meanings of "mine" are given? How many of these are sufficiently distinct in meaning to count as puns? What is the meaning of the abbreviations used (including the note "pred. only"), of the variations in type and of the punctuation used? How are the two distinct *derivations* of the two basic words here indicated in this entry?

(a) Look up the following words in a dictionary, and find at least two distinct meanings for each. Then compose one sentence using the word in each of these meanings, in such a way as to show its meaning. Study these examples, noting how one half of the sentence gives an indication of the meaning of the word in the other half.

132

(i)   Those books may be Joe's, but these are *mine*, and I intend to keep them.

(ii) When the local *mine* was closed down, there was still a considerable quantity of coal underground, but it was thought uneconomic to dig it out.

(iii) The unexploded *mine*, washed up on the beach, was probably laid during the war to protect the river estuary.

base	boil	founder	lock	pound
bill	fine	grave	pass	swift

(b) Explain the two meanings of the puns in the following sentences:

(i)   The strip cartoons on the backs of breakfast food packets are usually cereal stories.

(ii)   The explorer was fond of foreign climes and we can only wonder how he managed his great feat in view of the dissent of the other climbers.

(iii) The wealthy landowner loved the water where he rode for exercise, but he did not give a damn for conserving it.

(iv)   The motor boat was too dear, so we decided on a quick sail.

(v)   He arrived at the wedding reception in mourning clothes, having been formerly married himself: indeed, he knew all the rites of marriage.

(vi)   How much bread you make depends upon how much you need.

(vii) They scorned any higher purchase for they had worked in the bargain basement where there was always a cellar's market.

(viii) His friend found work sowing firs for lumberjacks.

(ix)   Many girls in this town are chased, for the young men rarely caught them.

(x)   It was a play about drug traffic, but the hero got the heroine in the end.

(c) Find at least one homonym or pun for each of the following and, if you can, make up a sentence that might equally well use either word [as in the examples in part (b)] in each case:

allowed	boar	isle	mail	oar
bear	buoy	key	mayor	pain
beer	dual	liar	muscle	sight

Exercise 2. Study the following two newspaper reviews of th
play "If His Lordship Pleases", and then discuss or writ
answers to the questions below:

1. Here at last. An honest, down-to-earth play about ordinary foll
A real slice of life served up with a spicy sauce of humour to help yo
forget your troubles—that's *If His Lordship Pleases* at the Crofto
Empire this week. His Lordship: none other than Tony Smithson
fresh from his success as *Our Tone* on TV.

Fans rocked with laughter from first scene to tenth curtain-ca
last night. The impossible scrapes he gets into turn mum and da
grey with despair. And when girl-friend one (Betty Buding) fac
girl-friend two (Sonia Harvey) in the Hansons' front parlour . . .!

This is the Tony we have all learned to love, now proving that h
goes over just as big in the live theatre. More, please.

2. The superficial domestic comedy *If His Lordship Pleases* (Crofto
Empire) serves as further proof that television material is unsuite
to the legitimate theatre. In the ITV series, Tony Smithson's role
the inadvertently disruptive adolescent is amusing enough for
twenty-minute sketch; two hours of this unrealistic nonsense is simpl
tedious, and the actors themselves showed signs of the strain. Bett
Buding and Sonia Harvey are accomplished young actresses in the
own right—it is painful to see them as mere foils for Mr. Smithson
formula comedy. No doubt the star's devoted following will ensu
this production a long West End run, but it can never be more tha
a light television show repeated *ad nauseam*.

(a) Taking information from both these reviews, what can yo
conclude about the plot and setting of this play?

(b) What do you think the first reviewer thinks of plays tha
had been recently produced, in contrast to this one? Ho
does he imply this?

(c) How does each reviewer inform his readers that this pla
presents Tony Smithson in a similar role to his televisio
one?

(d) What was the theatre audience's reaction to this play
How does each reviewer inform us of this?

(e) Which reviewer does more justice to the supporting cast
Is there any reason for the difference?

(f) What, apparently, is the second reviewer's objection t
this play? Does he use the play to illustrate a genera
principle of criticism?

(g) What does the second reviewer mean by the following
domestic comedy—the legitimate theatre—the inad
vertently disruptive adolescent—unrealistic nonsense—

mere foils—formula comedy—a long West End run—
repeated *ad nauseam*.

(h) Study the vocabulary of the two reviews. Which might
appear in a popular newspaper? In what ways do the
reviewers appeal to or flatter their respective readers?

(i) The publicity for a play (in posters, newspaper advertisements, handbills, etc.) often quotes a few words or phrases
from different reviews. What short quotations do you think
a publicity manager (especially if not scrupulously
honest) could take from these reviews?

(j) Study the sentence and paragraph structure of these
pieces. Notice all the incomplete sentences in the first: why
does this reviewer use them? Is there any effective balance
of ideas in the longer sentences of the second review?

(k) Would *you* want to see this play after reading these reviews?
Give full reasons for your decision.

Exercise 3. The extract from *A Resounding Tinkle* uses several
examples of absurd conclusions and twisted reasoning for
comic effect. When the second comedian says: "I just don't
get the air, Doctor," the reply: "Somebody must have it if
you don't" at first seems a logical argument. Circular arguments are also used:

"There's no reason at all, Mr. Avalanche, why given time
you shouldn't have a good twenty or thirty years in front
of you."

Dishonest and twisted arguments are, however, not confined
to comedy; in serious discussion they are more dangerous, since
they may appear convincing:

e.g. "I am quite impartial on this matter, but I am also quite
convinced, whatever they may say, that the government
are wrong about it."

This is an abuse of the word "impartial" (which should mean
"unbiased to either side") in order to make the condemnation
of the government sound fairer than it is.

Discuss the following arguments, or try to explain in writing
what is dishonest or illogical about them.

(a) A. Of course, I am against cruelty to animals.
B. But you go fox-hunting!
A. Yes, but I don't think that is cruel. The fox enjoys it.
B. Surely he doesn't enjoy being caught and killed?
A. Perhaps not, but he enjoys the chase, and anyway he usually
gets away.

(b) A. I believe that we should cut our expenditure on arms so tha we can give more help to underdeveloped countries.

  B. That is an unpatriotic suggestion: aren't you prepared t defend your country?

(c) In the three days of the Christmas weekend there have been si minor accidents on that corner, and three days before Christma I saw someone killed there. That's an average of an acciden every day—365 a year—and a death per week. What an appallin situation!

(d) Each of our air-liners carries 50 passengers on this 1600-kilo metre route; that means our air line can now claim to hav flown each of 1000 passengers over 1600 kilometres and we hav only had one serious crash. How many coach companies coul claim such a safety record?—One accident per 1 600 000 kilo metres!

(e) When we are ill we need strong medicine to clean us out and ri us of germs—it is the same with the country's economic difficul ties: get rid of all the unproductive people, like gamblers, th unemployed, civil servants and teachers, and you will solve th problem.

(f) Of course it is natural for men to fight, so there will always b wars: you have only to watch a couple of tom cats scrapping ove a mate, to see what I mean.

(g) Extremists are always dangerous—if I had my way I woul imprison them all and only tolerate reasonable people of moderat views.

(h) Randovia's typical man-in-the-street has one-and-a-half chil dren, earns 439·5 drotskis a month, marries ·8 times, smokes 2 cigarettes a day and spends 1·5% of his income on gambling; h is also 162·7 cm high and owns 1/6th of a dog.

(i) The Germans started two world wars within thirty years: wouldn't trust a German girl to help look after *my* children.

(j) The demonstrators began to get out of hand: some were threaten ing to attack the police and break into the Embassy. They wer behaving like mad dogs, and when a dog goes mad, you shoo him!

Topics for Written Work

1. Write a short story, if possible a humorous one, dependin on a misunderstanding, or on lack of communication betwee people. Reconsider first the basic humorous technique incongruous situations where dignified or pompous peopl become absurd, comic timing where events happen or fail t happen by a fraction of a second, comic muddles of words o meanings, satirical criticism of people or institutions made t

seem ridiculous, usually by exaggerating their faults or peculiarities.

To write effectively, you need to plan carefully so that characters and plot are fully worked out. The final form could be either a story or a short play.

2. Write a review of a play you have recently seen, heard or read. Write more fully than either of the journalists in *Exercise* 2 above. Try to give a fuller and more balanced view of the play of your choice, so that the reader understands (in a very *brief* summary) what the play is about, what kind of play it was intended to be, who performed in it and what kind of performance the leading actors gave, and how successful different aspects of the production (including scenery, costume, lighting and music, where these are important) were. Finally give a personal recommendation to your readers, saying how good a play this is, compared with others of its kind.

Oral Work

1. Groups of the class could attempt play-reading or acting of the extract from *The Resounding Tinkle*, or other parts of the same play, or other humorous short plays or extracts. Comedy, however, *must* be well-rehearsed: everything depends on timing and on polished acting. In most comedies, for instance, it is vital for the funniest characters to be completely serious themselves, and to give highly disciplined performances.

As an alternative to class-room acting, a group could attempt a tape-recorded version. In this case, look for clearly distinguished voices, and aim at extra clarity in the speaking, since the jokes will depend entirely on the spoken words.

2. Collect a number of different newspaper reviews of one play or television programme, and prepare a short talk reporting "what the papers said", with as much comment and contrast as possible to make this lively and interesting.

Activities and Research

1. Find out what you can about the "Drama of the Absurd". Look at some of the work of Eugene Ionesco, Harold Pinter and N. F. Simpson, and perhaps also Samuel Beckett and John Mortimer. Martin Esslin's book *The Theatre of the Absurd* (Eyre & Spottiswoode; Penguin) might also be useful. Refer also to the *Goon Show*, which was so popular on radio and later on television in Britain, and to the kind of satire to be found in magazines such as *Punch*, *Private Eye* and *Mad*. The same kind of absurd humour has also appeared in films.

2. Make a special analysis of newspaper coverage of the arts and entertainment, comparing the amount of space devoted over a week of issues, and trying to show any noticeable differences of emphasis in the kind of entertainment reviewed or the depth of criticism. This study could follow on from work done in Chapter 8.

3. Organise a play visit one evening for all members of the class who wish to come. Study the local press to see what is on in your district in the next few months, discuss a suitable choice, and enquire about possible reduced prices for a party, and reduced travel rates for the outing.

A Resounding Tinkle appears in the collection *The Hole—Plays and Sketches* by N. F. SIMPSON (French) (822.91)
The plays of N. F. Simpson are the dramatic counterparts to the nonsense literature and poetry of Lewis Carroll and Edward Lear. In addition to writing the film script of *The One Way Pendulum*, he has also created a large number of plays for television about the domestic tribulations of Bro and Middie Paradock, who appear in *A Resounding Tinkle*.

The Room and *The Dumb Waiter* by HAROLD PINTER (Methuen) (822.91)
If you enjoyed your first taste of the drama of the Absurd, these two short plays by another outstanding British playwright will provide a very suitable follow up. Pinter's style is not so "goonish" as Simpson's: although he too uses the clichés of everyday conversation as his basic ingredient, he usually combines them into what has been described as an "unnerving comedy of menace". Another volume, *A Slight Ache* (822.91), contains three one-act plays originally written for radio and television, and five revue sketches.

Waiting for Godot by SAMUEL BECKETT (Faber) (822.91)
Beckett is one of the most profound of the dramatists of the Absurd, and this play, first produced in 1952, earned him a world-wide reputation. In it, two tramps stand, talk, try to make a decision—and wait.

Absurd Drama (Penguin) (822.91)
This volume contains four plays. They are EUGENE IONESCO's first full-length play, Amédé, and three shorter pieces, ARTHUR ADAMOV's *Professor Taranne*, FERNANDO ARRABEL's *The Two Executioners*, and *The Zoo Story* by EDWARD ALBEE.

Supplementary Exercises

Revision Exercise 1

Each of the following sentences contains either *redundant* words (see page 33) or unnecessary *verbosity* or *circumlocution* (see page 45). Simplify them.

1. In the accident, the driver and passenger of a Jaguar car were fatally injured, and have both since died.
2. In the museum they kept one of the most valuable jewels in the world: a unique diamond quite unlike any other.
3. A disinterested, impartial observer, with no stake in the outcome of the contest, would certainly have expected the home team to win.
4. After a day's assiduous, hard, concentrated labour, he felt he deserved to spend the evening resting in the arms of Morpheus.
5. We have made a complete prognosis of the future course of his illness, and our forecast is that the patient will be walking again next week.
6. His impeccable sartorial taste in clothes, faultless in every detail, has earned him a reputation not unlike that of a dandy man about town.
7. One of the worthy guardians of the law rendered any escape down the corridor impossible by planting his corpulent frame firmly on the threshold of the room.
8. Whilst I was proceeding in a southerly direction down the thoroughfare known as the High Street, it came to my notice that what was obviously an inmate of one of Her Majesty's corrective establishments was lurking in the doorway of an emporium by the name of Banstead's.

Revision Exercise 2

(a) Find a *homonym* (a word of identical sound, though different meaning), that is spelt differently, for each of the following. In some cases there may be more than one. Be prepared to explain the different meanings.

e.g. cue—queue

canvas; compliment; faint; gamble; metal; palate; peak; rein; root; wrote.

(b) The following are *homographs*: each word has at least two quite distinct meanings. Write two sentences for each word to illustrate two distinct meanings:

band; boil; fleet; grate; kind; lark; mean; ring; skate; sound.

c) Form new words—adjectives—from the following by using the suffixes -able, or -ible, whichever is correct in each case.

e.g. combustion—combustible; despise—despicable.

access	compare	division	practice	service
admit	comprehend	envy	revoke	terror
agree	convert	ignite	sale	value
avoid	digest	justify	size	vision

Revision Exercise 3

a) Rewrite the following short passage, choosing the correct word for each context from the two given in brackets, one of which is a word frequently confused with the other.

As one thief ran down the narrow (allies, alleys), another followed (suit, suite). The police, however, were still (confidant, confident) that they were taking the right (coarse, course). for they had left the (principal, principle) part of their force (lying, laying) in (wait, weight) down by the river. The (currant, current) there was flowing very strongly after the (reign, rain) and only the most (masterly, masterful) or foolhardy of sailors would dare cross in such (averse, adverse) conditions. The (advice, advise) to the men was to (lie, lay) low and keep a (continuous, continual) close watch, for an arrest now seemed (eminent, imminent).

b) Compose sentences to illustrate the difference between the two words in each of the following easily confused pairs. Try to compose sentences that include a clear indication of meaning, as suggested on pages 44 and 132–3.

accept	access	fallible	imaginary
except	excess	fallacious	imaginative
industrial	notable	practice	proceed
industrious	notorious	practise	precede
metre		visual	
meter		visible	

Revision Exercise 4

a) Each of the following *proverbs* is equivalent to one of the statements printed below (although in a different order). Notice that the statement, being the literal meaning that the proverb embodied in a neat figurative form, tends to be longer, or indeed rather verbose. Pair them off correctly.

Hunger is the best sauce.
You cannot get blood out of a stone.
Don't burn the candle at both ends.
The pen is mightier than the sword.
Procrastination is the thief of time.
You cannot run with the hare and hunt with the hounds.
Blood is thicker than water.
Fools rush in where angels fear to tread.
One swallow doesn't make a summer.
Beggars cannot be choosers.

It is foolish to squander what little one has.
Putting off decisions is only a waste of valuable time.
Those who depend upon others' generosity cannot afford reject offers of help.
People are naturally sympathetic towards their own relatives.
One should not judge any situation on a single piece of evidenc
Being necessitous makes one appreciate what small favours or does receive.
Books and pamphlets have a greater influence upon men minds and the shape of society than do violence and force arms.
It is impossible to support and be friendly with two opposi sides in any dispute.
Only the foolhardy will interfere in a difficult situation witho thinking.
When faced with an impossible task, there is no point in attemp ing it.

(b) For each of the following ten *idioms* or sayings, first write a sentenc
to illustrate its correct use and imply its meaning, and then write
clear explanation (in non-figurative language) of that meaning

e.g. To feather one's own nest.

(i) The speaker accused the Board of Directors of feathering thei
own nests at the expense of the ordinary shareholders by raisin
their own salaries while the dividend on shares remained ur
changed.

(ii) To feather one's own nest = to look after oneself, usually fina
cially, regardless of others.

To put the cart before the horse.
To clutch at a straw.
To fish in troubled waters.
To stick to one's guns.
To be like a fish out of water.
To have a shot at something.

142

To get one's knife into someone.
To throw someone off the scent.
To back the wrong horse.
To rub someone up the wrong way.

Revision Exercise 5

(a) Each of the following two sentences can be punctuated in at least six different ways, so as to alter the meaning without altering the words or their order (except to change small to capital letters, where necessary). Write out the different versions:

1. he said that was how it was she thought
2. what jack said they did not fully understand

(b) The following sentences are already *ambiguous*, that is, they have two or more meanings as they stand. Rewrite each one at least twice, with sufficient alteration (of words, word order or punctuation) to give them one meaning only each time.

1. She thought she saw a ghost lying naked in her bubble bath.
2. Parsons are often found in prison or in hospital.
3. The shop steward refused to wear any clothes to distinguish him from the other workers.
4. Did the Romans want the Britons to be slaves or to keep the peace in that part of the world?
5. The murder weapon was found in the shrubbery by the victim.
6. They replied that they would like their stolen money back with considerable interest.
7. A naturalist should be able to climb trees fast enough to catch a monkey without a tail.
8. Primitive man regularly went hunting for his wife and family.
9. There were no free seats left for the excursion.
10. He told his father that he had dropped his hammer on the tiled floor and cracked it.

Précis Exercise 1

By cutting out redundancy and repetition, reduce the following passage from about 130 words to between 35 and 45. State at the end the number of words in your summary. The four sentences should be reduced to one single sentence. *(See Précis Rule 1, page 33.)*

All club members who have joined the club are asked and requested to pay over their money for their subscriptions as they arrive, on entering the club. All members of the club are asked and requested to please inform the person acting as the club's secretary beforehand and in advance if and when they, the club members, wish to bring one or more visitors or guests with them to the club. All members of the club are asked and requested to wear plimsols on their feet when they go into the games room,

whether to play games or for some other purpose. Finally a
members of the club are kindly requested to go away and leav
the building where the club is held promptly at 10.30 p.m., an
no later.

Précis Exercise 2

By applying Précis Rule 1 as well as 2, but again not omitting any ideas
re-write the passage below in between 70 and 85 words, instead c
about 190. State at the end the exact number of words you used
(For Précis Rule 2, see page 61.)

The number of car crashes and road accidents in which th
people involved have been killed has grown to a very considerabl
degree over recent months. In all probability this increase ca
be attributed in some part to the volume of traffic, since mor
and more cars and other vehicles are being sold and brought int
use on our roads and highways every year; but in some part i
can also be attributed to the fact, which seems most disturbing
that these new vehicles are now being designed by those wh
produce them to do the kind of high speed that is only suitable o
the new, fine motorways that are now being built. But the truth
which we all find so unfortunate, is that, in the whole of th
British Isles, we have only a few hundred miles of motorway
where these new vehicles that average such high speeds can b
safely driven at those speeds; and there remain hundreds c
miles of poor main road (at least they are called "main roads")
which are quite inadequate, and where it is criminally dangerou
to drive fast.

Précis Exercise 3

By stating the main facts and the main argument, and leaving ou
all the illustrations, re-write the following passage in 60 to 70 words
instead of about 225. State the number of words you use. *(For Préci
Rule 3, see page 90.)*

The various methods of advertising can have effects that ar
highly undesirable. When the manufacturers try to make th
ordinary men and women in the street associate their particula
products, such as a soap-powder, a shampoo, a box of chocolate
or a make of sports car, with a particular kind of success—succes
on the dance floor or in marriage or promotion in one's firm—
they are spreading a very poor set of values. On every side
through every mass medium, on our television screens, in ou
newspapers and magazines, on ugly hoardings in the streets, i
every shop window, we are being told repeatedly, over and ove
again, that buying things, owning things, purchasing ne
things, will bring us happiness, will solve all our persona

problems, and will guarantee success. People begin to take it for granted that, if they spend more and more, they will become happier and happier. They assume, for instance, that a holiday abroad is bound to be happier than one at home, or that a large expensive car is more desirable than a cheap one. In fact, however, the effect of all this advertising, urging us to buy more and own the newest and the latest, be it a washing machine, or a scooter, or a record player, is to make us increasingly discontented with ourselves, our homes and our incomes.

*Analysis Exercise 1

In this exercise we revise all the kinds of subordinate clauses dealt with in Book Three: various adjective clauses, adverb clauses of time, place, manner, cause, purpose, result, concession and condition, and noun clauses as subjects, objects and complements. Each sentence contains a main clause and one subordinate clause, and you should begin by noting the verbs and the introductory word; for example
(i) The old man *who* <u>used to tell</u> stories about the war <u>died</u> last week.
(ii) He <u>knew</u> *what* <u>makes</u> a good story.
(iii) *As* he <u>talked</u>, you <u>could</u> almost <u>smell</u> the gunpowder.
Then draw up columns, as we showed in Book Three, to set out the information clearly:

	CLAUSE	KIND	FUNCTION	RELATIONSHIP
1.A	the old man . . . died last week	Main clause		
a¹	who used to tell stories about the war	Subordinate clause	Adjective	Qualifies noun "man" in main clause "A"
2.A	he knew	Main clause		
a¹	what makes a good story	Subordinate clause	Noun	Object of verb "knew" in main clause "A"
3.A	you could almost smell the gunpowder	Main clause	ı	
a¹	as he talked	Subordinate clause	Adverb of time	Modifies verb "could smell" in main clause "A"

145

1. He was the sort of man whose opinions I respect.
2. No one that I have known could tell a better story.
3. He used to sit where the tree threw its shade.
4. All the local children would like to be soldiers when they grow up.
5. Until he came to our village, life was very dull for the children.
6. They all wept because they missed him so much.
7. He died peacefully as an old soldier should.
8. If he were still alive, he would be sitting by the green this morning.
9. Although he had been through twenty battles, he had never been wounded once.
10. He was so determined to be a soldier that he ran away from home.
11. He signed on quickly so that his father would not be able to stop him.
12. What he most wanted was to win a medal.
13. He always said that he had never deserved one.
14. His stories were what the children loved to hear.

*Analysis Exercise 2

Look at this sentence:
(i) It had been raining hard, *but* the house burnt fiercely, *when* it was well alight.

Three verbs mean three clauses and the introductory word "when" no doubt introduces a subordinate clause, probably an adverb clause of time. The conjunctions "and", "but", "or" (and the compounds "both . . . and", "neither . . . nor", etc.), however, always join phrases and clauses of equal importance – they are *coordinating conjunctions*. In the example (i) above, the word "but" joins *two main clauses*, and the word "when" introduces a subordinate adverb clause of time dependent on the second main clause—i.e. saying when it burnt fiercely.

The same coordinating conjunctions can join together two subordinate clauses, provided that they both have the same function and depend on the same word in the same main clause. Study these two examples:
(ii) The occupants were the kind of people *who* would leave the house unattended *and who* did not take sensible precautions.
(iii) Bill and Ted saw *what* seemed to be a red light shining in the window, *but what* was in fact a burning carpet.

All three examples are analysed in columns below; note the wording used and the way they are set out.

	CLAUSE	KIND	FUNCTION	RELATIONSHIP
1.A	it had been raining hard	Main clause		
B	but the house burnt fiercely	Main clause	Co-ordinate with main clause "A"	
b¹	when it was well alight	Subordinate clause	Adverb of time	Modifies verb "burnt" in main clause "B"
2.A	the occupants were the kind of people	Main clause		
a¹	who would leave the house unattended	Subordinate clause	Adjective	Qualifies noun "kind" in main clause "A"
a²	and who did not take sensible precautions	Subordinate clause	Adjective	Coordinate with sub. clause "a¹"
3.A	Bill and Ted saw	Main clause		
a¹	what seemed to be a red light shining in the window	Subordinate clause	Noun	Object of verb "saw" in main clause "A"
a²	but what was in fact a burning carpet	Subordinate clause	Noun	Coordinate with sub. clause "a¹"

Analyse the following in columns:
1. They saw the house on fire and they ran to give the alarm.
2. There was a phone-box in that road but it was out of order.
3. They neither panicked nor were paralysed but acted calmly and sensibly.
4. Each of them tried one of the houses to which telephone wires were fixed.
5. Bill was unlucky but Ted found a housewife who was willing to phone the brigade.
6. Then they walked back down the street so that they could direct the firemen and so that they could offer to help.

7. The fire officers said firmly that they wanted no help and that it was dangerous for people to come too close.
8. The police soon arrived and said that they must either move right back or leave the street altogether.
9. The reporters were also there looking for the people who had spotted the blaze first and who had reported it.
10. Bill and Ted, who wanted their names in the papers, hurried forward to talk to the reporters when they arrived.

*Analysis Exercise 3

We have already noted a number of examples where adverb or adjective clauses appear without the introductory word. What introductory word is "understood" in each of the following examples?
(i) <u>Were</u> I the King of China, I <u>could have</u> anything I <u>wanted</u>.
(ii) He <u>wanted</u> the book we <u>gave</u> him very much.
In Chapter Two, we have also noted a number of other variations on the normal "if" pattern of adverb clauses of conditions; e.g.
(iii) *Provided that* you <u>ask</u> politely, you <u>can have</u> it.
Here is the column analysis of these three examples:

	CLAUSE	KIND	FUNCTION	RELATIONSHIP
1.A	I could have anything	Main clause		
a¹	(that) I wanted	Subordinate clauses	Adjective	Qualifies pronoun "anything" in main clause "A"
a²	were I the King of China	Subordinate clause	Adverb of condition	Modifies verb "could have" in main clause "A"
2.A	He wanted the book ... very much	Main clause		
a¹	(which) we gave him	Subordinate clause	Adjective	Qualifies noun "book" in main clause "A"
3.A	you can have it	Main clause		
	provided that you ask politely	Subordinate clause	Adverb of condition	Modifies verb "can have" in main clause "A"

Analyse the following in columns; those marked (2) contain two subordinate clauses.

1. The man I want to see may arrive at any time.
2. The business I have with him is really very important.
3. It can only wait if he is prepared to take no action.
4. Were he to act alone, it would ruin the whole scheme.
5. I can only act if I have his full co-operation, which he may be unwilling to give. (2)
6. Should he arrive this morning, please send him straight in.
7. If he arrives after lunch, keep him waiting, unless he has to hurry back. (2)
8. Unless he comes and I can persuade him, we can do nothing. (2)
9. Provided that we get his agreement, we could complete the work this summer.
10. We should then have all the facilities we need here.

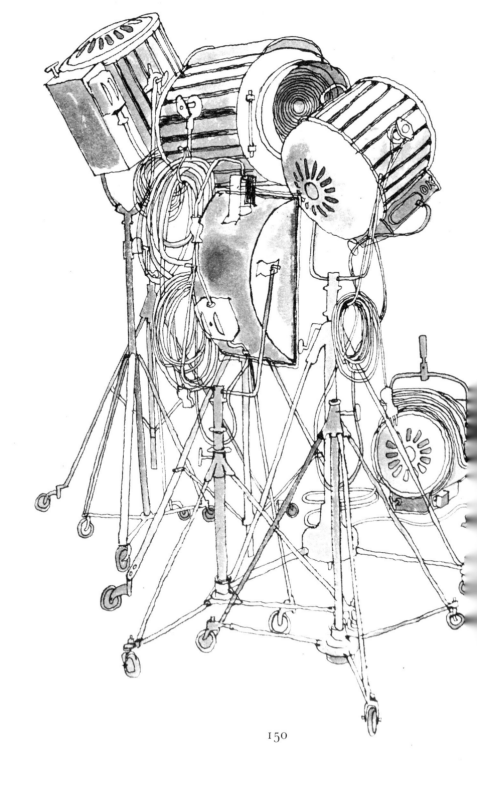

CHAPTER TEN

Television

Jim Raeder is taking part in a television "thrill show" contest, in which he risks his life to entertain viewers, for the sake of a big money prize. He is not a professional "stunt" man, but he has taken part in other, less dangerous, contests before.

He closed his eyes again and remembered, with mild astonishment, a time when he had been in no trouble. . . .

He had been a big pleasant young man working as a truck driver's helper. He had no talents. He was too modest to have dreams.

The tight-faced little truck driver had the dreams for him. "Why not try for a television show, Jim? I would if I had your looks. They like nice average guys with nothing much on the ball. As contestants. Everybody likes guys like that. Why not look into it?"

So he had looked into it. The owner of the local television store had explained it further.

"You see, Jim, the public is sick of highly trained athletes with their trick reflexes and their professional courage. Who can feel for guys like that? Who can identify? People want to watch exciting things, sure, but not when some joker is making it his business for fifty thousand a year. That's why organized sports are in a slump. That's why the thrill shows are booming."

"I see," said Raeder.

"It's a marvellous opportunity. Take you. You're no better than anyone, Jim. Anything you can do, anyone can do. You're *average*. I think the thrill shows would go for you." . . .

* * * * *

There was a heavy truck approaching. He kept on walking, pulling his hat low on his forehead. But as the truck drew near, he heard a voice from the television set in his pocket. It cried, "*Watch out!*"

He flung himself into the ditch. The truck careered past, narrowly missing him, and screeched to a stop. The driver was shouting. "There he goes! Shoot, Harry, shoot!"

Bullets clipped the leaves from the trees as Raeder sprinted into the woods.

"*It's happened again!*" Mike Terry was saying, his voice high-pitched with excitement. "*I'm afraid Jim Raeder let himself be lulled into a false sense of security. You can't do that, Jim! Not with your life at stake! Not with killers pursuing you! Be careful, Jim, you still have four and a half hours to go!*"

The driver was saying, "Claude, Harry, go around with the truck. We got him boxed."

"*They've got you boxed, Jim Raeder!*" Mike Terry cried. "*But they haven't got you yet! And you can thank Good Samaritan Susy Peters of twelve Elm Street, South Orange, New Jersey, for that warning shout just when the truck was bearing down on you. We'll have little Susy on stage in just a moment . . . Look folks, our studio helicopter has arrived on the scene. Now you can see Jim Raeder running and the killers pursuing, surrounding him . . .*" . . .

*   *   *   *   *

One week ago he had been on the *Prize of Peril* stage, blinking in the spotlight, and Mike Terry had shaken his hand.

"Now, Mr. Raeder," Terry had said solemnly, "do you understand the rules of the game you are about to play?"

Raeder nodded.

"If you accept, Jim Raeder, you will be a *hunted man* for a week. *Killers* will follow you, Jim. *Trained killers*, men wanted by the law for other crimes, granted immunity for this single killing under the Voluntary Suicide Act. They will be trying to kill *you*, Jim. Do you understand?"

"I understand," Raeder said. He also understood the two hundred thousand dollars he would receive if he could live out the week. . . .

"Very well!" cried Mike Terry. "Jim Raeder, meet your would-be killers!"

The Thompson gang moved on stage, booed by the audience.

"Look at them, folks," said Mike Terry, with undisguised contempt. "Just look at them! Antisocial, thoroughly vicious, completely amoral. These men have no code but the criminal's warped code, no honour but the honour of the cowardly hired killer. They are doomed men, doomed by our society which will not sanction their activities for long, fated to an early and unglamorous death."

The audience shouted enthusiastically.

152

"What have you to say, Claude Thompson?" Terry asked.

Claude, the spokesman of the Thompsons, stepped up to the microphone. He was a thin, clean-shaven man, conservatively dressed.

"I figure," Claude Thompson said hoarsely, "I figure we're no worse than anybody. I mean, like soldiers in a war, *they* kill. And look at the graft in the government, and the unions. Everybody's got their graft."

That was Thompson's tenuous code. But how quickly, with what precision, Mike Terry destroyed the killer's rationalisations! Terry's questions pierced straight to the filthy soul of the man. . . .

"We'll get him," Thompson said.

"And one thing more," Terry said, very softly. "Jim Raeder does not stand alone. The folks of America are for him. Good Samaritans from all corners of our great nation stand ready to assist him. Unarmed, defenceless, Jim Raeder can count on the aid and good-heartedness of *the people*, whose representative, he is. So don't be too sure, Claude Thompson! The average men are for Jim Raeder—and there are a lot of average men!" . . .

*   *   *   *   *

Raeder thought about it, lying motionless in the underbrush. Yes, *the people* had helped him. But they had helped the killers too.

A tremor ran through him. He had chosen, he reminded himself. He alone was responsible. The psychological test had proved that.

And yet, how responsible were the psychologists who had given him the test? How responsible was Mike Terry for offering a poor man so much money? Society had woven the noose and put it around his neck, and he was hanging himself with it, and calling it free will.

Whose fault?

"Aha!" someone cried.

Raeder looked up and saw a portly man standing near him. The man wore a loud tweed jacket. He had binoculars around his neck, and a cane in his hand.

"Mister," Raeder whispered, "please don't tell!"

"Hi!" shouted the portly man, pointing at Raeder with his cane. "Here he is!" . . .

The killers were shooting again. Raeder ran, stumbling over uneven ground, past three children playing in a tree house.

"Here he is!" the children screamed. "Here he is!"
Raeder groaned and ran on. He reached the steps of the building, and saw that it was a church.
As he opened the door, a bullet struck him behind the right kneecap.
He fell, and crawled inside the church.
The television set in his pocket was saying, "*What a finish, folks, what a finish! Raeder's been hit! He's been hit, folks, he's crawling now, he's in pain, but he hasn't given up! Not Jim Raeder!*"
Raeder lay in the aisle near the altar. He could hear a child's eager voice saying, "He went in there, Mr. Thompson. Hurry, you can still catch him!"
Wasn't a church considered a sanctuary, Raeder wondered.
Then the door was flung open, and Raeder realised that the custom was no longer observed. He gathered himself together and crawled past the altar, out the back door of the church.
He was in an old graveyard. He crawled past crosses and stars, past slabs of marble and granite, past stone tombs and rude wooden markers. A bullet exploded on a tombstone near his head, showering him with fragments. He crawled to the edge of an open grave.
They had deceived him, he thought. All of those nice average normal people. Hadn't they said he was their representative? Hadn't they sworn to protect their own? But no, they loathed him. Why hadn't he seen it? Their hero was the cold, blank-eyed gunman, Thompson, Capone, Billy the Kid, Young Lochinvar, El Cid, Cuchulain, the man without human hopes or fears. They worshipped him, that dead, implacable robot gunman, and lusted to feel his foot in their face.
Raeder tried to move, and slid helplessly into the open grave.

(from *The Prize of Peril*, a short story by R. Sheckley)

Appreciation and Discussion

1. What exactly did Jim Raeder have to do to win the "prize of peril"?
2. What would you imagine the Voluntary Suicide Act to be? Do you think the television companies might have tried to persuade the government to pass it? If so, why?
3. How did Jim Raeder come to be appearing as victim in thrill shows?
   (a) Who first suggested it?

(b) What qualifications had he required?

(c) What was Jim's main reason for agreeing to take up this kind of challenge?

4. (a) What, briefly, is the story of the Good Samaritan?

(b) Explain the television company's idea in encouraging their "Good Samaritans".

(c) What reasons, apart from simple kindness, might people have for helping a victim like Raeder?

5. What evidence is there that ordinary viewers did not really want Raeder to come through easily?

6. How responsible *were*:

(a) Jim Raeder;

(b) Mike Terry and the TV company; and

(c) the psychologists and the law that permitted him to take part? Was the viewing public also responsible?

7. Explain what "identification" means when we are discussing audiences' reactions to characters in books, on the stage or on the screen. Why should audiences find it easier to identify with "nice average guys"? In what ways was Jim "average"? (Was he average in his looks, too?)

8. What effect does "identification" already have on television programmes today?

9. Would it be true to say that even politicians and professors go out of their way to appear "ordinary" and "human" on television? Do popular newspapers try to make important people appear "just like us" in many ways?

10. This story is set in the future. What do television audiences today find thrilling about dangerous sports? (Give several examples.) Would such programmes be less thrilling if there were no danger to men taking part?

11. Discuss Mike Terry's commentary style. Why does he call his audience "folks"? What is Mike Terry's function on this programme? When he introduces the killer Thompson "with undisguised contempt", do you think his questions really "pierced straight to the filthy soul of the man"?

12. Is there some justification for the Thompsons and what they are doing? Would it be fair to say that the television company have "got their graft" too?

13. Is the end of this extract a satisfactory end to this story? What other endings would you suggest? If possible, read the whole story, and compare the end in the full version with this one.

Exercise 1. Study the following passage, and then answer the questions below:

A television director is ultimately responsible for the whole show, from the vetting of the script, through the casting, rehearsal and preparation of the scenes and sets, including filmed sequences, to the final selection of every camera shot that appears on the screen. He works first with the script-writer, whose material has to be adapted to the limitations (financial and technical) of the television medium. Filmed sequences are expensive, but if used they must merge smoothly with the parts of the play that are to be televised from the studio. Television plays need to have a few easily distinguished main characters, and must attract interest and attention quickly and tell a story clearly in a limited setting.

There will only be a few studio sets, and these must be realistic, even though cramped into a small space. Rear-projected film and much-enlarged still photographs are often used to give a background of movement or the appearance of space. If a film sequence is included, there is the added worry of ensuring continuity from set to film and back to the set. Careful attention must also be given to lighting and to arrangements for sound reproduction. The appearance of a microphone hanging near the top of his screen may completely spoil a viewer's involvement in a particular scene; so may a distracting thump or squeak from the studio equipment, or any noise from the technicians at work during the performance.

The director is responsible for casting the play and rehearsing the actors. Good television actors learn to work with the ·cameras, responding at the right moment in close-up, and often delaying their reactions to give time for the cameras to switch to them. They may have to move quickly (and silently) from set to set, and change their moods (or even their clothes) in a few seconds. Yet the rehearsal period is often short—perhaps less than a week.

The director's work reaches its climax during the actual transmission. He now has indirect control of the cameras, by means of the headphones each cameraman wears, and personally decides which of the cameras' shots to use at any given moment. He watches several monitor screens, each showing one camera's pictures, and switches from one to another, and across to titles or film sequences, at appropriate moments. This editing of shots is an extremely subtle art. Too much cutting from picture to picture becomes distracting, yet at precisely the right moment the viewers must move from one speaker to another, or from long shot to close-up, and the cameras must track in or pan round to help the audience follow any movement by the actors, or any new development in the story. "Establishing shots" o the whole scene are important, and the viewer must never be confused or annoyed by a sudden jump to an unfamiliar view of the action.

(a) Discuss the technical terms used here, e.g.: the vetting of the script; sets; rear-projected film; continuity; casting the play; transmission; monitor screens; editing; cutting; track in; pan.

(b) Compare and contrast the work of the television director, as described here, with that of (i) a film director, and (ii) a theatrical producer or director.

(c) Discuss whether television makes greater demands upon actors than (i) film or (ii) plays in the theatre.

(d) Suggest a title for this passage, summing up its main theme in more than one but fewer than seven words.

(e) Choose a short sub-title to sum up each of the five paragraphs.

(f) Make a short summary in note form of the whole passage, using your title and sub-titles as a framework for the notes.

Exercise 2. In summarising, it is necessary to omit details and examples. Such details, however, often convey an important part of the information in the passage to be summarised. If the details are left out, the general point they illustrate must still be retained.

To do this, you must learn to generalise. This means finding one term to cover many details. Here is an obvious example:

In the course of one typical evening's television viewing, we may see a travel film, a further instalment of a regular "soap opera", two or three cartoons, a Western film, a crime serial, a comedy programme, a competitive quiz and a panel game. Serious news or comment and anything making intellectual demands on the viewer will form a comparatively small part of the evening's viewing. (65 words)

This could be summarised:

Most of a typical evening's television programmes are light entertainment; serious items are comparatively few. (15 words)

Generalise from the detail in the following passage, so that the three main impressions of London are clearly expressed. Remember to apply Précis Rules 1 to 4. Reduce the passage from about 262 words to between 75 and 95 words, stating the exact number you have used.

The documentary programme about London presented a wealth of impressions of Britain's capital city. Three features, however, seemed to stand out particularly. From the shots of stations like Victoria, the viewers gained a vivid impression of the London rush-hour—that mass of people, old, young, fast, slow, smart, and dowdy, merging into a vast, depressing crowd, each person in a dark suit and carrying raincoat or rolled umbrella and evening paper, hurrying on relentlessly with blank faces, apparently without thinking what they were doing or why. They showed neither joy nor disgust at it, simply acceptance. In contrast, the film gave a relaxed picture of the great parks right in the centre of London. There ducks waddled unconcerned, lovers strolled, children played, old men slept, and a few rowers plied their oars in a leisurely way. All was peaceful and soothingly green, especially the grass, though people could walk freely over it. The film emphasised, too, the extraordinary architectural contrasts. London was not built to a pattern, like Paris, nor was it several different cities alongside one another, like Rome. Here old shouldered new; one turned a corner by a new block of óffices to meet a crazy, half-timbered Elizabethan house. There were also contrasts of size, so that vast cathedrals dwarfed parish churches, and near sky-scrapers towered above the twisting, narrow streets. Then there were ugly Victorian houses staring at graceful Georgian fronts over the road, and beautiful tree-lined squares beside grim-looking business houses. For the director of this documentary, this inextricable mixture of styles was the special attraction of London.

Précis Rule 5. GENERALISING:

Sum up all unimportant detail, so that the general point is clearly stated, but the details are omitted.

Exercise 3. In Chapter Eight we noted that *adjective clauses* and *noun clauses* can be easily confused when they are both introduced by the word "that", or when both appear without any introductory word:
   (i) Do you understand the rules of the game *(that) you are about to play?* (Adjective clause).
   (ii) Do you understand *(that) you are about to play a dangerous game?* (Noun clause).
Do you remember the simple test to see whether a clause like this is an adjective clause or a noun clause? (See p. 117).
   The same kind of difficulty applies to clauses introduced by the words "where" and "when". They can obviously introduce *adverb clauses* of place or of time:
   (iii) *When Jim Raeder was a truck driver's mate* he went *where the firm told him to go.*

But as soon as the place or the time is itself mentioned in the main sentence, the "where" and "when" clauses become *adjective clauses,* describing the time or the place. What nouns are qualified by the adjective clauses in this example?

(iv) At the time *when Jim Raeder was a truck driver's mate,* he went to all the places *where the firm told him to go.*

Notice that in this example (iv), "when" could easily be replaced by "at which" and "where" by "to which"—the word "which" can again be used as a test to show that these are adjective clauses.

Thirdly, "when" and "where" can be used to introduce *noun clauses.* Whenever such a clause follows a verb of saying or thinking, it is more likely to be *what* someone is saying, rather than when or where he is saying it. For example:

(v) Mike Terry asked Jim *where he had been a truck driver's mate.*

(vi) He told Jim *when he would receive the prize money.*

Here the "where" and "when" clauses are the *objects* of the verbs "asked" and "told".

(a) In the following sentences, the "where" and "when" clauses have been printed in italics. Decide whether each is an adverb, an adjective, or a noun clause. State what verb it modifies, or what noun (or pronoun) it qualifies, or what verb it is subject, object or complement of, in each case.

(i) Jim's life was much happier *when he was simply a truck driver's mate.*

(ii) Jim remembered a time *when he had been in no trouble.*

(iii) He remembered *where he was.*

(iv) *When the dare-devil is a professional "stunt-man",* people are not very interested.

(v) People do not enjoy a programme *where the thrills are carefully rehearsed.*

(vi) Viewers will sympathise more *when the victim is just an ordinary person.*

(vii) Jim did not know *where he could go for shelter.*

(viii) He found a church *where he might be safe from the gunmen.*

(ix) *When he opened the church door,* a bullet struck him.

(x) At the very moment *when he entered the church,* he was shot down.

(b) Complete the following sentences so that you have made up a sensible "where" or "when" clause for each. Make sure that your clause contains its own subject and verb, and that it has the function indicated in brackets in each case.

> e.g. We all know when. . . . (Noun cl.)
> We all know *when the schools programmes begin.*

(i) Television programmes where . . . are often very funny. (Adj. cl.)

(ii) You can thank Susy Peters for that shout just when . . . (Adj. cl.)

(iii) They do most of their viewing when . . . (Adv. cl.)

(iv) The director decides where . . . (Noun cl.)

(v) When . . ., there will probably be many angry letters. (Adv. cl.)

(vi) On an occasion when . . ., we see B.B.C. television at its best. (Adj. cl.)
(vii) Where . . ., there you will find added difficulties. (Adv. cl.)
(viii) The government have just announced where . . . (Noun cl.)

Topics for Written Work

1. First, keep a record of your own television viewing for a continuous period, perhaps a week. For each programme, make a separate entry. Note the following information:
   (a) Date, time, duration, number of breaks.
   (b) Channel, title, credits (as given in the *Radio Times*, for instance), including director or producer, etc.
   (c) Kind of programme (see the categories suggested in *Activities and Research*, 1 (a).), its aims and purpose (including the kind of audience that it was meant for).
   Give a very *brief* account of its theme or story, etc.
   (d) Success of the script, acting, and use of humour, tension, personality, or whatever is relevant.
   (e) Technical details: use of music, film, camera-work, background, editing, and so on.

2. Now, choose one or two programmes, or a particular series, for fuller consideration. Similar headings will be a useful frame-work, but you will now be probing deeper into the success of the programme under (d) and (e). Having established what it is trying to achieve, compare the programme with others of a similar kind, and try to measure its strengths and weaknesses. If it sets out to portray real people, for instance, ask yourself how convincing their lives are, how careful has been the attention to realistic detail, and what kind of example this study of people offers to the rest of us. Be alert for any clichés of situation or dialogue. Finally sum up with your own honest opinion of the success of the programme.

Oral Work

1. Prepare a brief explanation of some or all of the following technical terms (or *jargon*) from the world of television production. Make notes where necessary so that you can give a brief oral report to the class when required:
   (a) commentator; compère; floor manager; interviewer; news-caster; script-writer; sports-caster;
   (b) animation; live or recorded; soap opera; sound effects; tele-cine; test card; videotape;

160

(c) boom; camera-script; captions; dissolve; fade-out; mixer; on location; outside broadcast;

(d) close-up; long shot; medium shot; pan; track; traverse; wide-angle; zoom;

(e) adapted by; devised by; dramatised by; edited by; introduced by; narrated by; presented by.

2. During the many hundreds of hours of television broadcasting every week, certain formulas and clichés emerge all too often. Stock situations, stock characters, stock questions and stock responses often indicate a depressing lack of originality and sincerity. Sometimes just a typical sentence or phrase is enough to indicate the whole standard situation or the all too familiar character. Take some or all of the following, for instance, and either describe the character or situation, or continue the dialogue or monologue in the expected way.

(a) Five, four, three, two, one, blast off!

(b) I can't take any more, Jim.

(c) And how does it feel to be the first man to . . .

(d) O.K. This is it!

(e) Nobody talks to me like that . . .

(f) Will she be all right, doctor?

(g) Very clever, Mr. Bolkov, very clever indeed . . .

(h) He's no fool, you know.

(i) I'd be the last person to want to . . .

(j) How about that, eh? How about that?

(k) You can say that again, brother.

(l) Her Majesty, wearing a bright blue beret trimmed with . . .

Make your own list of popular current clichés, and discuss these with the class.

3. Discuss the influence of television on various parts of the community. Can children watch too much television? What harmful effects could it have on them? Are programmes you would consider unsuitable for (say) children of 11 or younger shown at times when they are still likely to be viewing?

Do people learn much from television, or is it too superficial to make any impression or change people's attitudes?

Do you think there is too much violence shown on television? What harmful effects could this have? Is some violence more harmful than other kinds of violence? How far can we blame television for the increase in crime?

Has television discouraged reading and more creative and active hobbies and recreations?

Activities and Research

1. (a) Make a survey of the kinds of programme offered on a typical day, or during a typical week, by all the channels available in your area. In order to draw some comparisons and contrasts, it will be necessary to decide on certain categories into which nearly all programmes can be fitted. Limit the number of these categories, extending them to include all programmes if possible; here is a suggested list of headings:

More Serious
News and background
Discussions, talks, etc.
Documentaries
Serious plays and films
Serious music, opera, ballet
Educational programmes
   (for schools, adults, etc.)
Religious programmes

Lighter Entertainment
Sports news, comment, etc.
Light plays, comedy series
Travel and nature films
Western, crime and spy films
Light and pop. music, dancing, etc.
"Magazine" programmes, etc.
   (for women, children, the deaf)

First, add up the broadcast time devoted to each category on each channel. Then note how much of this time is "live" broadcasting, how much is television recording, how much is film; and, in the case of smaller commercial television companies, how much time is given to their own programmes, and how much is "networked".

(b) Where different channels broadcast similar programmes, attempt some comparison of their styles. Here the judgement is bound to be largely a matter of personal opinion, but it should be interesting to note differences in the way in which news, documentaries, quiz shows, etc. are presented.

2. Find out about the B.B.C. and the independent television companies. How are they financed? How are they controlled? How much influence has the government on the B.B.C. or the advertisers on the commercial companies? What principles and codes of practice do the B.B.C. and I.T.A. lay down for themselves, for instance about violence or standards of advertising? What geographical areas do the broadcasts cover? Find out how much a short advertisement costs with the big companies at different times of the week.

3. If possible, arrange for the class or a small group to visit a television studio, to see a broadcast as part of a studio audience, or to be shown round. Tickets for shows are usually free; but not always easy to obtain! Make a report on what you saw, and learned from the visit.

Further Reading

The Prize of Peril by ROBERT SHECKLEY appeared in *Second Orbit* edited by G. DOHERTY (Murray)

Robert Sheckley is one of the most talented of science fiction writers. In an original and intriguing way, his short stories examine human values, institutions, and patterns of behaviour to be found in contemporary society. And, although it is a fair criticism that the use of words by many science fiction writers is on the same level as popular journalism, Robert Sheckley's style often rises considerably above this level.

The anthology in which this chapter's story is to be found, and its forerunner, *Aspects of Science Fiction*, provide a good introduction to worthwhile science fiction.

Listed below are other anthologies that contain stories of considerable merit in the quality of values implied, in manipulation of plot, and in invention of incident.

Penguin Science Fiction Omnibus, edited by BRIAN ALDISS (Penguin)
Best S.F., series edited by EDMUND CRISPIN (Faber)
Connoisseur's S.F., edited by TOM BOARDMAN (Dobson)

CHAPTER ELEVEN

Defeat

Annie was a conductress on a Midland tram service in the First World War. John Thomas Raynor was an impudent young inspector who flirted with one after another of the girls on the tram-cars.

There was no mistake about it, Annie liked John Thomas a good deal. She felt so rich and warm in herself whenever he was near. And John Thomas really liked Annie, more than usual. The soft, melting way in which she could flow into a fellow, as if she melted into his very bones, was something rare and good. He fully appreciated this.

But with a developing acquaintance there began a developing intimacy. Annie wanted to consider him a person, a man: she wanted to take an intelligent interest in him, and to have an intelligent response. She did not want a mere nocturnal presence, which was what he was so far. And she prided herself that he could not leave her.

Here she made a mistake. John Thomas intended to remain a nocturnal presence; he had no idea of becoming an all-round individual to her. When she started to take an intelligent interest in him and his life and his character, he sheered off. He hated intelligent interest. And he knew that the only way to stop it was to avoid it. The possessive female was aroused in Annie. So he left her.

It is no use saying she was not surprised. She was at first startled, thrown out of her count. For she had been so *very* sure of holding him. For a while she was staggered, and everything became uncertain to her. Then she wept with fury, indignation, desolation, and misery. Then she had a spasm of despair. And then, when he came, still impudently, on to her car, still familiar, but letting her see by the movement of his head that he had gone away to somebody else for the time being, and was enjoying pastures new, then she determined to have her own back. . . .

*   *   *   *   *

Annie went round to all the girls John Raynor had been out with, and

"Who're you going with tonight, John Thomas?" asked Muriel Baggaley coolly.

"Tonight?" said John Thomas. "Oh, I'm going home by myself tonight—all on my lonely-o." . . .

"Nay," said Muriel. "Don't leave us all lonely, John Thomas. Take one!"

"I'll take the lot, if you like," he responded gallantly.

"That you won't either," said Muriel. "Two's company; seven's too much of a good thing." . . .

He turned his head away. And suddenly, with a movement like a swift cat, Annie went forward and fetched him a box on the side of the head that sent his cap flying and himself staggering. He started round.

But at Annie's signal they all flew at him, slapping him, pinching him, pulling his hair, though more in fun than in spite or anger. He, however, saw red. His blue eyes flamed with strange fear as well as fury, and he butted through the girls to the door. It was locked. He wrenched at it. Roused, alert, the girls stood round and looked at him. He faced them, at bay. At that moment, they were rather horrifying to him, as they stood in their short uniforms. He was distinctly afraid.

"Come on, John Thomas! Come on! Choose!" said Annie.

"What are you after? Open the door," he said.

"We shan't—not till you've chosen!" said Muriel.

"Chosen what?" he said.

"Chosen the one you're going to marry," she replied.

He hesitated a moment.

"Open the blasted door," he said, "and get back to your senses." He spoke with official authority.

"You've got to choose!" cried the girls.

"Come on!" cried Annie, looking him in the eye. "Come on! Come on!"

He went forward rather vaguely. She had taken off her belt, and swinging it, she fetched him a sharp blow over the head with the buckle end. He sprang and seized her. But immediately the other girls rushed upon him, pulling and tearing and beating him. Their blood was now thoroughly up. He was their sport now. They were going to have their own back, out of him. Strange, wild creatures, they hung on him and rushed at him to bear him down. His tunic was torn right up the back. Nora had hold of him at the back of his collar, and was actually strangling him. Luckily the button burst. He struggled in a wild frenzy of fury and terror, almost mad terror. His tunic was simply torn off his back, his shirt sleeves were torn away, his arms were naked. . . .

Annie knelt on him, the others girls knelt and hung on to him. Their faces were flushed, their hair wild, their eyes were all glittering strangely. He lay at last quite still, with face averted, as an animal lies when it is defeated and at the mercy of the captor. Sometimes his eye glanced back at the wild faces of the girls. His breast rose heavily, his wrists were torn. . . .

"Do you hear—do you hear?" said Annie. And with a sharp movement, that made him wince, she turned his face to her.

"Do you hear?" she repeated, shaking him.

But he was quite dumb. She fetched him a sharp slap on the face. He started, and his eyes widened. Then his face darkened, with defiance, after all.

"Do you hear?" she repeated.

He only looked at her with hostile eyes.

"Speak!" she said, putting her face devilishly near his.

"What?" he said, almost overcome.

"You've got to *choose*!" she cried, as if it were some terrible menace, and as if it hurt her that she could not exact more.

"What?" he said, in fear.

"Choose your girl, Coddy. You've got to choose her now. And you'll get your neck broken if you play any more of your tricks, my boy. You're settled now."

There was a pause. Again he averted his face. He was cunning in his overthrow. He did not give in to them really— no, not if they tore him to bits.

"All right, then," he said. "I choose Annie." His voice was strange and full of malice. Annie let go of him as if he had been a hot coal.

"He's chosen Annie!" said the girls in chorus.

"Me!" cried Annie. She was still kneeling, but away from him. He was still lying prostrate, with averted face. The girls grouped uneasily around.

"Me!" repeated Annie, with a terrible bitter accent.

Then she got up, drawing away from him with strange disgust and bitterness.

"I wouldn't touch him," she said.

But her face quivered with a kind of agony, she seemed as if she would fall. The other girls turned aside. He remained lying on the floor, with his torn clothes and bleeding, averted face.

"Oh, if he's chosen—" said Polly.

"I don't want him—he can choose again," said Annie, with the same rather bitter hopelessness.

"Get up," said Polly, lifting his shoulder. "Get up."

He rose slowly, a strange, ragged, dazed creature. The girls eyed him from a distance, curiously, furtively, dangerously.

"Who wants him?" cried Laura, roughly.

"Nobody," they answered, with contempt. Yet each one of them waited for him to look at her, hoped he would look at her.

All except Annie, and something was broken in her.

(from *Tickets, Please*, a short story by D. H. Lawrence)

Appreciation and Discussion

1. How many girls were assembled to teach John Thomas his lesson that Sunday? What were their names, as far as you can tell from this extract?

2. Is there any distinction here in the attitudes of the various girls to John Thomas? Is Annie at all different in the violence of her words or actions?

3. Is there any difference between the way the girls first attack him, and the way they set about him again? Can you account for any change of mood?

4. Why (and in what way) did he "not give in to them really?"

5. When he chose Annie, his voice was "full of malice". Why? What was cunning or malicious about this choice?

6. What details in this story suggest that Annie was really in love with John Thomas?

7. What do you think Polly was going to say about his choice of Annie, when Annie interrupted her?

8. What was the difference between Annie's liking for John Thomas, and the way he liked her? In your opinion, is this difference a normal difference between a girl's and a boy's attitude to a boy-girl friendship? Could it just as easily happen the other way round?

9. Discuss the phrase "the possessive female". Is it fair to generalise about girls and women like this? Was John Thomas himself being possessive or selfish in his own way?

10. Why didn't Annie accept John Raynor at the end? What

does Lawrence mean by "something was broken in her"?

11. What divides Annie from the other girls at the end? Is her attitude to John, and his choice of girl, fundamentally different from theirs?

12. Where do the sayings "all on my lonely-o" and "Two's company; seven's too much of a good thing" come from?

13. Notice D. H. Lawrence's use of *several* adjectives, nouns or adverbs together: does each add a different suggestion in these contexts?

    (a) "She felt so *rich* and *warm* in herself";

    (b) "Annie wanted to consider him a *person*, a *man*;"

    (c) "She wept with *fury, indignation, desolation* and *misery*."

    (d) "The other girls rushed upon him, *pulling* and *tearing* and *beating* him."

    (e) "His voice was *strange* and *full of malice*."

    (f) "A *strange, ragged, dazed* creature . . ."

    (g) "The girls eyed him . . . *curiously, furtively, dangerously*."

14. In the opening of this story, Lawrence emphasises the tough independence of these conductresses, who are well able to look after themselves among the rough miners on the trams. Does this view of the girls help make this incident more convincing? Do you feel that Annie herself is *more* or *less* tough than her fellow-conductresses?

15. Do you think John Raynor deserved this punishment? Is it right to carry on a series of flirtations with different girls as he did? Is it possible, in your opinion, to do this without making some of them jealous, and without some of them wanting the boy to become "an all-round individual"? Is it worse when a boy behaves like this than when a girl does, for any reason?

Breakfast

He put the coffee
In the cup
He put the milk
In the cup of coffee
He put the sugar
In the *café au lait*
With the coffee spoon
He stirred
He drank the *café au lait*
And he set down the cup
Without a word to me
He lit
A cigarette
He made smoke-rings
With the smoke
He put the ashes
In the ash-tray
Without a word to me
Without a look at me
He got up
He put
His hat upon his head
He put his raincoat on
Because it was raining
And he left
In the rain
Without a word
Without a look at me
And I took
My head in my hand
And I cried.

JACQUES PRÉVERT,
translated by LAWRENCE FERLINGHETTI

Discussing the Poem

1. Explain simply why the person speaking here ("I") cried. What kind of person does "he" appear to be, or what mood is he in at this breakfast?
2. What difference would it make to this poem to punctuate it throughout? Can it be argued that the division into short lines is already a kind of punctuation? What effects does this line division have?
3. Discuss the repetition. Does it add to the sense that "he" is deliberately ignoring the other person?

Techniques

Exercise 1. (a) Look again at the punctuation and sentence structure in the passage from *Tickets, Please*. The sentences generally are short and dramatic, and simply constructed, and there is considerable use of commas. In the following examples these are used mainly to divide up lists. Rewrite each, inserting the commas wherever they seem necessary, and then compare your version with the punctuation of the original:

(i) The soft melting way in which she could flow into a fellow as if she melted into his very bones was something rare and good.
(ii) Then she wept with fury indignation desolation and misery.
(iii) But at Annie's signal they all flew at him slapping him pinching him pulling his hair though more in fun than in spite or anger.
(iv) Roused alert the girls stood around and looked at him.
(v) Their faces were flushed their hair wild their eyes were all glittering strangely.
(vi) He rose slowly a strange ragged dazed creature.
(vii) The girls eyed him from a distance curiously furtively dangerously.

(b) Elsewhere in the passage, the commas are used to set apart parallel words or phrases that are *in apposition* to an existing noun or other part of speech. Thus in:

Annie wanted to consider him a person, a man.

the nouns "person" and "man" are clearly parallelled, each word being another way of expressing the other. What is in apposition to what in the following further examples?

He struggled in a wild frenzy of fury and terror, almost mad terror.

Strange wild creatures, they hung on him and rushed at him to bear him down.

Two nouns are said to be in apposition when they are similar in meaning and identical in grammatical function—thus, "person" and "man" in the first example were *both* object complements of the infinitive "to consider", and yet, of course, not two separate objects.

Rewrite the following, inserting all the necessary commas, especially those that mark nouns or phrases in apposition. Be prepared to say which nouns are in apposition, and whether they are subject, object, object of a preposition, etc., in the sentence.

(i) Annie a conductress had grown to like John Thomas the young inspector very much.

(ii) The trams run up hill and down through the ugly mining villages from Nottingham the big city to their terminus the last cold little place of industry the little town on the edge of wild open country beyond.

(iii) The other conductresses Muriel Laura Polly Emma and Nora were all waiting that evening in their little room at the depot a rough cosy place with a fire an oven and some simple furniture.

Exercise 2. (a) A number of words we have used in the last two or three chapters illustrate the different, and rather confusing, ways in which English forms nouns for "doers" or "operators":

inspect + -or = inspector; produce + -er = producer;
technique + -ian = technician; satire + -ist = satirist.

Adding these *suffixes* often involves spelling changes, and doubling the previous consonant (in short words) is quite common: e.g. run + -er = runner. There are very few rules to help with the spelling of these words. You must learn by practice and reference to the dictionary.

Add the appropriate suffix (-or, -er, -ian, -ist) to the following words, making any other necessary changes:

advertise	biology	economy	photography	telephone
advise	council	edit	physics	theology
assess	counsel	examine	politics	trap
astrology	create	guarantee	report	violin
biography	direct	logic	telegraph	wait

(b) The -tion, -sion suffixes, which usually form abstract nouns, present similar difficulties; study the following examples:

desert—desertion: submit—submission:
destroy—destruction: oppose—opposition.

Find the correct abstract nouns, ending in -tion or -sion, to correspond to the following verbs:

abolish	commit	disperse	exert	part
add	compose	dispose	expose	permit
admit	construct	divert	ignite	recognise
afflict	convert	edit	inhibit	repeat
assert	demolish	evict	omit	revert

*Exercise 3. Look at this sentence from the passage:

He lay at last quite still, with face averted, *as an animal lies* when it is defeated.

The "as" clause here is an *adverb clause of manner*—it indicates *how* he lay.
There are also a number of "as if" clauses in the passage, e.g.

She could flow into a fellow *as if she melted into his very bones*.

This could be regarded as another adverb clause of manner (how she would "flow"), but in fact it also implies a *condition*; it means:

She could flow into a fellow *as she would if she melted . . .*

This then is analysed:

A She could flow into a fellow—main clause.
a^1 as (she would)—subordinate adverb clause of manner, modifying verb "could flow".
a^2 if she melted into his very bones—subordinate adverb clause of condition, modifying verb "would" in the adverb clause.

(a) Break the following sentences down into clauses in this way. They include adverb clauses of time and of cause, introduced by "as", as well as adverb clauses of manner (and condition) to be analysed as in the example above.

(i) They were rather horrifying to him as they stood in their short uniforms.
(ii) He suddenly started to struggle as an animal might.
(iii) She cried as if it were some terrible menace.
(iv) She talked as if it hurt her.
(v) Annie let go of him as if he had been a hot coal.
(vi) She seemed as if she would fall.
(vii) As he had treated Annie so badly, perhaps he deserved it.
(viii) The girls certainly behaved as if they now hated him.

(b) Make up "as if" clauses of your own, to complete the following sentences, and then analyse them:

(i) The sky went black, as if . . .
(ii) As if he . . ., he marched up to the Headmaster.

(iii) Some animals will feign a limp, as if . . .
(iv) It is not as if she . . .
(v) He spent that day as if . . .

Topics for Written Work

. If life is to proceed smoothly and people are to remain on good terms with one another, we have to learn to accept defeat sometimes, to acknowledge we are wrong, and to apologise. There are occasions when this is a sign of strength of character, not weakness. Nora says at the end of *Tickets, Please*:

> "Tit for tat, old man . . . show yourself a man and don't bear a grudge."

f you were John Thomas, how would *you* take the girls' attempt o teach you your lesson?

Letters of apology are, of course, difficult to write. They have o ring true, and so they must not be too coldly formal, nor hould they be too exaggerated in their obsequiousness. Certainly one should appear to take trouble over them (setting 1em out formally and writing them neatly and well), or they ·ill appear grudging and insincere.

Try to write an honest, plain, effective letter of apology, nagining yourself in one of the following predicaments:

1) You are John Thomas Raynor, and you now realise how adly you have treated Annie Stone. Write to apologise (after 1e incident in our extract), giving an imaginary Nottingham-1ire address.

)) You are Annie, and you bitterly regret the way you and 1e other girls treated John Thomas at the Depot on Sunday. Vrite to him trying to put things right.

:) You have quarrelled with a favourite older person (perhaps 1 uncle or aunt) and made some very hurtful remarks about 1ults in general and him in particular. Now you want to)ologise, without appearing simply to be interested in the nd of presents or other help he can give you.

t) You have quarrelled with someone your own age about ligion or politics. You have not changed your mind, but you) not see why you cannot remain friends in spite of a funda-ental difference of outlook.

) You have done something you know was quite wrong 'borrowed" something valuable without the owner's per-ission, for instance, and then damaged it). Now you have to face the consequences, and write to offer to make the damage good.

2. Everyone has some experience of failure, defeat and shame, and an *honest* record of how it feels to be in this position should make an effective free-verse poem. Begin by recalling a particular incident in detail. Try to re-live the experience step by step, with all the circumstances, and above all your personal feelings, and all the associations that surround the memory of the shame itself. Make a few notes, trying to be honest and to re-live the situation as vividly as you can.

Then begin to *select* the striking details and associations, and to search for the right words and comparisons to convey what you really felt. Finally, arrange your thoughts step by step, varying the lines to suit your ideas, as was done in the poem *Breakfast*, and has been done by a fourth former in the following poem:

WHY?

Casually strolling across
That soft carpet of cheerful, earthy grass
Which was the common,
In the clean, clear freshness
Of the Sunday morning.
Then, I slowly, reluctantly, remembered,
Remembered the fight.
I didn't want to,
No,
But I had to, had to.
Why?
Why had I fought so badly?
Without confidence,
Without courage,
And let my team down.

I searched my brain for an answer,
One which I knew I wouldn't find,
An impossible excuse.
My mind could never be at rest
Until I could know why;
Forcing,
Forcing me to ponder over this,
As I walked across that common.

JOHAN

174

1. Dramatise the incident in the extract, or the whole short story *Tickets, Please*. Probably a tape-recorded production depending on a narrator with several actors and sound effects will prove most convenient and successful. Even an all-male group might be able to tackle the dramatisation on tape.

2. Find, or if necessary invent, examples of different ways of proposing marriage from history and literature. Act II, Scene 1 of *The Taming of the Shrew*, and the last act of *Henry V* are obvious examples in Shakespeare's plays. Mr. Collins' proposal to Elizabeth Bennet in *Pride and Prejudice* is a deliciously absurd incident in Jane Austen's novel. Different groups in the class might each present a contrasting example from fact, fiction or imaginative improvisation, ranging from the age of the caveman to the most up-to-date approach, and including both the serious and the ludicrous.

Activities and Research

1. Find out more about D. H. Lawrence, poet and novelist, who was one of the controversial figures in English Literature in the first half of the twentieth century. Nearly all his work is available as Penguin paperback books. *The White Peacock* and *Sons and Lovers* are the most closely autobiographical of his novels. His animal poems, particularly *Snake*, are frequently included in anthologies; why, do you think? Many of his stories and novels reflect closely the working-class life of the mining community where he was brought up, and this is an interesting field of study.

2. Trams and trolley-buses are obsolescent forms of transport, but were of course very common in our main cities. Make a full study of the history of the tramcar, horse-drawn and electric, illustrated with photographs and sketches. Find out what museums preserve specimens of them and what cities, at home or abroad, still have trams either as regular services or as tourist attractions.

Include sections on the mechanisms that were used in trams and trolley-buses, together with an anthology of references to them in songs or contemporary accounts.

Selected Tales by D. H. LAWRENCE (ed. Serraillier) (Heinemann) "Tickets, Please" is included in this selection, as are other stories reflecting Lawrence's own experiences at home in the Nottingham area. "Odour of Chrysanthemums" reflects the quiet acceptance of tragedy in a miner's home, "Strike-Pay" the exuberance of the miners even in the face of poverty and unemployment. But above all his stories are concerned with the relationships between people, and the effects of environment on them.

Sons and Lovers and *The White Peacock* by D. H. LAWRENCE (Heinemann; Penguin) Lawrence was himself the son of a miner and lived at East-wood, near Nottingham. His mother was better educated than his father and encouraged her children's intellectual interests. Both these novels draw on the Lawrences' family life and its tensions, and show the author's very accurate observation of people and nature. *Sons and Lovers*, particularly, is closely autobiographical and traces in fascinating detail Paul Morel's relationships with Miriam, with his possessive mother, and with Clara.

Pride and Prejudice by JANE AUSTEN (various publishers) The polite, middle-class world of the 1790's seems very different from the mining villages that D. H. Lawrence knew, but Jane Austen understood people and loved to poke fun at their foolishness and vanity, their snobbish pride and their blind prejudice. The high-born, rather shy Fitzwilliam Darcy seems no proper match for shrewd, vivacious Elizabeth Bennet, and her family have neither money nor enough good sense. Yet Jane Austen contrives to bring them together in a novel that is full of delicate, ironical good humour.

CHAPTER TWELVE

Political Satire

Napoleon and Snowball, two young boars on Manor Farm, had led the animals in a rebellion and overthrown the cruel and incompetent farmer, Jones. But Napoleon trained some fierce dogs as a bodyguard, drove Snowball off the farm and made himself dictator. Squealer, another pig, has the job of persuading the animals (including Boxer and Clover, who are hard-working farm-horses) that Snowball is to blame for all their troubles.

But Boxer was still a little uneasy.

"I do not believe that Snowball was a traitor at the beginning," he said finally. "What he has done since is different. But I believe that at the Battle of the Cowshed he was a good comrade."

"Our Leader, Comrade Napoleon," announced Squealer, speaking very slowly and firmly, "has stated categorically—categorically, comrade—that Snowball was Jones's agent from the very beginning—yes, and from long before the Rebellion was ever thought of."

"Ah, that is different!" said Boxer. "If Comrade Napoleon says it, it must be right."

"That is the true spirit, comrade!" cried Squealer, but it was noticed he cast a very ugly look at Boxer with his little twinkling eyes. He turned to go, then paused and added impressively: "I warn every animal on this farm to keep his eyes very wide open. For we have reason to think that some of Snowball's secret agents are lurking among us at this moment!"

Four days later, in the late afternoon, Napoleon ordered all the animals to assemble in the yard. When they were all gathered together, Napoleon emerged from the farmhouse, wearing both his medals (for he had recently awarded himself "Animal Hero, First Class", and "Animal Hero, Second Class"), with his nine huge dogs frisking round him and uttering growls that sent shivers down all the animals' spines. They all cowered silently in their places, seeming to know in advance that some terrible thing was about to happen.

Napoleon stood sternly surveying his audience; then he uttered a high-pitched whimper. Immediately the dogs bounded forward, seized four of the pigs by the ear and dragged them, squealing with pain and terror, to Napoleon's feet. The pigs' ears were bleeding, the dogs had tasted blood, and for a few moments they appeared to go quite mad. To the amazement of everybody, three of them flung themselves upon Boxer. Boxer saw them coming and put out his great hoof, caught a dog in mid-air, and pinned him to the ground. The dog shrieked for mercy and the other two fled with their tails between their legs. Boxer looked at Napoleon to know whether he should crush the dog to death or let it go. Napoleon appeared to change countenance, and sharply ordered Boxer to let the dog go, whereat Boxer lifted his hoof, and the dog slunk away, bruised and howling.

Presently the tumult died down. The four pigs waited, trembling, with guilt written on every line of their countenances. Napoleon now called upon them to confess their crimes. They were the same four pigs as had protested when Napoleon abolished the Sunday Meetings. Without any further prompting they confessed that they had been secretly in touch with Snowball ever since his expulsion, that they had collaborated with him in destroying the windmill, and that they had entered into an agreement with him to hand over Animal Farm to Mr. Frederick. They added that Snowball had privately admitted to them that he had been Jones's secret agent for years past. When they had finished their confession, the dogs promptly tore their throats out, and in a terrible voice Napoleon demanded whether any other animal had anything to confess. . . .

When it was all over, the remaining animals, except for the pigs and dogs, crept away in a body. They were shaken and miserable. They did not know which was more shocking—the treachery of the animals who had leagued themselves with Snowball, or the cruel retribution they had just witnessed. In the old days there had often been scenes of bloodshed equally terrible, but it seemed to all of them that it was far worse now that it was happening among themselves. Since Jones had left the farm, until today, no animal had killed another animal. Not even a rat had been killed. . . .

The animals huddled about Clover, not speaking. The knoll where they were lying gave them a wide prospect across the ountryside. Most of Animal Farm was within their view—the ong pasture stretching down to the main road, the hayfield, the pinney, the drinking pool, the ploughed fields where the oung wheat was thick and green, and the red roofs of the farm uildings with the smoke curling from the chimneys. It was a lear spring evening. The grass and the bursting hedges were ilded by the level rays of the sun. Never had the farm—and vith a kind of surprise they remembered that it was their own arm, every inch of it their own property—appeared to the nimals so desirable a place. As Clover looked down the hillside er eyes filled with tears. If she could have spoken her thoughts, t would have been to say that this was not what they had imed at when they had set themselves years ago to work for he overthrow of the human race. These scenes of terror and laughter were not what they had looked forward to on that ight when old Major first stirred them to rebellion. If she erself had had any picture of the future, it had been of a ociety of animals set free from hunger and the whip, all equal, ach working according to his capacity, the strong protecting he weak, as she had protected the lost brood of ducklings with er foreleg on the night of Major's speech. Instead—she did lot know why—they had come to a time when no one dared peak his mind, when fierce growling dogs roamed everywhere, nd when you had to watch your comrades torn to pieces after onfessing to shocking crimes. There was no thought of ebellion or disobedience in her mind. She knew that, even as hings were, they were far better off than they had been in the lays of Jones, and that before all else it was needful to prevent he return of the human beings. Whatever happened she would emain faithful, work hard, carry out the orders that were iven to her, and accept the leadership of Napoleon. But still, t was not for this that she and all the other animals had hoped nd toiled. It was not for this that they had built the windmill nd faced the bullets of Jones's gun. Such were her thoughts, hough she lacked the words to express them.

(from *Animal Farm* by George Orwell)

Appreciation and Discussion

1. (a) Why does Squealer "cast a very ugly look at Boxer"
   during the earlier discussion here?
   (b) Could this be connected at all with the dogs' attack
   on Boxer?
   (c) Why is everybody "amazed" by this attack?
2. What seemed so terrible about these executions to the
   other animals?
3. Why was Clover determined to go on obeying Napoleon
   even after this slaughter?
4. What do you assume "Sunday Meetings" were, before
   Napoleon abolished them? Why might he have wanted to
   stop them?
5. (a) Who had been blamed for the destruction of the windmill? (See the 8th paragraph.) (b) Who had built this
   windmill? (See the last paragraph of this extract.)
6. Old Major was an old boar who had first expounded the
   idea that one day the animals would revolt and take over

from men. What kind of society do you think he had looked forward to?

7. What do the following words and phrases mean in this passage? (Remember to give your answer in the same part of speech—"Categorically" has to be explained by an adverb or adverb equivalent.) (a) categorically; (b) to change countenance; (c) tumult; (d) collaborated; (e) retribution; (f) knoll; (g) a wide prospect; (h) spinney; (i) gilded; (j) according to his capacity.

8. Boxer, the hard-working cart-horse, is chiefly noted for his unquestioning loyalty to the leaders of the animals' rebellion. Why should he have such doubts about Snowball's guilt? What two methods does Squealer use (here) to persuade Boxer?

9. Things had gone badly for the animals: they were short of food and finding it difficult to compete with neighbouring farmers (like Mr. Frederick). Why did Napoleon blame Snowball, rather than accept responsibility himself?

10. Why did Napoleon award himself medals?

11. Squealer's propaganda had made the animals fearful and hysterical. Do you think the pigs who "confessed" were really guilty? Could there be any reason for them to say what they knew Napoleon wanted them to say?

12. Are there any signs in this passage of the way the pigs (with the dogs) were becoming a separate "ruling class"? Is it significant that the first four animals to be executed as traitors were pigs?

13. Can you suggest reasons why Clover and the others felt so attached to Animal Farm at this time particularly?

14. In this book, George Orwell satirises the history of real revolutionary movements by imagining a similar situation among animals.
    (a) What political creed looks forward to a "society of (men) set free from hunger and (oppression), all equal, each working according to his capacity . . ."?
    (b) Which dictators does Napoleon remind you of?
    (c) Can you find parallels for Jones, Snowball, Boxer, the dogs and Squealer in (for instance) the history of the Russian Revolution and the U.S.S.R.?

15. Do you agree that sudden revolutions always lead to political oppression and dictatorship, instead of liberating the people who support them?

This Excellent Machine

This excellent machine is neatly planned,
A child, a half-wit would not feel perplexed:
No chance to err, you simply press the button—
At once each cog in motion moves the next,
The whole revolves, and anything that lives
Is quickly sucked towards the running band,
Where, shot between the automatic knives,
It's guaranteed to finish dead as mutton.

This excellent machine will illustrate
The modern world divided into nations:
So neatly planned, that if you merely tap it
The armaments will start their devastations,
And though we're for it, though we're all convinced
Some fool will press the button soon or late,
We stand and stare, expecting to be minced—
And very few are asking *Why not scrap it?*

JOHN LEHMANN

Discussing the Poem

1. In what ways *is* this machine like nations with their armaments, in the modern world? What does the poem mean by "Some fool will press the button"?

2. This poem was first published in 1932. Was it in fact prophesying the Second World War? Is its message now out of date, or would you say that it is even more true today? Why don't we "scrap it"?

3. What is so "excellent" and "neatly planned" about the machine? Is the poem itself in a neat and regular form? Mark the rhyme scheme (beginning: a, b, c, b . . .). What is different about the rhyme "button—mutton"? Is this kind of rhyme used with special effect in either or both the verses?

Exercise 1. Study the punctuation of the conversation that opens the extract from *Animal Farm*. Can you explain why the words "he said finally" in the opening sentence are followed by a capital letter ("What . . ."), while in the reply by Squealer, the words "announced Squealer . . ." are followed by a small h- ("has stated categorically . . .")? Explain also the use of dashes in that second speech, and the way commas are used, particularly before and after "Comrade Napoleon" in the same speech, and in "categorically, comrade—". Why is the word comrade sometimes given a capital C and sometimes not? Finally, why does the phrase "Animal Hero, First Class" have double inverted commas round it, and when would it be printed with single inverted commas?

(a) Rewrite the following passage (which is adapted from an earlier excerpt from the same conversation), adding all the necessary punctuation. Paragraphing, capital letters and apostrophes are already correct. Both single and double inverted commas were originally used, in addition to the usual commas, full stops, exclamation marks and question marks.

I do not believe you Boxer said Snowball fought bravely at the Battle of the Cowshed I saw him myself Did we not give him Animal Hero First Class immediately afterwards

That was part of the arrangement cried Squealer Jones's shot only grazed him . . . And do you not remember too that it was just at that moment when panic was spreading and all seemed lost that Comrade Napoleon sprang forward with a cry of Death to Humanity and sank his teeth in Jones's leg surely you remember *that* comrades exclaimed Squealer frisking from side to side

(b) The following sentence is from the same conversation; Squealer says:

> "For we know now—it is all written down in the secret documents that we have found—that in reality he was trying to lure us to our doom."

Here, a pair of dashes have been used to indicate the clauses that are in parenthesis, or aside from the main sentence. What other punctuation marks could have been used instead of dashes? What other use for a dash have you learnt about?

Write as many different versions of this sentence as you can make by altering the position of a dash or dashes. Discuss the changes in meaning that result. Here is *one* alternative as an example:

> "For we know now it is all written down in the secret documents—that we have found—that in reality he was trying to lure us to our doom."

Exercise 2. Napoleon in *Animal Farm* used Squealer as his propaganda chief. Squealer was clever at manipulating facts and choosing words to disguise the blunt truths about the régime the pigs had set up. When he had to announce a reduction in the animals' rations, he called it a "readjustment", spoke of it as temporary, and persuaded the animals that they would be much worse off if Jones (the farmer) came back. It was Squealer who altered the "Seventh Commandment" of "Animalism" from "All animals are equal" to "All animals are equal, but some are more equal than others."

Pair off the statements in the left-hand column below with those of similar basic meaning in the right-hand column (at present they do not match). Discuss which of the two seems to be more honest and straightforward, in each case, and the reasons why the other one is less satisfactory.

Any state is justified in taking firm action to eliminate undesirable elements in the interests of the majority.	An automatic outcome of the competition inherent in a free economy is the elimination of relatively inefficient business organisations.
In the border war we invaded the enemy before they could attack us.	We want a decision on better pay.
We were driven back by a successful enemy attack.	The rodent prevention officer found the premises in a condition somewhat below current standards of public health and hygiene for human habitation.
Anyone would prefer a noble struggle enduring hardship to abject slavery even in physical comfort.	A government can murder its opponents provided it was elected by more than half the voters.

A free capitalist system always puts some men out of business.	Unemployment is bound to result from this policy.
The rat-catcher found the house too filthy for people to live in.	Heavily outnumbered, we made a tactical withdrawal to our own positions.
We can state categorically that we are desirous of seeing a satisfactory outcome to the negotiations at present in progress over the amelioration of rates of remuneration.	A certain readjustment of food allocations became necessary as a temporary delay in production continued.
We shall have to accept a certain amount of redeployment of labour as an inevitable price of progress in this direction.	Certain factors not unconnected with our financial difficulties compel us to decline this offer.
	You would prefer poverty and independence to comfort in subjection.
We cannot afford it.	
Rations had to be reduced because of the prolonged famine.	In an outbreak of hostilities on the frontier, our men made certain incursions into hostile territory as a purely defensive manoeuvre.

Exercise 3(a). If you have to make a summary, or précis, of a passage such as the one in the *Animal Farm* extract, where Clover compares her ideals with the actual state of affairs on the farm under Napoleon, you should first make notes setting out the main points of the argument. Take the passage beginning "If she herself had had any picture of the future . . ." and ending ". . . faced the bullets of Jones's guns." (in the last paragraph of the extract), and try to work out your own notes. Then compare them with those suggested below:

1. Clover hoped to see animals well-fed, equally free, each working for all.
2. Instead: fear, oppression and distrust.
3. Still better than Jones's régime, therefore she would support Napoleon.
4. But animals had worked and suffered for something better.

(b) Make notes summing up the main points of the following argument against compulsory school uniform. Be careful to distinguish the main points from examples of them.

Firstly, the speaker argued that compulsory uniform denied the adolescent his rightful freedom of choice. Indeed, he added, such freedom was vital to the young man or woman's developing personality. Compulsory uniform denied the pupil the opportunity of exercising his own discretion in choosing what he should wear from day to day. The pupil might make mistakes, but it was essential that he should be free to exercise responsibility. He also argued that it was a kind of regimentation, forcing everybody to be the same, which seemed more appropriate to a totalitarian state, and quite out of place in a democracy where people valued personal freedom and allowed for individualists.

Moreover, in Britain's variable climate there was the practical point that the same uniform was unlikely to be comfortable for two weeks together—it was bound to seem too hot or too cold, and to have to be varied by the addition or subtraction of sweaters or cardigans. Even those schools which relaxed the rule about wearing ties in hot weather invariably seemed to do so just after the only heat wave of the summer was over.

But his most serious attack was not on its impractical sameness, but on the quite unfashionable nature of the traditional school uniform for boys, and even more so for girls. The dull colours, the clumsy cut, the coarse, cheap materials, the complete lack of style—all were fiercely attacked. For instance, he said, girls were at that time absolutely forbidden to wear the currently fashionable black stockings, while their mothers had been equally firmly forbidden to wear any other colour of stocking at school.

(c) Now, using your notes, write a complete summary in continuous form, using complete sentences suitably linked into *one* paragraph of about 90 words. The passage now contains 270 words; state in brackets at the end of your summary the exact number you have used.

Précis Rule 6. PLANNING:
Before summarising longer passages, make a list of the main points made, paying particular attention to the logical development of any argument to a conclusion.

Topics for Written Work

1. The passage set for précis in Exercise 3(b) of this chapter (opposite) gave several arguments against compulsory school uniform for young people of your age. Here are several arguments *for* compulsory school uniform:

(a) Uniform distinguishes the pupils from a particular school in public. This helps teachers (especially on outings) and gives pupils a sense of "belonging".

(b) Younger pupils like to associate themselves with older ones, and to remember the school's tradition of former pupils (some distinguished, no doubt) who wore the same dress.

(c) In most schools uniform sets a certain standard of dress—with complete freedom, wealthier children could dress better than the others, who would feel inferior and resentful.

(d) With freedom in dress, it is difficult to draw the line as to what is appropriate for school; and some pupils would always want to wear rather daring fashions in clothes, or styles that are associated by the general public with hooligans or young people who get into trouble.

If you are asked to write a composition discussing the subject of school uniform you can either take one particular side, or write a balanced argument giving both points of view. But in either case it is best to begin by making notes of arguments on *both* sides of a controversial question—you will argue better if you take account of your opponent's point of view.

Write a composition on a controversial subject. School uniform (i) is one possible topic. Here are some others:

(ii) Should the age when people can vote be lowered?
(iii) Should some countries, including our own, give up most of their armed forces to show their desire for peace?
(iv) Should people in prosperous countries be forced to give help to underdeveloped countries where people are poor or starving?
(v) Should hitch-hiking, and all forms of begging, be made illegal?
(vi) What arguments are there for and against an international army to "police" the world?
(vii) Should there be an international language, made a compulsory subject in all schools throughout the world?
(viii) What are the advantages and disadvantages of changing to a decimal system (for coinage and all weights and measures) from a non-decimal one?

(ix) Is it wrong to make children learn subjects that will not be "useful" to them, like art or music, or "dead" languages, or religious instruction?

(x) What are the advantages and disadvantages of spending time and effort on out-of-school activities and societies (to the pupils and the staff of a school)?

2. The full report of the speaker's views on school uniform in Exercise 3(b) (on page 186), and even more so the summary you made of this, might well have formed part of the "Minutes" of a discussion on school uniform which would have been kept by the secretary to a discussion group or debating society.

Minutes are a record of all the important decisions and transactions of any committee or group. It is usual to make such a record and read it out at the next meeting for members to agree that it is an accurate record of what took place, and the chairman then signs the minutes to show they have been accepted. The time and place and number of members present are always recorded, together with the matters discussed and decisions reached. How much detail of individual speeches is recorded varies according to the customs of the group.

Imagine you have to write the minutes of a School Council meeting when the subject was School Uniform. Begin by copying the opening set out below, and continue by inventing other arguments, including some from other speakers. End by recording a decision.

Minutes of the Meeting of the Wendle School Council held at 3.15 p.m. on Wednesday, 21st February, in the School Library; Pat Smith, U6Sc, in the Chair.

The Secretary read the Minutes of the meeting on 14th January, which were passed as correct.

The Chairman reported briefly on her discussions with the Headmaster about the provision of seats in the quadrangle. This matter would now be put before the School Governors at their next meeting.

Jim Brown of 5A then rose to propose that the School Council should recommend the abolition of school uniform for boys and girls in the 5th and 6th forms. He argued that senior pupils should be trusted by the school to choose their own clothes and that freedom in this very personal matter was important to their development as young adults . . .

Oral Work

1. Arrange for a formal debate on a controversial subject taken from politics, current affairs or problems for young people at home or at school. The topics suggested for composition on pages 187–8 might be suitable, or might suggest some similar ideas; remember to select a subject that will divide the group fairly evenly, with plenty of support for both sides.

A formal debate requires a strict chairman, and in this case it would be interesting to have a secretary, or to appoint a number of people to try to keep minutes of the discussion, which could be read out for approval later. Certain others need to be appointed beforehand: a proposer and his seconder (who will speak first and third, respectively), an opposer and his seconder (to speak second and fourth respectively), and two tellers (to count votes at the end).

Discuss and agree procedure before you begin: how much time will be allowed to the main speakers? Will either or both be allowed to sum up before the vote is taken? Will speakers "from the floor" be limited to one speech or to any limit of time? How will "points of order" and "points of information" be treated? How will speakers refer to one another if they are to "address the Chair"? (In Parliament, speakers *refer* to "the "Honourable Member for . . ." instead of giving names).

2. Holding a realistic *Mock Election* can be very interesting, particularly if this is organised at about the same time as any national or local elections are taking place. Instead of a deposit of money, each candidate can perhaps be asked to produce a certain minimum number of supporters' signatures. One of his supporters will then act as his agent. A returning officer and certain polling clerks will also be required. Candidates supporting existing political parties can, of course, obtain literature and information from local constituency parties, and base their campaigns upon this. A full campaign may not be practicable at school, but at least arrange for an "eve-of-the-poll" confrontation of the candidates, in which each speaker can put his case to the rest of the voters, and answer their questions.

Try to make the polling arrangements as realistic as possible: the instructions to voters that used to be displayed in every polling station are shown on page 190. Note that the ballot papers shown would also have counterfoils with serial numbers which also appear on the back of the ballot papers.

PARLIAMENTARY ELECTION

DIRECTIONS

FOR THE

GUIDANCE OF THE VOTERS

IN VOTING

1. The Voter may vote for not more than **ONE** Candidate.

2. The Voter should see that the ballot paper, before it is handed to him, is stamped with the official mark.

3. The Voter will go into one of the compartments, and with the pencil provided in the compartment, place a **cross** on the right-hand side of the ballot paper, opposite the name of the Candidate for whom he votes, thus **X**

4. The Voter will then fold up the ballot paper so as to show the official mark on the back, and leaving the compartment will, without showing the front of the paper to any person, show the official mark on the back to the presiding officer, and then, in the presence of the presiding officer, put the paper into the ballot box, and forthwith leave the polling station.

5. If the Voter inadvertently spoils a ballot paper, he can return it to the officer, who will, if satisfied of such inadvertence, give him another paper.

6. If the Voter votes for more than **ONE** Candidate, or places any mark on the ballot paper by which he may be afterwards identified, his ballot paper will be void, and will not be counted.

7. If the Voter fraudulently takes a ballot paper out of the polling station, or fraudulently puts into the ballot box any other paper than the one given him by the officer, he will be liable on conviction to imprisonment for a term not exceeding six months.

EXAMPLES OF BALLOT PAPER,

and of the manner of marking.

1	ALPHA (John Alpha, of 52, George Street, Bristol, Merchant)	
2	BETA (William Beta, of High Elms, Wilts, Esquire)	X

Note. The above names, etc., are for purposes of illustration only.

1	ALPHA (John Alpha, of 52, George Street, Bristol, Merchant)	X
2	BETA (William Beta, of High Elms, Wilts, Esquire)	
3	GAMMA (Henry John Gamma, of Beeches Avenue, Carshalton, Surrey, Auctioneer)	

The names, etc., of the actual Candidates are printed on the ballot paper supplied to the Voter.

A ballot box can easily be made out of cardboard and a register of electors can be based on school class lists. Each voter has to answer to his name and give his address (or form) to one polling clerk, who then ticks the name on the register and reads out the voter's polling number to the other polling clerk (seated beside him), who writes this number on the counterfoil, tears off one ballot paper, and stamps it on the back. The voter makes his choice by putting a cross against one candidate in the privacy of a polling booth, and then folds his ballot paper once and places it in the ballot box, in such a way as to allow the polling clerks to see the official stamp on the back (but not, of course, the cross indicating his vote).

Ballot boxes are sealed when empty, and the seals are only broken at the official counting station, in the presence of the candidates or their representatives at the count. All the counting has to be done under the strict supervision of the returning officer, whose job it is to announce the result after the count, or to decide whether any re-count can reasonably be asked for.

Activities and Research

1. Members of the class could make studies of the lives of various dictators in modern history: e.g. Napoleon, Lenin, Stalin, Hitler, Mussolini, Mao-Tse-Tung, General Franco. Report back on the advantages of dictatorship in building up strong government, and on the price people have had to pay by losing their freedom, suffering cruel oppression in many cases, and perhaps being led into disastrous wars.

2. Make a study of how Britain's Parliamentary democracy functions. Look first at the member of Parliament and how he is elected: what is a constituency, and how much do these vary? Who can put up a candidate, and what is a deposit? What are agents, canvassing, hustings? What are the party manifestoes, party political broadcasts, election promises, public opinion polls, psephologists, returning officers, polling stations and booths, ballot papers and boxes, and the count?

Then look at the workings of Parliament itself: what is the difference between the powers of the Lords and those of the Commons? Who are the Speaker and Black Rod? What are a session, an adjournment, question time, lobby correspondents, committees of the House? What are white papers, a royal commission, a parliamentary commissioner, parliamentary privilege, a precedent, a speech from the throne and a loyal address? Find out how a bill passes through its various stages (or "readings"), with "amendments", until it receives the "royal assent" and becomes law. Who are the party "whips", what do they do, and what is a "three-line whip"?

Further Reading

Animal Farm by GEORGE ORWELL (Secker & Warburg; Penguin
By substituting animals for humans, Orwell is satirising in the
form of a fable the course that so many political revolutions have
taken. The animals, after driving away the men from their
farm, set up their own "democracy", based on seven Com
mandments, one of which is "All animals are equal". Bu
their leaders, the pigs, soon become "more equal" than the
other animals; they copy the manners of men, and rule with
the help of the ferocious dogs. And so we have the revolution
resulting not in a democracy but in a different, though equally
oppressive form of dictatorship.

Nineteen Eighty Four by GEORGE ORWELL (Secker & Warburg
  Penguin)
This is an adult and terrifying book. The world is governed
by three totalitarian states, perpetually at war. Nobody is
allowed to think or to act for himself; all information is
twisted to suit the political viewpoint of the moment; all
records are systematically altered so that they conform with
this. Everybody is spied upon by the police (there are tele
screens in every room). Men and women who rebel—as
Winston Smith, the "hero" of this story does—are "converted"
by physical and mental torture. The story seems to hold ou
no hope for Man, but it should be remembered that it wa
meant as a warning, not a prediction.

Down and Out in Paris and London (920 ORW), *The Road to Wigan
  Pier* (331.7) and *Collected Essays* (824) (Secker & Warburg
  Penguin) all by GEORGE ORWELL.
These are some of his most interesting non-fiction writings
Orwell's real name was Eric Blair. From Eton he went to
Burma, and the essays "Shooting an Elephant" and "A
Hanging" date from that experience. Then he lived in Paris
and returned to make contact with working-class people in
England in the 1930s. His record of experience is factual
often shocking, but always humane and direct.

CHAPTER THIRTEEN

Crime

The narrator of this story is a Borstal boy, convicted of breaking into a bakery and stealing the cashbox, who takes the opportunity presented to him through his prowess as a cross-country runner to demonstrate his hatred of authority.

I'm in Essex. It's supposed to be a good Borstal, at least that's what the governor said to me when I got here from Nottingham. "We want to trust you while you are in this establishment," he said, smoothing out his newspaper with lily-white workless hands, while I read the big words upside down: *Daily Telegraph.* "If you play ball with us, we'll play ball with you." (Honest to God, you'd have thought it was going to be one long tennis match.) "We want hard honest work and we want good athletics," he said as well. "And if you give us both these things you can be sure we'll do right by you and send you back into the world an honest man." Well, I could have died laughing, especially when straight after this I hear the barking sergeant-major's voice calling me and two others to attention and marching us off like we was Grenadier Guards. And when the governor kept saying how "we" wanted you to do this, and "we" wanted you to do that, I kept looking round for the other blokes, wondering how many of them there was. Of course, I knew there were thousands of them, but as far as I knew only one was in the room. And there *are* thousands of them, all over the poxeaten country, in shops, offices, railway stations, cars, houses, pubs—In-law blokes like you and them, all on the watch for Out-law blokes like me and us—and waiting to phone for the coppers as soon as we make a false move. And it'll always be there, I'll tell you that now, because I haven't finished making all my false moves yet, and I dare say I won't until I kick the bucket. If the In-laws are hoping to stop me making false moves they're wasting their time. . . .

As I run and see my smoky breath going out into the air as if I had ten cigars in different parts of my body I think more on the little speech the governor made when I first came. Honesty. Be honest. I laughed so much one morning I went ten minutes down in my timing because I had to stop and get rid of the stitch in my side. The governor was so worried when I got back late that he sent me to the doctor's for an X-ray and heart check. Be honest. It's like saying: Be dead, like me, and then you'll have no more pain of leaving your nice slummy house for Borstal or prison. Be honest and settle down in a cosy six pounds a week job. Well, even with all this long-distance running I haven't yet been able to decide what he means by this, although I'm just about beginning to—and I don't like what it means. Because after all my thinking I found that it adds up to something that can't be true about me, being born and brought up as I was. Because another thing people like the governor will never understand is that I *am* honest, that I've never been anything else but honest, and that I'll always be honest. Sounds funny. But it's true because I know what honest means according to me and he only knows what it means according to him. I think my honesty is the only sort in the world, and he thinks his is the only sort in the world as well. That's why this dirty great walled-up and fenced-up manor house in the middle of nowhere has been used to coop-up blokes like me. And if I had the whip-hand I wouldn't even bother to build a place like this to put all the cops, governors, posh whores, penpushers, army officers, Members of Parliament in; no, I'd stick them up against a wall and let them have it, like they'd have done with blokes like us years ago, that is, if they'd ever known what it means to be honest, which they don't and never will so help me God Almighty. . . .

Our doddering bastard of a governor, our half dead gan-grened gaffer is hollow like an empty petrol drum, and he wants me and my running life to give him glory, to put in him blood and throbbing veins he never had, wants his potbellied pals to be his witnesses as I gasp and stagger up to his winning post so's he can say: "My Borstal gets that cup, you see. I win my bet, because it pays to be honest and try to gain the prizes I offer to my lads, and they know it, have known it all along. They'll always be honest now, because I made them so." And his pals will think: "He trains his lads to live all right, after all; he deserves a medal but we'll get him made a Sir"—and at this very moment as the birds come back to whistling I can tell myself I'll never care a sod what any of his chinless spineless

In-laws think or say. They've seen me and they're cheering now and loudspeakers set around the field like elephants' ears are spreading out the big news that I'm well in the lead, and can't do anything else but stay there. But I'm still thinking of the Out-law death my dad died, telling the doctors to scat from the house when they wanted him to finish up in hospital (like a bleeding guinea-pig, he raved at them). He got up in bed to throw them out and even followed them down the stairs in his shirt though he was no more than skin and stick. They tried to tell him he'd want some drugs but he didn't fall for it, and only took the painkiller that mam and I got from a herb-seller in the next street. It's not till now that I know what guts he had, and when I went into the room that morning he was lying on his stomach with the clothes thrown back, looking like a skinned rabbit, his grey head resting just on the edge of the bed and on the floor must have been all the blood he'd had in his body, right from his toenails up, for nearly all of the lino and carpet was covered in it, thin and pink. . . .

I'm slowing down now for Gunthorpe to catch me up, and I'm doing it in a place just where the drive turns in to the sportsfield—where they can see what I'm doing, especially the governor and his gang from the grandstand, and I'm going so slow I'm almost marking time. . . . But even so, I say, I won't go for that last hundred yards if I have to sit down cross-legged on the grass and have the governor and his chinless wonders pick me up and carry me there, which is against their rules so you can bet they'd never do it because they're not clever enough to break the rules—like I would be in their place—even though they are their own. No, I'll show him what honesty means if it's the last thing I do, though I'm sure he'll never understand because if he and all them like him did it'd mean they'd be on my side which is impossible. By God I'll stick this out like my dad stuck out his pain and kicked them doctors down the stairs: if he had guts for that then I've got guts for this and here I stay waiting for Gunthorpe or Aylesham to bash that turf and go right slap-up against that bit of clothes-line stretched across the winning post. As for me, the only time I'll hit that clothes-line will be when I'm dead and a comfortable coffin's been got ready on the other side. Until then I'm a long-distance runner, crossing country all on my own no matter how bad it feels.

from *The Loneliness of the Long Distance Runner* by Alan Sillitoe)

Appreciation and Discussion

1. What is (or was) a "Borstal"? What do you imagine a Borstal Institution to be like, after reading this extract?
2. Why does Smith (the Borstal boy who is the narrator in this book) say "I could have died laughing" about the Governor's remarks, and about the way they were followed by the "barking sergeant-major's voice"?
3. What various types of people are classed as "In-laws" by Smith (in this extract)?
4. What would Smith do to these "In-laws" if he had the power? What reason does he give for this?
5. How did Smith's father die? Why did he die in this way?
6. What indications are given in this passage that Smith and his family form a small minority, on their own against authority?
7. Smith's view of the Governor is highly emotional. List the adjectives and other descriptive words he chooses (e.g. "with lily-white workless hands"), and comment on the impression they are intended to give.
8. Throughout Smith's thoughts runs a clear division of people into "them" and "us". What other terms does he use for the two classes of people? Does this correspond to a social class division, in your opinion?
9. What exactly is Smith criticising about the Governor's "honesty"? He calls him "hollow like an empty petrol drum"—this seems to imply he is a hypocrite. How does Smith justify such an idea?
10. What is Smith's own kind of "honesty"? Clearly he does not mean always telling the truth and never stealing, so what *does* he mean?
11. What would "hitting that bit of clothes line" (i.e. winning the race) really mean to Smith? Why does he say he will never do it, until he dies, whatever the cost?
12. Is it true that the Governor and his friends can never understand what Smith thinks about "honesty"? Can *you* understand it, and sympathise with young criminals like Smith?
13. Is Smith typical of young offenders? If many criminals are rebels against a prosperous, middle-class society, does this suggest that we should try to *prevent* crime or *reform* criminals, instead of mainly punishing them? What treatment could have changed Smith's mind?

14. Discuss the style in which this passage is written. Does it succeed in conveying Smith's personality and the way he might talk? Does it also convey his ideas adequately? How unconventional do his comparisons seem? (e.g. "as if I had ten cigars stuck in different parts of my body"; "hollow like an empty petrol drum"; "loudspeakers like elephants' ears").

My Friend Maloney

My friend Maloney, eighteen,
    Swears like a sentry,
Got into trouble two years back
    With the local gentry.

Parson and squire's sons
    Informed a copper.
The magistrates took one look at Maloney.
    Fixed him proper.

Talked of the crime of youth,
    The innocent victim.
Maloney never said a blind word
    To contradict him.

Maloney of Gun Street,
    Back of the Nuclear Mission,
Son of the town whore,
    Blamed television.

Justice, as usual, triumphed.
    Everyone felt fine.
Things went deader.
    Maloney went up the line.

Maloney learned one lesson:
    Never play the fool
With the products of especially a minor
    Public school.

Maloney lost a thing or two
　　At that institution.
First shirt, second innocence
　　The old irresolution.

Found himself a girl-friend
　　Sharp suit, sharp collars.
Maloney on a moped
　　Pants full of dollars.

College boys on the corner
　　In striped, strait blazers
Look at old Maloney,
　　Eyes like razors.

You don't need talent, says Maloney.
　　You don't need looks.
All I got you got, fellers.
　　You can keep your thick books.

Parson got religion
　　Squire, in the end, the same,
The magistrate went over the wall.
　　Life, said Maloney, 's a game.

Consider then the case of Maloney
　　College boys, parson, squire, beak.
Who was the victor and who was the victim?
　　Speak.

CHARLES CAUSLEY

Discussing the Poem

1. What two classes or groups of people are represented on the one hand by Maloney, his mother, his girl-friend, and on the other by "the local gentry", the "college boys, parson, squire and beak"? In what ways are the terms used emotionally toned?

2. Discuss the language of this poem: do words like "copper" and "beak", and phrases like "Fixed him proper" and "went up the line" place the poem more on one side than the other in the clash between Maloney and authority? Discuss the meanings of any words or phrases that are not immediately clear. Is the idea of a "Nuclear Mission" hall in the slums of the town meant to be ironic?

3. What simple device emphasises the challenge in the last line? Did Maloney win? How was he justified in living life by his wits and for his own profit? Compare his philosophy with Smith's in the prose extract.

Techniques

Exercise 1. (a) The simplest use of the apostrophe (') is to indicate a letter or letters left out when we abbreviate words or run them together as contractions, as we often do in spoken English. The extract from *The Loneliness of the Long Distance Runner* opens with "I'm", short for "I am". Check that you understand this use of the apostrophe in the following examples taken from the opening paragraph of the extract:

(i) It's; that's; we'll; you'd; we'll; it'll; I'll; haven't; won't; they're.

As further revision, make contractions or abbreviations of the following, using apostrophes:

(ii) It is; she has; do not; cannot; I have; would not; I had; it would; she could have; they might not.

(b) In earlier books we have studied also the use of the possessive apostrophe. Basically, the apostrophe is added to the noun naming the "owner" of some thing or quality. An -s is also added after the apostrophe unless that noun already had a single -s as its last letter. Thus (in the extract) "the barking sergeant-major's voice" indicates that the voice belongs to the sergeant-major (and not the governor or Smith), and "like elephants' ears" indicates ears of elephants, that is, of many or any elephants, and not one particular elephant. There are a

few exceptional nouns ending in a single -s which take a further
-s after the possessive apostrophe: bus's, rhinoceros's, octopus's,
thesis's are all examples, most of them being words of foreign
origin. Other exceptions to the rules are proper names, like
Jones's, James's, Lewis's; and a few words ending in -ce, as in
"for conscience' sake". Perhaps the safest guide in all these
cases is to write what sounds correct.

Possessive adjectives and pronouns (my, his, hers, theirs,
etc.) do *not* have apostrophes. But some indefinite pronouns *do*
take a possessive apostrophe, with or without the -s, as if they
were nouns:

> Smith appropriated others' property as if it were his, and
> had no hesitation in spending someone else's hard-earned
> cash.

But remember that "it" is a personal pronoun, and so "its" is
the possessive form (meaning "of it"), which should *not* be
confused with "it's", meaning "it is, it has".

Thirteen apostrophes are required to complete the punctuation of the following passage. Rewrite it with the apostrophes
correctly placed:

> Look at the Princesss necklace: its made of hundreds of
> sharks teeth. I dont believe theyve all come from one
> sharks mouth; its makers mustve caught many sharks in
> their islands lagoon. Collecting enough sharks teeth for
> everyones needs must take many months hunting, in which
> ones risking ones life repeatedly.

(c) Since we manage reasonably well without any equivalent
to the apostrophe when speaking, it can be argued that we
could do without the apostrophe in written English. It is
already commonly omitted in names like "Blankton Boys
School"; and where there is confusion, as in:

> Both the girl and the money were his best friend's.

it is better style to rephrase the sentence:

> Both the girl and the money belonged to his best friend.

Comment on the use of the possessive, especially the position
of the apostrophe and how it affects meaning, in the following
sentences:

1. Their son and daughter's birthday was in June.
2. Their son's and daughters' birthdays were in June.
3. He bribed the brother of the King's guard.
4. He bribed the guard of the King's brother.

5. Messrs. Shadrak's and Duxbury's funeral service was conducted with dignity and solemnity.
6. Messrs. Shadrak and Duxbury's funeral service was conducted with dignity and solemnity.
7. The Queen's Mothers' Help Scheme was supported out of the previous year's fund-raising campaigns.
8. The Queen Mother's Help Scheme was supported out of the previous years' fund-raising campaigns.
9. John and Jane's uncles are not as generous as Bill's and Betty's uncles.
10. The debutants' parties were held at each of the Duchess's residences, and different duchesses' daughters were invited to each.
11. They hope to stay at two of their brother and sister's houses next holiday.
12. They hope to stay at two of their brother's and sister's houses next holiday.
13. They hope to stay at two of their brothers and sisters' houses next holiday.
14. Jack's invitation to join the professional sports club was a challenge to his team loyalty.
15. Jack's invitation to join the professionals' sports club was a challenge to his team's loyalty.

Exercise 2. (a) The story of Smith's life and his feelings about running in the inter-borstals' race is told in a colloquial style to suggest that the young man writes as he would talk or think. Spoken with a Nottingham accent, the narrative is dramatic and realistic. Most of his idiomatic phrases are widely used, and can easily be paraphrased in more formal English:

e.g. "We'll play ball with you" means:
"we shall co-operate, and be fair to you"

when the governor says it at the beginning of our extract.

Paraphrase each of the following examples from the extract in a similar way:

1. make a false move;
2. kick the bucket;
3. it adds up to something;
4. to coop up blokes like me;
5. if I had the whip hand;
6. let them have it;
7. to scat from the house;
8. he didn't fall for it;
9. I know what guts he had;
10. I'll stick this out.

(b) A number of traditional sayings or idioms, taken originally from crime and the administration of justice, have passed into general use in the language, where they are used figuratively. Thus the phrase:

"To make one's case"

may simply mean to argue in favour of something (not necessarily in a court), as in:

He made an excellent case for co-education when this was discussed by the class.

Explain the following idioms in this way, (i) saying what each means, and (ii) giving an example of its use as an idiom (not literally):

1. to be as thick as thieves;
2. to make a hue and cry;
3. to go scot free;
4. to hold no brief for;
5. to lay down the law;
6. a moot point;
7. to be null and void;
8. to laugh something out of court;
9. special pleading;
10. one might as well be hung for a sheep as a lamb.

Exercise 3. (a) One conspicuous feature of the style of the extract, which emphasises its colloquial flavour, is the frequent use of "like", and particularly where "like" is used in constructions where Standard English normally uses "as". The basic rules for Standard English (though not for American English) are to use "as" when introducing a clause, i.e. a group of words containing a verb, and keep "like" as a preposition (i.e. preceding a noun or pronoun), or as a verb or (rarely) a noun.

Discuss each of the following examples from the extract or the poem in this chapter. For instance, when Smith says:

"marching us off like we was Grenadier guards"

he is wrongly using "like" as a conjunction, and should have said;

"marching us off as if we were Grenadier guards"

More than half of the following are correct, others are incorrect, and so you should be prepared to justify any changes you wish to make, and should explain what correct use of "like" the others represent.

1. In-law blokes like you and them, all on the watch for Out-law blokes like me and us . . .
2. . . . and I don't like what it means.
3. I'd let them have it, like they'd have done with blokes like us.

4. Loudspeakers set around the field like elephants' ears are spreading out the big news.
5. He was lying on his stomach, looking like a skinned rabbit.
6. They're not clever enough to break the rules—like I would be in their place.
7. If he and all them like him did (understand) it'd mean they'd be on my side.
8. I'll stick this out like my dad stuck out his pain.
9. My friend Maloney swears like a sentry.
0. College boys . . . look at old Maloney (with) eyes like razors.

b) We saw in *Book Three* that a number of words (e.g. before, after, since, until, for) can be *conjunctions,* when they introduce a *clause* (i.e. when followed by a subject and verb), or *prepositions,* when they "govern" nouns or pronouns, and so introduce a *phrase.* "As" is normally a conjunction:

e.g. He is just as good at it as I (am).

"Like" is normally a preposition:

e.g. Like me, he is good at it.

Explain the difference in meaning between sentences in the following pairs, stating whether the words in italics are prepositions or conjunctions in each case.

e.g. (i) He stole the cash box *for* his mother.
     (ii) He stole the cash box, *for* his mother needed the money.

Here (i) means that he stole the box so that his mother could have it, and at her suggestion; (ii) means that he only decided to steal the box because his mother needed the money it contained. In (i) "for" is a preposition (governing "mother"), and in (ii) "for" is a conjunction, introducing the clause "his mother needed the money".

1. (i) Do you have many other friends *like* Smith?
   (ii) Do you have as many other friends *as* Smith (has)?
2. (i) You will never find a friend *like* George.
   (ii) You, *like* George, will never find a friend.
3. (i) *Before* them ran the victorious winners of the race, waving to the crowd.
   (ii) *Before* they ran, the victorious winners of the race waved to the crowd.
4. (i) The police were there *after* him.
   (ii) The police were there *after* he had left.

5.   (i) He lay low *until* dark, in the cellars.

    (ii) He lay low *until* it was dark in the cellars.

(c) Certain words (and phrases) are normally followed by particular *prepositions*: thus one suffers from an illness or disability, not with it (although one may suffer with other people from the same complaint). Decide which preposition each of the following is normally followed by, and illustrate each with a short sentence of your own:

aim	comment	deprive	in comparison
averse	comply	different	in search
believe	decide	indifferent	rely

Topics for Written Work

1. All over the world, at this moment, there are people in prison or in some form of detention. For some, prison is almost home, a refuge from the responsibilities of life outside. For many it is no better and no worse than the slums in which they were brought up. Many prisoners will feel bitter, resentful, ill-treated, frustrated and cooped up. Some are terrified of further violence or torture: in many countries there are people under sentence of death, or detained indefinitely without trial or hope of freedom. Some are innocent and wrongfully held; some are martyrs suffering for their political or religious views.

Read Oscar Wilde's *Ballad of Reading Gaol*, or George Orwell's essay entitled *A Hanging*, or Brendan Behan's account of his cell in *Borstal Boy* (pages 50–53 in the Corgi edition), or all of these. Try to imagine yourself imprisoned, confined, and completely under other people's authority. Try to express what you would think or feel, or to describe exactly your restricted environment and routine.

Here is a free-verse poem on this theme by a pupil at school:

This Prison

These four walls,
These four blank walls.
That black iron-fingered door.
These cold flagstones,
And that damned stool.

Squatting round
and prim and low in the corner
(I hate that stool more than anything else).
Placed beside it, the utility table,
On which there stands

A bowl of water,
A piece of yellow soap,
A coarse oblong towel,
Which I must always keep
Neatly folded, and in its proper place.

There is the same smell
Of disinfectant every day
Sweet and sickly, and mixed
With the same smell of sweat, and there is
The same ache in the air every day.

Man-made prison,
Man-made objects,
Man-made atmospheres,
And to make it complete:
Me—a man.

COLIN

2. The subject of crime and punishment is a broad one that raises problems that baffle the wisest experts. Here are some of the bigger questions, set out in note form:

(a) How to define crime? Does law allow large-scale dishonesty, exploitation, in commerce or between countries, yet punish petty thieves? Is violent robbery worse than profiteering? Worse to take money than a girl-friend or a reputation? Drunken driving criminal? Murder by jealous lover criminal?

(b) Can we divide criminals into types? Some "incurable"? Many too stupid to know better? Any embittered, unable to understand or sympathise? Is crime an illness? Some driven to crime by poverty, boredom, frustration?

(c) How to decide punishments? Aim at (i) revenge, (ii) deterring others, (iii) locking dangerous men up, or (iv) curing criminals? Can punishments do all these at once? How much to be spent? Should prisoners earn their keep? Learn an honest trade? Compensate their victims?

(d) Do confinement and harsh treatment embitter men, or change them? Does putting them together encourage crime? Could we *prevent* crime by helping disturbed, anti-social children? Make sure young people not frustrated, unwanted, nor given sense of failure? Why has crime (including juvenile and violent crime) increased, when living standards have risen?

Before writing your own views on some or all of these questions, in a full composition, it might be useful to consider and discuss both the extract and poem, and the *Oral Work* in this chapter.

Oral Work

Discuss all or some of the following provocative remarks and quotations on the subject of crime and punishment:

1. "All punishment is mischief: all punishment in itself is evil." (Jeremy Bentham, 1748–1832)

2. Punishments should be designed to fit the criminal, not the crime.

3. "I and all the people I know would prefer the cat to a long sentence any time. After three days it doesn't hurt any

more, and the scars soon heal, except those on your mind. What you feel is anger, resentment, and, most of all, a determination somehow to get your own back. But being deterred? The idea never gets a look in." (R. Allerton, a hardened criminal, as recorded by T. Parker in *The Courage of his Convictions.*)

4. "Criminals are the butts on to whom the rest of us can discharge our own angry feelings . . . To discharge them upon our friends and neighbours is not permissible . . . The criminal has given us plenty of excuse. We can hate him and punish him with a positive sense of virtue." (*Crime in a Changing Society* by Howard Jones.)

5. "The main thing (punishment in a detention centre) does, I think, is to reinforce your attitude towards authority: . . . it's always 'Them' and 'Us', you know, like in *Loneliness of the Long Distance Runner*, and you're just you running your own separate race, and you don't care what anybody does. The first thing you want to do is to get out and live your own life, but you come up feeling they're all bastards, they hate me." (From a B.B.C. interview with a young offender.)

6. Criminals are made, not born.

7. "Crime can in fact be regarded as essentially an expression of immaturity, a continuation into adult life of modes of feeling and patterns of behaviour that are characteristic of a childish stage of development." (*The English Penal System* by Winifred Elkin.)

8. When there is such widespread dishonesty, petty theft, cheating over taxes, fiddling of public money, and a general resort to violence, both in entertainment and in international affairs, who can blame criminals for looking after themselves?

9. We shall never get anywhere in the fight against crime until we can make informers completely acceptable, and get rid of the idea that the only mistake a criminal makes is to be found out.

10. "Through tatter'd clothes small vices do appear;
Robes and furr'd gowns hide all. Plate sin with gold,
And the strong lance of justice hurtless breaks;
Arm it in rags, a pigmy's straw does pierce it.
None does offend, none, I say, none."
                    (the mad King Lear in Shakespeare's play)

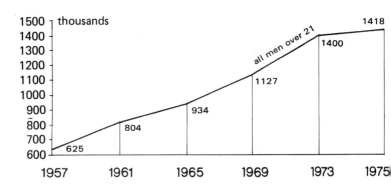

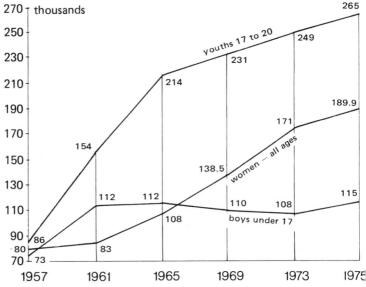

PERSONS FOUND GUILTY OF OFFENCES IN ENGLAND AND WALES (figures are to the nearest thousand)

Activities and Research

1. How grave a state of affairs do the graphs above indicate? Study them carefully, noting the scales used, and write down the conclusions you think can be drawn from them.

The graphs were based on figures in the *Annual Abstract of Statistics* issued by the Central Statistical Office. Borrow this in a reference library and bring the figures up to date. Study any other figures given; for instance, those for prisoners serving a second, third (or more) term in jail, or for the strength of the police. Reproduce them in diagram form.

Find out what you can about crime and the treatment of criminals in other countries. Is it true that *all* countries (whatever their political systems) with rising standards of living also have a rising rate of crime?

Further Reading

The Loneliness of the Long Distance Runner by ALAN SILLITOE
(W. H. Allen; Longman)
The edited version printed in this chapter is much shorter than the original story, which is the title piece of a remarkably good collection. The other stories are on more or less related themes, all of them evoking very vividly the atmosphere of poverty and rebellion. Particularly recommended are "Uncle Ernest" (which is about a lonely, middle-aged man who finds friendship, only to have it torn away by the hand of authority) and "On Saturday Afternoon" (which is told by a young boy who watches a man trying to hang himself).
In *Saturday Night and Sunday Morning* (W. H. Allen; Longman) he has created another rebel against authority raring for adventure.

One Day in the Life of Ivan Denisovich by ALEXANDER SOLZHENIT-
SYN (translated by Ralph Parker) (Gollancz; Penguin)
A disturbing, realistic account of life in the Siberian labour camps of Stalinist Russia, this is also an excellent introduction to the work of a great modern Russian author.

The Man Inside edited by TONY PARKER (Joseph) (365.6) and
The Courage of His Convictions by TONY PARKER and ROBERT
ALLERTON (Arrow) (920 ALL)
Both these books give vivid, first-hand accounts of criminals' attitudes to life, society, crime and punishment, from tape-recordings of their own conversations.

Borstal Boy by BRENDAN BEHAN (Hutchinson; Corgi) (920 BEH
or 365.42)
A thoroughly unconventional book by an unconventional, overwhelming writer, this is a record of Behan's experience in English prisons and in a Borstal as an I.R.A. extremist. It records ugly conditions and characters, and also warm humanity, with extraordinary sympathy and understanding.

In this short story we are projected into the future, when to deviate from the universally accepted pattern of leisure time behaviour is to invite more than curiosity.

CHAPTER FOURTEEN

All the Same

To enter out into that silence that was the city at eight o'clock of a misty evening in November, to put your feet upon that buckling concrete walk, to step over grassy seams and make your way, hands in pockets, through the silences, that was what Mr. Leonard Mead most dearly loved to do. He would stand upon the corner of an intersection and peer down long moonlit avenues of sidewalk in four directions, deciding which way to go, but it really made no difference; he was alone in this world of A.D. 2053, or as good as alone, and with a final decision made, a path selected, he would stride off, sending patterns of frosty air before him like the smoke of a cigar. . . .

On this particular evening he began his journey in a westerly direction, toward the hidden sea. There was a good crystal frost in the air; it cut the nose and made the lungs blaze like a Christmas tree inside; you could feel the cold light going on and off, all the branches filled with invisible snow. He listened to the faint push of his soft shoes through autumn leaves with satisfaction, and whistled a cold quiet whistle between his teeth, occasionally picking up a leaf as he passed, examining its skeletal pattern in the infrequent lamplights as he went on, smelling its rusty smell.

"Hello, in there," he whispered to every house on every side as he moved. "What's up tonight on Channel 4, Channel 7, Channel 9? Where are the cowboys rushing, and do I see the United States Cavalry over the next hill to the rescue?" . . .

"What is it now?" he asked the houses, noticing his wrist watch. "Eight-thirty p.m.? Time for a dozen assorted murders? A quiz? A revue? A comedian falling off the stage?" . . .

He came to a cloverleaf intersection which stood silent where two main highways crossed the town. During the day it was a thunderous surge of cars, the gas stations open, a great insect rustling and a ceaseless jockeying for position as the scarab-beetles, a faint incense puttering from their exhausts, skimmed homeward to the far directions. But now these highways, too, were like streams in a dry season, all stone and bed and moon radiance.

He turned back on a side street, circling around toward his home. He was within a block of his destination when the lone car turned a corner quite suddenly and flashed a fierce white cone of light upon him. He stood entranced, not unlike a night moth, stunned by the illumination, and then drawn toward it.

A metallic voice called to him:

"Stand still. Stay where you are! Don't move!"

He halted.

"Put up your hands!"

"But——" he said.

"Your hands up! Or we'll shoot!"

The police, of course, but what a rare, incredible thing; in a city of three million, there was only *one* police car left, wasn't that correct? Ever since a year ago, 2052, the election year, the force had been cut down from three cars to one. Crime was ebbing; there was no need now for the police, save for this one lone car wandering and wandering the empty streets.

"Your name?" said the police car in a metallic whisper. He couldn't see the men in it for the bright light in his eyes.

"Leonard Mead," he said.

"Speak up!"

"Leonard Mead!"

"Business or profession?"

"I guess you'd call me a writer."

"No profession," said the police car, as if talking to itself. The light held him fixed, like a museum specimen, needle thrust through chest.

"You might say that," said Mr. Mead. He hadn't written in years. Magazines and books didn't sell any more. Everything went on in the tomb-like houses at night now, he thought, continuing his fancy. The tombs, ill-lit by television light, where the people sat like the dead, the gray or multi-colored lights touching their faces, but never really touching them.

"No profession," said the phonograph voice, hissing. "What are you doing out?"

"Walking," said Leonard Mead.

"Walking!"

"Just walking," he said simply, but his face felt cold.

"Walking, just walking, walking?"

"Yes, sir."

"Walking where? For what?"

"Walking for air. Walking to *see*."

"Your address!"

"Eleven South Saint James Street."

"And there is air *in* your house, you have an air *conditioner*, Mr. Mead?"

"Yes."

"And you have a viewing screen in your house to see with?"

"No."

"No?" There was a crackling quiet that in itself was an accusation.

"Are you married, Mr. Mead?"

"No."

"Not married," said the police voice behind the fiery beam. The moon was high and clear among the stars and the houses were gray and silent.

"Nobody wanted me," said Leonard Mead with a smile.

"Don't speak unless you're spoken to!"

Leonard Mead waited in the cold night.

"Just *walking*, Mr. Mead?"

"Yes."

"But you haven't explained for what purpose."

"I explained; for air, and to see, and just to walk."

"Have you done this often?"

"Every night for years."

The police car sat in the center of the street with its radio throat faintly humming.

"Well, Mr. Mead," it said.

"Is that all?" he asked politely.

"Yes," said the voice. "Here." There was a sigh, a pop. The back door of the police car sprang wide. "Get in."

"Wait a minute, I haven't done anything!"

"Get in."

"I protest!"

"Mr. Mead."

He walked like a man suddenly drunk. As he passed the front window of the car he looked in. As he had expected, there was no one in the front seat, no one in the car at all.

"Get in."

He put his hand to the door and peered into the back seat, which was a little cell, a little black jail with bars. It smelled of riveted steel. It smelled of harsh antiseptic; it smelled too clean and hard and metallic. There was nothing soft there.

213

"Now if you had a wife to give you an alibi," said the iron voice. "But——"

"Where are you taking me?"

The car hesitated, or rather gave a faint whirring click, as if information, somewhere, was dropping card by punch-slotted card under electric eyes. "To the Psychiatric Center for Research on Regressive Tendencies."

He got in. The door shut with a soft thud. The police car rolled through the night avenues, flashing its dim lights ahead.

They passed one house on one street a moment later, one house in an entire city of houses that were dark, but this one particular house had all of its electric lights brightly lit, every window a loud yellow illumination, square and warm in the cool darkness.

"That's *my* house," said Leonard Mead.

No one answered him.

The car moved down the empty river-bed streets and off away, leaving the empty streets with the empty side-walks, and no sound and no motion all the rest of the chill November night.

(from *The Pedestrian*, a short story by Ray Bradbury)

Appreciation and Discussion

1. What are the other inhabitants of the city doing while Mr. Mead walks? Why, do you think, is he the only one to enjoy an evening walk?

2. Why are so few police needed? What sort of comment is this on the society Mead lives in?

3. Why is a writer counted as having no profession? Is Mead's lack of a job, a wife and a television screen significant?

4. What kinds of television programmes were apparently popular? Remembering how far into the future this is, comment on this choice of programmes.

5. Why is Mead surprised by the arrival of the police car, and in what ways does he become "stunned" like a moth or museum specimen?

6. Were you surprised, when reading, to find that the police car was remote-controlled? Where is it first hinted that the voice was not that of a policeman actually present?

7. Where does the story imply that the "remote-controller" of the car is itself an electronic brain?

8. What are "regressive tendencies", and what do you think is going to happen to Leonard Mead?

9. What is different about Mead's house as the car passes it? Why is this detail important?

10. Examine the part played by moonlight throughout this description.

11. Pick out the words and phrases that make the police car seem utterly impersonal.

12. How much about the city, the period in time, the way of life there, and the character of Mr. Mead can be deduced from the opening two paragraphs alone?

13. Discuss the effectiveness of the following quotations from this story:
    (a) sending patterns of frosty air before him like the smoke of a cigar;
    (b) There was a good crystal frost in the air: it cut the nose and made the lungs blaze like a Christmas tree inside;
    (c) picking up a leaf . . . examining its skeletal pattern . . . smelling its rusty smell;
    (d) highways . . . like streams in a dry season, all stone and bed and moon radiance;
    (e) a crackling quiet that in itself was an accusation.

14. What repels or sickens Mead about his neighbours' addiction to television entertainment? Is there a danger that people might become so addicted to passive enjoyment that they sit "like the dead, the gray or multi-colored lights touching their faces, but never really touching them"?

15. Do some people already seem to need light, noise and company and ceaseless entertainment from television or transistor radio? How often do people of your acquaintance enjoy being quiet, alone, and getting away from a wholly man-made environment?

Little Boxes

Little boxes on the hillside,
Little boxes made of ticky tacky,
Little boxes, little boxes, little boxes all the same.
There's a green one and a pink one
    and a blue one and a yellow one,
And they're all made out of ticky tacky
And they all look just the same.

And the people in the houses all go to the university,
And they all get put in boxes, little boxes all the same.
And there's doctors and there's lawyers
    and business executives,
And they're all made out of ticky tacky
And they all look just the same.

And they all play on the golf course
And drink their martini dry,
And they all have pretty children
    and the children go to school,
And the children go to summer camp
    and then to the university,
And they all get put in boxes.
And they all come out the same.

And the boys go into business
    and marry and raise a family,
And they all get put in boxes, little boxes all the same.
There's a green one and a pink
    one and a blue one and a yellow one,
And they're all made out of ticky tacky,
And they all look just the same.

MALVINA REYNOLDS

Discussing the Poem

If possible, hear a recording of this poem being sung, before discussing it.

1. How many meanings seem to be attached to the word "boxes" in the course of this poem?
2. What do you think is the implication behind the words "ticky tacky"? Do you think these words were made up especially for this poem?
3. Is this poem obviously based on American life? Is it attacking only one class of people? Could it be called a "protest" song, and if so, what is it protesting about?
4. What features of the verses and their lines seem particularly suited to a "traditional" or "ballad" type of song?

Techniques

Exercise 1. What is the subject word of the first sentence of the passage from *The Pedestrian?* Does this long and complex sentence in fact make an effective opening to the story? The simplest sentence structure in English is, of course,

SUBJECT — VERB — OBJECT, OR ADVERBS.

e.g. He would stand upon the corner of an intersection. This is varied for questions to

VERB — SUBJECT — OBJECT, OR ADVERBS.

e.g. Do I see the U.S. cavalry over the next hill?

But these basic patterns can and should be varied to add interest, variety or emphasis.

(a) Discuss the following variations on the same basic sentence. What difference do the changes make, in meaning or emphasis?

(i) Everything went on in the tomb-like houses at night now, he thought.

(ii) He thought everything went on in the tomb-like houses at night now.

(iii) In the tomb-like houses everything went on at night now, he thought.

(iv) At night now everything went on in the tomb-like houses, he thought.

(v) Now everything went on in the tomb-like houses at night, he thought.

(vi) Now, he thought, everything went on in the tomb-like houses at night.

(vii) He thought now everything went on in the tomb-like houses at night.

(b) Alter the order of words and phrases in each of the following so that each is expressed in at least *two more* possible ways. Discuss your answers and the effect on the meaning:

1. Mr. Mead was alone in the empty streets.
2. Occasionally he picked up a leaf as he passed.
3. The cloverleaf intersection was a thunderous surge of cars during the day.
4. The moon was high and clear among the stars.
5. The police car rolled through the night avenues, flashing its dim lights ahead.

(c) Combining several ideas into one complex sentence always adds interest and depth to writing. A pattern of cause and effect and of ideas interacting is suggested. In the passage these three statements:

He came to a cloverleaf intersection.

This intersection stood silent.

At this intersection two main highways crossed the town.

become:

He came to a cloverleaf intersection which stood silent where two main highways crossed the town.

Combine the following groups of short statements into *one* sentence in each case. You must not use "and", "but" and "so" as linking words. You may alter the wording or order, but not omit any of the ideas.

1. Leonard Mead loved to walk alone. He is the central character of this short story. All the people were comfortably watching the television screens at that time. These people lived in his town.

2. Leonard Mead despises his fellow-townspeople. He considers them only half alive. They do not read. Nor do they take exercise. Nor do they do anything active in their leisure at all.

3. The police found him. The police at once challenged him. But by our standards he was doing nothing wrong. He was taking his walk.

4. The police car was remote-controlled. The police car was quite capable of making an arrest. The police car was obviously armed. But the police car had no human occupants.

5. The police car arrested Mr. Mead. At the same time the police car admitted something. The police car was going to take Mr. Mead to a centre. At this centre he would lose his eccentric habit. His habit was walking alone at night.

Exercise 2. (a) Read the following passage carefully and make notes of the main points as suggested in Précis Rule 6 (see page 186).

The function of the machine is to save work. In a fully mechanized world all the dull drudgery will be done by machinery, leaving us free for more interesting pursuits. So expressed, this sounds splendid. It makes one sick to see half a dozen men sweating their guts out to dig a trench for a water-pipe, when some easily devised machine would scoop the earth out in a couple of minutes. Why not let the machine do the work and the men go and do something else? But presently the question arises, what else are they to do? Supposedly they are set free from "work" in order that they may do something which is not "work". But what is work and what is not work? Is it work to dig, to carpenter, to plant trees, to fell trees, to ride, to fish, to hunt, to feed chickens, to play the piano, to take photographs, to build a house, to cook, to sew, to trim hats, to mend motor bicycles? All of these things are work to somebody, and all of them are play to somebody. There are in fact very few activities which cannot be classed either as work or play according as you choose to regard them. The labourer set free from digging may want to spend his leisure, or part of it, in playing the piano, while the professional pianist may be only too glad to get out and dig at the potato patch. Hence the antithesis between work, as something intolerably tedious, and not-work, as something desirable, is false. The truth is that when a human being is not eating, drinking, sleeping, making love, talking, playing games, or merely lounging about – and these things will not fill up a lifetime – he needs work and usually looks for it, though he may not call it work. Above the level of a third- or fourth-grade moron, life has got to be lived largely in terms of effort. For man is not, as the vulgarer hedonists seem to suppose, a kind of walking stomach; he has also got a hand, an eye, and a brain. Cease to use your hands, and you have lopped off a huge chunk of your consciousness.

(from *The Road to Wigan Pier* by George Orwell, 1st pub. 1937)

(b) Compare your list of main points with ours:
1. Machines could remove drudgery of work.
2. But what are work and play?
3. Many activities can be either, for different people.
4. No clear contrast between work and other activity.
5. We all want to make effort, and must use bodies and minds to live fully.

With such a skeleton of ideas, you can now make a summary *in your own words* of the original passage. When you are asked to use your own words, this does not of course mean avoiding every word of the original, but it does mean paraphrasing all unusual words or phrases the author may have used, and it certainly means you must not borrow whole sequences from the original. It would therefore be quite wrong to begin the summary:

"The function of the machine is to save work . . ." or to use words like "antithesis" and "not-work".

Make a summary of the passage using not more than 100 words. It now contains about 370 words, but much of it is taken up with examples, which can easily be cut out. Apply all the Précis Rules you have been given.

Précis Rule 7. YOUR OWN WORDS:
After making notes of the main points, build up the summary
from them in your own words. Refer back to the original passage, but never copy whole phrases or sentences from it.

Exercise 3. We noticed in Chapter Three (page 47) that *present
participles* (ending in "-ing") and *past participles* (usually ending
in "-ed" or "-t") are *non-finite* parts of verbs – i.e., when by themselves (without a finite part of the verbs "to be" or "to have"),
they often act as adjectives, instead of being verbs limited in
person and tense by a subject. Thus in:
     . . . upon that buckling concrete walk . . .
"buckling" is a present participle, acting as an adjective to
describe the concrete walk. And in:
     . . . long moonlit avenues of sidewalk . . .
"moonlit" is a past participle acting as an adjective to describe
the avenues of sidewalk. And in:
     . . . he would stand . . . and peer . . . deciding which
     way to go : . .
"deciding" is an adjective, describing "He"—if it were to be a
finite verb, it would have to be written:
     . . . he would stand . . . and peer . . . and decide
     which way to go . . .

(a) Pick out the present and past participles (ten in all) acting
as adjectives in the following examples from the passage. In
each case say which noun (or pronoun) they describe.

1. He would stride off, sending patterns of frosty air before
   him. . . .

2. He began his journey in a westerly direction, toward the
   hidden sea.

3. You could feel the cold light going on and off, all the
   branches filled with invisible snow. (2)

4. He whistled a cold quiet whistle between his teeth, occasionally picking up a leaf as he passed, examining its skeletal
   pattern in the infrequent lamplights as he went on, smelling
   its rusty smell. (3)

5. "What is it now?" he asked the houses, noticing his wrist
   watch. "Eight-thirty p.m.? Time for a dozen assorted
   murders? A quiz? A revue? A comedian falling off the
   stage?" (3)

(b) The third non-finite part of verbs is the INFINITIVE, which is normally the form of the verb preceded by the word "to". This is most often a noun:

> *To enter* out into that silence . . . *to put* your feet upon that buckling concrete walk . . . *to step* over grassy seams and *(to) make* your way, hands in pockets, through the silences, that was what Mr. Leonard Mead most dearly loved to do.

The *infinitives* in italics here are all *nouns*, all in apposition to the subject word "that" of the verb "was"—these were the things (or actions) he loved. Yet as non-finite verbs, they can still have adverb phrases (e.g. "out into that silence") and objects (e.g. "your feet") attached to them.

Pick out the ten infinitives acting as nouns in the following examples, and say whether they are subjects or objects of the sentences.

1. To see men sweating at work makes one sick.
2. To dig a trench for pay is work, but to dig one's own garden is pleasure. (2)
3. Some men want to carpenter, to fell trees, to ride, to fish or to play the piano for their own amusement. (5)
4. To mend motor-cycles may be play to one person and work to another.
5. A human being needs food, drink and rest, but he also needs to work.

(c) The "-ing" form of the non-finite verb can also be a noun, but if it is acting as a noun, it is always called a GERUND, and never a present participle. In several of the examples in (b), we could easily substitute a *gerund* for the infinitive:

> *Entering* out into that silence . . . *putting* your feet upon that buckling concrete walk . . . *stepping* over grassy seams and *making* your way, hands in pockets, through the silences, that was what Mr. Leonard Mead most dearly loved to do.

Rewrite examples 1, 2 and 4 from exercise (b). replacing infinitives by gerunds.

Try to decide whether the "-ing" form of the verb in italics in each of the following sentences is (i) part of a finite verb, (ii) a present participle, or (iii) a gerund:

1. Crime was *ebbing*; there was no need now for the police, save for this one lone car *wandering* the empty streets.

2. The car ... gave a faint *whirring* click as if information, somewhere, was *dropping* card by punch-slotted card under electric eyes.

3. The labourer, set free from *digging* may want to spend his leisure, or part of it, in *playing* the piano.

4. When a human being is not *eating, drinking, sleeping,* etc., he needs work.

5. Man is not a *walking* stomach, he enjoys *doing* things with his hands.

6. *Living* a full life involves some effort.

(d) Note that, when the "-ing" form is a gerund, a noun, it takes a possessive adjective. We therefore say:

> I dislike him; I dislike his piano; and I dislike *his* playing it so loudly.

Choose the correct word from the two or three given in brackets in each of the following:

1. (Them, Their, They're) giving all that money to charity was just meant to impress us.

2. This will not prevent (us, our) helping as far as we can.

3. (You're, You, Your) going out this evening is rather inconvenient.

4. I quite enjoy (his, him, he's) acting the fool at parties, but (his, he's) doing it in the street is really rather embarrassing.

Topics for Written Work

1. What do you see as the biggest problems facing mankind, and your generation, during your lifetime? Consider these possibilities; perhaps you would want to alter or add to these notes?

(a) Increased powers of destruction: H-bombs, missiles, armed satellites, germ warfare.

(b) Population increases: people must live closer together, parents must limit families, no room for adventure or aggression, food and housing shortages.

(c) Differences in living standards: richer nations becoming richer, poorer majority becoming poorer.

(d) Complexity of knowledge: leaving decisions to computers that may then go wrong, using chemicals (e.g. fertilisers, cleaning fluids) without knowing long-term effects (e.g. poisoning wild life, etc.).

(e) Increased leisure: people may be bored and lose their mental or physical powers.

(f) Old age: medicines keep people alive, but old people are lonely and under-employed.

(g) Mass production: food, entertainment, clothes, houses, etc. all the same throughout the world.

Take some or all of these as a theme, and plan a discussion essay on them. Use a basic pattern that begins with a general paragraph, treats each of several specific points in a separate paragraph, and ends with a general summing up. Make it clear whether, on the whole, you are pessimistic or optimistic about mankind's future happiness.

When you have planned your essay and assembled your information and evidence, write the finished piece entitled:

SOME PROBLEMS OF THE FUTURE

2. *Either* (a) Imagine you are a complete stranger to our society today, and have to form your opinion of what we are like—how we eat, work, spend our leisure, dress and look after ourselves, where we live and how we treat one another and our children, pets, etc.—*entirely* from television or other advertisements. If you want to know what a typical modern mother is like, for instance, you have only the ones you see on television advertisements to go by. Are people going to seem richer, healthier, happier, more polite, better dressed or more attractive than they are in real life? Write a full description of the typical family from the world of television advertisements.

Or (b) Write a short story set in the future, imagining some present tendency, such as increased television entertainment, or mass-production, or shorter working hours, carried on to an ultimate extreme. "The Pedestrian" is clearly such a story. Here is another example composed by a pupil:

The Demonstrators

To a stranger from the previous century, particularly the depression years of the 1930's and 1970's, a crowd of people, such as these, marching with their posters, would not have been an uncommon sight. If he had glanced at the posters they would have seemed very familiar. These people were marching on London over the shortage of work

224

Posters like "Strike Now – More Work", "Reintroduction of Over-time" or "Longer Hours" were dotted amongst the crowd like boats on a sea. But there was a vast difference between this and past workers' demonstrations. Ever since the Revolution of Automation, seventeen years before, working hours for men and women had been cut more and more. The Revolution had begun officially in the South, when the giant computer X32L was completed, and had spread its tentacles over the country in a matter of months. London had become the nucleus of automation, with its moving pavements, and roads, lifts and all types of independent automatic machines in the shops and offices. By 2035 the old face of London had almost completely disappeared; only Big Ben, St. Paul's and the Houses of Parliament remained. London had become a gigantic area of automated sky-scrapers and towering office-blocks, every one of which completely overshadowed the decaying G.P.O. building built in the 1960's.

At first, people had been delighted to do less work for the same money, but gradually their three-day week had become a two-, then a one-day week. When work was abolished completely, people began to realise that the machines, hideous, efficient and blank, were not only taking over their jobs but ruling their whole lives. They began to go back to work in order to preserve their self-respect and their sanity. Having to create jobs for people caused difficulties, and so the Government charged a fee for the privilege of going to work. Rates soon became exorbitant. People neglected their homes and families, mortgaged their houses and pawned their clothes in order to find enough money to buy a job.

When the Employment Societies decided to increase their interest rates to 29%, it was the last straw for many people. A crowd formed in a street in Newcastle and quite spontaneously marched, angrily determined, towards London. Even a small mob cannot march without being noticed, of course. Reports were flashed to London. First they were thought to be exaggerated, but later reports showed that, if anything, the earlier ones had been understatements. As soon as it became clear that the mob meant business, desperate attempts to turn them back were made. All moving pavements and other forms of transport were immobilized. It made no difference. Traffic control machines and alien blockade units were adapted and sent to deal with the crowd. These were overcome easily and the now vicious crowd moved on to the outskirts of London.

It was on the seventh day of their march that the mob reached North London. Desperate attempts were made to pacify them, but the now near-frenzied mob paid little heed. As the crowd moved, so they smashed and destroyed, burnt and plundered. All attempts to stop them were overrun as they moved on to the heart of London. They were determined to get what they had come for – the abolition of automation and free work for all. At long last the head of the mob came to Westminster. The Houses of Parliament were surrounded by a thick belt of tranquilizer gas. The crowd halted for a moment and the Prime Minister appeared overhead in a magnetic hovercraft, amid a chorus of jeers and boos. After a while they stopped and listened. The P.M. refused to *ban* automation, but he said he would cut down the amount of it. The crowd began to listen more closely.

He went on to say that free work would be reintroduced. The crowd began to calm. He had won them over.

Most of the crowd went to Battersea Park and burnt all their posters in a gigantic bonfire, and quietly began the march home. They had won. They had got what they came for. They were happy.

But the Prime Minister was not at all satisfied. He wrote in his diary that night: "Where will today's concessions end? There is only one logical outcome. The people will demand to be *paid* for working. The economy of the country will be ruined."

ALAN

Oral Work

In his book *Journey Down a Rainbow*, J. B. Priestley coined a new word for a world in which we tend to become "all the same":

"*Admass*. This is my name for the whole system of an increasing productivity, plus inflation, plus a rising standard of material living, plus high-pressure advertising and salesmanship, plus mass communications, plus cultural democracy and the creation of the mass mind, the mass man . . .

"In this empire are many kingdoms. One I propose to call *Nomadmass*. This is the land of the new nomads, dominated by the internal combustion engine . . .

"It is good for people to travel, to leave their homes now and again and discover how other people live, to spend their days in wildly unfamiliar surroundings, to make every meal an experiment, to sit behind exotic drinks and listen to foreign tunes and unimaginable lyrics, to try to understand alien habits, customs, values, to be half-repelled, half-enchanted; and then, with bursting bags and memories, to find themselves back home once more. But this is the opposite of *Nomadmass* life, which offers movement without any essential change. It is a street three thousand miles long. At each end are the same cigarettes, breakfast foods, television programmes, movies, syndicated columns, songs and topics of conversation. You burn a hundred and fifty gallons of gasoline to arrive nowhere. You are never really at home nor away from home. You neither cultivate your own garden nor admire other people's: the gardens have gone. So has the Past, for everything here is brand-new, just unpacked from the factory, with gadgets replacing old skills, endless entertainment and no art, filled with the devices of second-rate men and utterly removed, perhaps for ever, from the noble passions, the tragic insights, the heroic laughter, of great minds. Ten miles of it will not show you a bookshop. Books belong to yesterday. *Nomadmass* is nearly tomorrow."

Discuss this passage, first to see that you agree as to what Priestley is criticising and warning us about, then to see how far you agree with him. It is quite common for people to regret modernisation and the mass-production of new comforts and other aids to a higher standard of living. People will criticise the passing of steam locomotives, the demolition of Victorian buildings, the building of new housing estates by industrialised construction methods, the advent of supersonic passenger aircraft, and so on. Are they simply opposing progress? Is there a real danger that, in order to give *everyone* food, housing and leisure, we shall have to live in a monotonous, mass-produced environment eating the same tasteless food and without any opportunity to cherish individual or national differences? Priestley blames "high-pressure advertising and salesmanship"—in fact our modern industrial system—for persuading us to accept this second-rate world; do you?

Discuss the question of design. Study the series of pictures on page 228. How does one decide on questions of style? Does an article have to be simply functional, or is its appearance, in relation to the materials it is made of, important too? What, if anything, is wrong with putting false "Tudor" beams on the front of a brick-built, twentieth-century house? Can machines make *better* articles than skilled men can make with their hands? If so, is there any virtue in traditional hand-made articles? D. H. Lawrence wrote:

Things men have made with wakened hands,
    and put soft life into
are awake through years with transferred
    touch, and go on glowing
for long years.
And for this reason, some old things are lovely
warm still with the life of forgotten men
    who made them.

Do you agree?

Activities and Research

Make a study of popular culture today, with special reference to the teenage market. The following headings and suggestions might be useful:

1. *"Pop" Music:* What are the leading songs, singers and musicians at present? Who "measures" their popularity and how? How long have the currently popular artists been well-known? Study the style of music and the words of the songs. Note any popular fashions in instruments, rhythm or melody, and try to discover how, or from what influences, they have arisen. Are there any common trends in the themes or words of the songs, and do they compare or contrast with earlier fashions?

2. *"Pop" Stars:* If you can, find out some of the true biographical details about the leading stars of today. Do these contrast with the "image" of their publicity? Enquire into their education, who "discovered" and "manages" them, how much they earn, etc. Discuss their real musical talent, as opposed to the "gimmicks" or the technical skill with which their songs or music are recorded.

3. *Commercialism:* Examine current teenage fashions in clothes, transport, hair-styles, etc. Which of them are tied up with pop-stars? Find examples of stars' names (or pictures) being used to sell goods to teenagers.

4. *Boys' Magazines, etc.:* Collect examples of comics, picture-books and general magazines (as opposed to those connected with particular pastimes) and make generalisations about the kinds of heroes and the stories in them. Do they tend to follow certain well-worn patterns? Collect examples of the ends of stories or the central incidents. Are the same interests reflected in advertising in the magazines? What kind of boy would read each of the magazines?

5. *Girls' Magazines:* Make the same kind of study, and ask the same questions, as in (4). Draw some contrasts between the material popular with boys and girls.

6. *Teenage Leisure Habits:* Survey the different ways of spending free time in your own area, and attempt to assess how popular each is. What are the popular clubs, coffee-bars, dance-halls, etc.? Are sporting activities or facilities for hobbies flourishing? Do particular places or ways of spending time seem to be confined to particular age-groups?

The Pedestrian from *The Golden Apples of the Sun* by RAY BRADBURY
(Rupert Hart-Davis; Corgi)
To describe this collection of short stories as science fiction is
rather misleading. It is true that there are a number of stories
which, like *The Pedestrian*, are set in worlds of the future and
which pass comment on the social conditions and attitudes to
be found there. But there are also many tales of fantasy, and
others, such as *The Garbage Collector*, dealing with incidents
which take place in the present. This chapter's extract provides
a fair example of Bradbury's style, which is sometimes rather
sentimental, but always poetic.

Farenheit 451 by RAY BRADBURY (Hart-Davis; Corgi)
In this science fiction novel, firemen are people who do not
put out fires but set fire to every habitation which still contains
books. Against this world, where private thought or action is
criminal, the hero, Montag, rebels. He hides a book. The
account of his rebellion and pursuit is not only exciting but
thought-provoking, warning us, as many of Bradbury's stories
do, against the continual assaults that are made upon the world
of our imaginations.

Other books by RAY BRADBURY are *The Illustrated Man* (Hart-
Davis; Corgi), *The Day it Rained Forever* (Hart-Davis; Penguin),
The Silver Locusts (Hart-Davis; Corgi), *The October Country*
(Hart-Davis)

CHAPTER FIFTEEN

Advertising

This is an extract from a book of advice to consumers on how to obtain value for money. In a chapter on "The Impact of Advertising", the author considers some of the methods of advertising and their results.

Life would be much less convenient if one could not find out from advertisements the programme at a local cinema, the date of Harrod's sale, or the details of a cheap excursion ticket to Ryde on Sundays. Consumers may be glad the people concerned have had the initiative to announce these things by advertising; but sorry that, for every useful advertisement, there are so many which seem intent not on bringing good news about wares or services, but on pulling out every stop on the emotional organ, or on using every illusion in their pseudo-scientific conjuring box, or even on sailing as near to the edge of truth as they dare, in order to sell something neither better nor worse than a dozen alternative brands . . .

Certainly advertising by manufacturers is diminishing retailers' responsibility and therefore detracts from the expertise which the consumer needs from them. This is undoubtedly so, and is at the heart of the matter in other chapters of this book. Questioned by the writer about the merits of various brands of furniture polish, the buyer in a leading department store recommended two or three, giving good reasons. Asked why he also stocked brands he had found inferior, he said that shoppers insisted on having these makes because they had seen them regularly advertised. The Drapers' Chamber of Trade has found that "high-powered advertising of corsetry has compelled retailers to stock a particular product which quite often did not sell after the initial impact". Advertising can mean that too many shops all stock the same brands, and overall demand in the locality, when thus divided up, does not warrant any one of them carrying a full range of, say, sizes and colours – to the disadvantage of the consumer.

Advertising agents seem especially sensitive on the subject of emotional manipulation in advertising. Of course emotional satisfactions are real, and of course they can be well-founded. The love of a woman for a man, that of a mother for a child, are as obviously genuine as they are valuable. But the manipulation of these profound and fundamental values merely to sell a deodorant or a bag of toffees must cause some uneasiness. If advertising indeed influences people's habits as much as the advertising agents would have the manufacturers believe, then theirs is a very grave responsibility indeed, particularly in the case of advertisements specifically aimed at the young, and particularly when the product advertised is alcohol or tobacco. Educationists, doctors, and others have been protesting at the rapid increase in advertising of this kind.

On one page of a newspaper one may read of the increase in venereal disease, illegitimate babies, and abortions amongst teenage girls; on another an advertisement showing such a girl delighted at being "picked up" (I use the expression advisedly) by a stranger in a train as the result of using so-and-so's soap. When such advertisements and other similar influences are multiplied ten-thousandfold, surely only the wilfully obtuse cannot see the connexion between these two facts. While teachers and parents struggle to turn young barbarians into reasonably polite and considerate people, a confectionery firm apparently sees nothing amiss in an advertisement with a child saying "I've got mine – you get your own."

Furthermore, advertisements exploit that most potent emotion of all, fear; not least fear of "what people will think". I didn't find the company of my friends any less agreeable *before* that "Somebody isn't using Amplex" series than I do now; yet presumably (since it has been running some time) a number of people are indeed persuaded to think they might get shunned if they don't use Amplex. Is it, therefore, real need or only fear that created this market? Any reader can multiply instances of this kind by looking at newspapers or posters with an analytical eye. The less critical reader is influenced without realising it.

Then there are the advertisements which blind by what goes as science; these are too numerous to mention, though the many toothpaste advertisements referring to "miracle" ingredients of one kind or another are a classic example. So is the TV soap advertisement: "Doctors in over a thousand skin tests proved X makes your skin younger, softer, lovelier than ever." (How does one "test" loveliness?) And in a 1959 issue of

Shopper's Guide the following commentary on detergent manufacturers' claims was made after chemical analyses:

"New magic ingredient"	Carboxymethylcellulose – no doubt new to this product —is in all synthetic detergents.
"Fabulous new ingredient"	Fluorescer: is also in other detergents.
"Special ingredient . . . oxygen bubbles ease out stains."	Perborate: is also in other detergents.

It has been said that advertising is the more potent, the greater the consumer's ignorance.

The last-ditch stand of copy-writers, when they are challenged about some of their least probable claims, is often the happy thought that "no one takes that literally". The advertiser seems to claim a sort of poetic licence – once safely outside the territory of the Merchandise Marks Acts, that is. Where does this tolerance end? Journalists, politicians, teachers, clerics – all (and rightly) are sharply criticized when they get their data wrong, indulge in wild generalization, or let opinion masquerade as fact. On what grounds may an advertiser claim immunity from the ordinary responsibility of any spokesman to respect facts? Yet the temptation not to do so is extra strong if the advertiser who sticks to the exact truth is in lively fear that a less scrupulous competitor will steal some of his market. Thus some British refrigerator manufacturers now seem to be departing from the practice of quoting their sizes "net" simply because continental firms misleadingly always quote "gross" figures.

(from *Your Money's Worth* by Elizabeth Gundrey)

1. Sum up the kinds of advertisements that the author seems to approve of. She gives examples in the first paragraph – generalise from these.
2. What two different effects is advertising said to have on retailers' stocks, according to the second paragraph?
3. What kinds of advertising could be said to represent "emotional manipulation" (3rd paragraph)? Make a list of the emotions (or feelings) that these paragraphs (the 3rd, 4th and 5th of this extract) suggest are being exploited by advertisers.
4. What points is the author making about the use of "science" in advertisements?
5. What is the advertiser's excuse for not sticking to the exact truth (according to this passage)? Is this a fair argument, or can you think of any obvious answer to his excuse?
6. Explain the point of quoting "gross" instead of "net" figures for refrigerator sizes, showing what the terms mean.
7. What distinction is the author making between "useful" advertisements and those that "pull out every stop on the emotional organ", "use every illusion in their pseudo-scientific conjuring box" or "sail as near to the edge of truth as they dare"? What parts of this passage expand these faults in advertising more fully?
8. What is a retailer's "responsibility" to his customer? What does the author mean by "the expertise which the consumer needs from them" (2nd paragraph)?
9. What is the function of a "buyer" in a department store? How was advertising altering the buyer's policy in the example in the second paragraph? Was this "detracting from his expertise"?
10. Is the author's argument about a connection between advertising and the increase in sexual immorality (or irresponsibility) really fair? Has she *proved* that the wider use of sex appeal in advertisements has *caused* the increase in these problems? Could both increases perhaps have a common cause? Do you personally think she might be right, even if she has not altogether proved it here?
11. What assumption is the author making in her parenthesis "since it has been running some time" (5th paragraph)? Considering how expensive advertising campaigns are,

and how much work is done on "market research", do you agree with the assumption?

12. What is "poetic licence"? Can you give further examples from current advertisements of (a) "getting data wrong", (b) "indulging in wild generalisation", and (c) "letting opinion masquerade as fact"?

13. What is wrong with the advertisement showing a child saying: "I've got mine – you get your own."? Do you think advertising is to blame for a growth in acquisitiveness and materialism? (What do those terms mean?)

Techniques

Exercise 1. Why do manufacturers advertise? Basically, they have information to give to the public, but how many advertisements on television, in newspapers or on hoardings do in fact contain much information? In industrialized countries, firms must be sure of a vast market before investing large sums of money in machinery. Yet there is not an unlimited demand for products. If many families already have a car or quite serviceable furniture, advertisers must try to persuade them to buy replacements before they really need them. And if the products of different firms are really much the same, sales will depend only on the appeal of the advertisements, not on the quality of the goods.

(a) Most of us can be tempted to give way to our basic desires. Traditionally, there are seven "deadly sins" which tempt us all. At least six of them are today frequently exploited by advertisers. Cut out from a newspaper or magazine one advertisement that seems to make each of these appeals, and stick this into a book or file where you can add a few words of comment to show which part of the advertisement you have in mind:

1. *Gluttony:* Look for an advertisement that appeals to your greed for food or drink, especially one that tries to reassure you that the product will do you good as well.
2. *Avarice:* Products are often sold as bargains, or with free gifts, money-saving coupons, or the chance of winning a prize.
3. *Envy:* Look for advertisements that suggest you need the product to make you as happy, beautiful, successful or prosperous as your more fortunate friends and neighbours.
4. *Sloth:* Find an example of a product offering you ease, comfort or leisure.
5. *Pride:* All advertisements that emphasise how exclusive and superior the product is, showing it in an expensive or upper-class setting, include this appeal.
6. *Lust:* Perhaps sex-appeal is the most obvious advertising technique of all, but look for an example where the product really has no direct connection with the pretty girl or the handsome man.
7. *Anger:* Probably the most difficult category to find an example of, but you occasionally see an advertisement intended to make you so furious with someone or something that you will spend money to relieve your feelings.

(b) Certain other feelings and fears are common to most of us, and advertisers have been quick to exploit them. Find examples of the following appeals:
8. *Conformity:* Many people hate to be conspicuous, and gain pleasure from following fashions and trends. Find examples of the "Thousands of housewives use it" type of advertisement.
9. *Personal success:* Much advertising promises easier personal relationships and success in making friends. Elizabeth Gundrey referred in the passage to the Amplex campaign to make people worry about bad breath. Find similar examples from current advertisements.

10. *Security:* Look for advertisements offering a cosy and safe home life, or playing on fears of unforeseen disaster.
11. *Identification:* Hero-worship is often exploited: if the sports-man or pop-star approves of the product, so will his admirers.
12. *Respect:* Famous personalities, scientists, doctors, nurses, etc., are all used to sell things. Why?
13. *Mother love:* Pictures of children have an immediate appeal, and any mother can easily be made to wonder if she is doing the best for her children.
14. *Health:* Look for an advertisement that first creates a fear of some illness (probably an unlikely one), and then offers a cure.

(c) Many advertisements attempt to do more than simply appeal to our feelings or fears. Their aim is to build up an IMAGE of the product that will make it attractive and satisfying at a sub-conscious level. Psychologists are employed to analyse people's feelings about the goods and the way they are packed and presented. In *The Hidden Persuaders,* Vance Packard describes the process of "motivation research", which uses word association tests and other techniques to understand people's deep-seated desires, fears or sense of guilt. He refers particularly to the work of Dr. Dichter, who was once called in to help boost falling sales of Californian prunes. He found that prunes were associated sub-consciously with "decrepitude and devitalization", with strict parents and stingy landladies, with black witches, and above all with constipation.

"He felt that what was needed was a top-to-bottom surgery job on the public's image of the prune so that the public could 'rediscover' it as a brand-new fruit. The prune, he decided, would be the new 'wonder fruit'. The whole concept of the prune as a dried-out fruit for people in need of a laxative was recast into a more 'dynamic' image under his guidance by the California prune people. The aim in stressing 'new wonder fruit' was to reassure housewives that it was now perfectly acceptable to serve people prunes.

"Overnight the prune became a delightful, sweet fruit, almost a candy, if you were to believe the ads. The new imagery showed prunes in a setting as far away as you could get from the dark, murky, old-maidish look of old in which four black prunes were shown floating in a dark fluid. In the new ads gay, bright colours were used, and childish figures were shown playing. Later the image figures of 'youth' gradually changed from children to pretty girls figure-skating or playing tennis. And where prunes were shown they were in bright, gay-coloured dishes or shown against white cottage cheese. With the pictures were jingles saying 'Put Wings on Your Feet' and 'Get That Top of the World Feeling'. One ad said, 'Prunes help bring colour to your blood and a glow to your face'. In its public image the prune became a true-life Cinderella!

"As for the laxative angle it was now mentioned in passing near the bottom of the message. One ad showing the cute figure skater concluded with these words: '– and, a gentle aid to regularity. When you feel good, good things happen to you. So start eating prunes today till you have energy to spare.'

"The rediscovered prune soon was enjoying a spurt in sales. . . ."

Try to analyse any similar full advertising campaign designed to build up a particular image for a product. If possible, select a variety of advertisements (perhaps from *different* newspapers and magazines) for one product, and study them all.

Exercise 2. The use of English in advertisements includes all the stylistic techniques that can be employed to help persuade the public.

(a) Find examples from the advertisements you collected in answering Exercise 1, or from others in newspapers and magazines, of each of the following:

1. Emotive words (e.g. beauty, gay, mother, wonderful, tension, tragedy, pain, success, soft, sweet);
2. repetition of names, slogans or phrases;
3. scientific and technical jargon;
4. made-up or distorted language (e.g. "Drinka Pinta Milka Day");
5. exclamations and questions (especially *rhetorical questions*, where no answer is expected);
6. alliteration and rhyme;
7. puns and other uses of humour;
8. proverbs or sayings adapted for the advertisement;
9. exaggeration;
10. "headline" language, incomplete sentences, etc.

(b) Study the following advertisement from the point of view (i) of its "image" and its emotional appeal (as discussed in Exercise 1), and (ii) of its style and vocabulary (the kind of points listed in (a) above). Then write a short analysis of the advertisement, stating what market you think it is aimed at, and how it seeks to give the product an appeal and to make the reader remember the brand-name.

Now

NU-LUX set the trends in brightness

Is there a bright, warm welcome in your home?

NU-LUX, the most popular paint on the market, will give your family the luxury they deserve.

NU-LUX paint is based on the newest formula known:

* *Do it yourself?*—NU-LUX is thixatropic and the paint won't run!

* *Brighten that bathroom?*—NU-LUX is hygroscopic and just absorbs condensation!

* *Impress the neighbours?*—NU-LUX range of colours is expansive but not expensive. Every shade is uniquely blended by expert consultant designers to bring you that exclusive elegance!

And remember: dirt harbours disease! Only NU-LUX is germicidal, and offers lasting protection.

You save on every pint of this one-coat wonder paint!

NU-LUX is a home's best friend

NU-LUX PAINTS LIMITED

(By appointment paint manufacturers to H.R.H. the Duke of Wendle since 1894)

Exercise 3. A number of words used by Elizabeth Gundrey in the passage can have two quite distinct common meanings:

> e.g. "warrant" as a verb often means "justify" (as here in the 2nd paragraph);
> "warrant" as a noun means a document certifying or authorising something (as in "search warrant").

(a) What meaning have the following words in the passage? In each case give a second distinct meaning, and write a short sentence to illustrate this different meaning clearly:

e.g. Although in plain clothes, the police officer produced a genuine *warrant* for Smith's arrest, and took him into custody.

In paragraph 3:	grave; case;
In paragraph 4:	page; train; obtuse; firm;
In paragraph 5:	company;
In paragraph 6:	blind;
In paragraph 7:	respect; net.

(b) The examples in (a) are of words which, spelt and pronounced in the same way, still have two or more distinct meanings or functions. A number of English words, however, shift their pronunciation slightly when they change meaning or function. Thus the one word "protest" might be given the following dictionary entry for its two meanings:

protest, 1. (protĕst′), *v.t.* & *i.* Solemnly affirm; make a p., express disapproval.
2. (prōt′ĕst), *n.* Formal expression of disagreement or disapproval.
prot′estant, *adj.* Belonging to any Western Church except the Roman Catholic: *n.* member of such a Church. [PRO+TESTAMENT, L. *testis* witness]

Discuss all the abbreviations and symbols used here. How is the word pronounced in each case? Which pronunciation fits the word "protesting" as used in the third paragraph of the passage? In the fourth paragraph the word "in′crease" is used as a noun; what part of speech would it be if pronounced "increase′", with the STRESS on the *second syllable*?

Show, by marking the stress with an accent mark and then giving a brief definition, the *two* different pronunciations and meanings (or functions) of each of the following: subject (3rd paragraph); exploit (5th paragraph); exact (7th paragraph); compound; content; contest; contrast; desert; extract; present; produce; project.

Topics for Written Work

1. Mr. David Ogilvy in his book *Confessions of an Advertising Man* gives the following advice on wording the "copy" of advertisements. He is referring particularly to the "headlines" of advertisements, but the advice applies also to smaller print.

(1) The headline is the "ticket on the meat". Use it to flag down the readers who are prospects for the kind of product you are advertising. If you are selling a remedy for bladder weakness, display the words BLADDER WEAKNESS in your headline; they catch the eye of everyone who suffers from this inconvenience. If you want *mothers* to read your advertisement, display MOTHERS in your headline. And so on.

Conversely, do not say anything in your headline which is likely to *exclude* any readers who might be prospects for your product. Thus, if you are advertising a product which can be used equally well by men and women, don't slant your headline at women alone; it would frighten men away.

(2) Every headline should appeal to the reader's *self-interest*. It should promise her a benefit, as in my headline for Helena Rubinstein's Hormone Cream: HOW WOMEN OVER 35 CAN LOOK YOUNGER.

(3) Always try to inject *news* into your headlines, because the consumer is always on the lookout for new products, or new ways to use an old product, or new improvements in an old product.

The two most powerful words you can use in a headline are FREE and NEW. You can seldom use FREE, but you can almost always use NEW – if you try hard enough.

(4) Other words and phrases which work wonders are HOW TO, SUDDENLY, NOW, ANNOUNCING, INTRODUCING, IT'S HERE, JUST ARRIVED, IMPORTANT DEVELOPMENT, IMPROVEMENT, AMAZING, SENSATIONAL, REMARKABLE, REVOLUTIONARY, STARTLING, MIRACLE, MAGIC, OFFER, QUICK, EASY, WANTED, CHALLENGE, ADVICE TO, THE TRUTH ABOUT, COMPARE, BARGAIN, HURRY, LAST CHANCE.

Don't turn up your nose at these clichés. They may be shopworn, but they work. That is why you see them turn up so often in the headlines of mail-order advertisers and others who can measure the results of their advertisements.

Headlines can be strengthened by the inclusion of emotional words, like DARLING, LOVE, FEAR, PROUD, FRIEND, and BABY. One of the most provocative advertisements which has come out of our agency showed a girl in a bath-tub, talking to her lover on the telephone. The headline: *Darling, I'm having the most extraordinary experience . . . I'm head over heels in* DOVE.

(5) Five times as many people read the headline as read the body copy, so it is important that these glancers should at least be told what brand is being advertised. That is why you should always include the brand name in your headlines.

(6) Include your selling promise in your headline. This requires long headlines. When the New York University School of Retailing ran headline tests with the co-operation of a big department store,

they found that headlines of ten words or longer, containing news and information, consistently sold more merchandise than short headlines.

Using this advice and all you have already learnt from study of advertising in this chapter, set about writing the "copy" for the most unlikely sales campaign you can imagine. For instance, selling refrigerators to Eskimos or central heating in the Congo, brown soap, slow cars, hand-operated mangles, coloured drinking water, odd socks, or do-it-yourself kits for producing pure salt from sea-water. Choose your own unlikely subject and work out at least one advertisement for it.

2. Few of us will become advertising agents but all of us will be consumers. We are all likely to have cause for complaint about goods or services that we have paid for, and occasionally will need to put the complaint politely but firmly in writing.

(a) Here is a brief, clear business letter on these lines. As practice in setting out and punctuation, rewrite it neatly on a clean page. The letter itself should be in three paragraphs.

10 Edge Terrace Westford Kent DA172ML 16th March 19—Ronald Smith and Co Ltd (Dept F6) 113 High Way Saint Martins Yorkshire HX7 3AX Dear Sirs On 21st February I wrote for one of your Excel Pedometers as advertised in the "Views of the World" and on 10th March I received one in a very poorly packed parcel The pedometer's case was scratched but the damage appeared to be superficial However when I tried it out by walking a known distance of 3 kilometres I found that it registered 4 kilometres on one occasion 3½ on another and 4½ when my sister carried it over the same journey Your advertisement clearly states that the pedometer is accurate to 0·25 of a kilometre I am therefore returning this one in a separate parcel and I trust you will either replace it with an accurate and undamaged one or refund the £7 I paid for it together with the 60p I have spent on postage and packing Yours faithfully Peter Brown

(b) You now have a "model answer" on which to base a letter complaining about any poor goods or services you may imagine you have received. Choose a real and feasible situation, even if it is imaginary, and let your complaint sound reasonable. Rudeness and exaggeration are not likely to prove effective, and you should save threats for the very last stage of a struggle to obtain your rights. Always use a business letter format, and begin with clear references to the goods in question, to dates when you bought and received them, and any reference or serial numbers that may help the firm identify these goods.

As an alternative to another letter of complaint, try to write what you think could be the reply from Ronald Smith and Company to Peter Brown's complaint.

1. If groups of members of the class work on collecting different kinds of advertisements (on the lines suggested in Exercise 1 and 2), this will give an excellent opportunity for some reporting back to the class, with illustrations cut from newspapers and magazines as a display or mounted on sheets to be passed round. A member of the group should analyse and criticise each advertisement, showing what techniques are being employed and commenting on any unfair exploitation of feelings or use of persuasion.

2. After studying advertising and analysing particular examples, hold a discussion or debate where the arguments for and against free advertising can be summed up. Here are some of the possible points to argue about:

For:

(a) Advertising boosts sales and so helps reduce prices of goods.
(b) It keeps the public informed of new products.
(c) In a free country, manufacturers must be free to compete by persuading customers to buy.
(d) Advertisements for new and better products help raise people's standards of hygiene, comfort and design.
(e) Advertisements are often interesting, witty or gay.

Against:

(a) Advertisements add to the cost of goods.
(b) They use persuasive techniques, instead of simply relying on quality of goods.
(c) They unfairly persuade people to buy goods they do not want or need.
(d) Advertisements repeatedly suggest that one can *buy* success and happiness, if only one is rich enough.
(e) They are unsightly and tedious and waste newspaper space and television time.

3. Make up some comic advertisements that you can record on tape, with appropriate music or sound effects. Some of those written as Topic for Written Work, 1 may be suitable. Work in groups to put several short advertisements together on tape, perhaps linked by music or clashing cymbals.

1. Consumer protection organisations are our best answer, as customers, to advertising and high-powered sales promotion. Find out what the following do: The Consumer Council, The Consumers Association, the British Standards Institution, the Council of Industrial Design, the Good Housekeeping Institute. Which of them are completely independent? Are any supported by industry or by the Government? Do any allow their recommendations to be used in a firm's own advertising? Examine copies of the magazine *Which* — nearly all public libraries keep files of back numbers of these. Choose a particular product and see how they set about testing it and what particular makes are recommended and why. The magazine publishes a cumulative index of all products that have been investigated and tested: try looking up any particular article you might want to buy or recently have bought, such as a record player, or equipment for your own sport or hobby, and study the entry for it if there is one, to see what they recommended as "best buy" in that case.

2. We print below a "scenario" for a short "mock advertisement" film worked out by a pupil as a *parody* of television advertisements. Notice how it is divided into two columns, with vision on the left and sound on the right, and yet treated shot by shot. In this case, Geoffrey was working out a scenario that could easily be shot by members of the class as a short film of their own. All the "locations" therefore are simple ones to do in school, and the sound track is to be a tape-recorded commentary, and not "synchronised" conversation.

SCENARIO FOR A MOCK FILM ADVERTISEMENT

VISION (with silent, 16 mm. camera)	SOUND (tape-recorded)
1. Close-up of "WANDSWORTH SCHOOL" notice.	*Interviewer:* Recently Plasman's Super Tonic team visited Wandsworth School.
2. Long shot of school gate with boys leaving at 3.50 p.m.	*Interviewer:* We asked some of the pupils whether any of the staff had been showing signs of strain and taking it out on the boys.
3. Medium shot of interviewer calling boy from crowd, shot over interviewer's shoulder.	(Background noise of boys leaving school)

244

4. Close-up of boy talking (to interviewer).

Boy: Well, yes. We've had a lot of extra work from our English master lately, and he has been keeping us all in for nothing after school.

5. Medium shot of interviewer shaking hands with boys.
(Fade out)

Interviewer: We decided to go into this a bit further. We took our cameras in to film that English master in the class-room.

6. Medium pan-shot of class-room of boys round to a very depressed master at the front.

7. Medium shot of master looking up, shot over interviewer's shoulder.

Interviewer: We asked that English master if he had been feeling depressed and irritable lately. He replied:

8. Master turns in chair towards blackboard looking surprised.

Master: Yes, I must admit that this class have rather been getting me down lately.
(Background class noise)

9. Medium front shot of interviewer in front of blackboard, with a complicated formula written up, holding bottle of Plasman's Super Tonic in one hand and stick of chalk in other.

Interviewer: So we told him just how lucky he was that we had the very thing to cure that anti-social feeling: Plasman's Super Tonic – a spoonful a day makes you feel years younger! Cures back-ache, deafness, hiccups, and is ideal for rubbing into sore corns.

10. Close-up of Tonic bottle in hand.

Interviewer: And it's only 30p a bottle.

11. Medium shot of interviewer pointing to formula on board, and explaining it to master.
(Fade out)

Interviewer: As we showed in this simple diagram, Plasman's Super Tonic, with H_2SO_4 and thiamin, works to sooth the nerves.

12. Pan shot of school gate with boys leaving at 3.50 p.m.

Interviewer: Two weeks later, after treating that English master with Plasman's Super Tonic, our Wandsworth schoolboy had a very different story!

13. Repeat shot 3.

14. Repeat shot 4.

Boy: Oh yes, we have had less homework, and he's really been quite nice to us.

15. Repeat shot 5. (Fade out)

Interviewer: So Plasman's Super Tonic really works! Large bottles only 30p, and the 15p size for minor ailments.

16. Close-up of 2 tonic bottles with prices.

GEOFFREY

245

After studying the way this scenario has been set out and worked out, try to compose a short one of your own.

Members of the class might then try to select the most suitable scenario and film it, if a cine-camera is available. The following officials are useful for class film-making projects: a director, to be generally in charge; two cameramen, one of whom should be responsible for the focus adjustment, two distance measurers (with a long tape-measure), one continuity man (assisted by properties men if necessary), one light-measurer (to read the light meter), lighting men for any extra indoor lighting, and a secretary to keep a shot-by-shot log (including information about camera setting, duration of shot, the reading of the feet-counter on the camera, etc.).

If there is equipment for editing, and some cutting and splicing are necessary, these jobs can be done by other members of the team, as can the work on any tape-recorded sound-track that may be included.

Further Reading

Your Money's Worth by ELIZABETH GUNDREY (Penguin) (659) Although this book was written in 1962, and some of its information (particularly prices) is therefore out of date, Part 1 deals with safeguards for customers, warns us of many unfair sales practices and explains what rights we have. Part 2 gives basic advice on what to consider when buying various particular fitments, machines or items of furniture. **Elizabeth Gundrey has also written *You and Your Money* and *You and Your Shopping* (Evans) and *Making Ends Meet* (Arrow)** (332).

Which? is the magazine of the Consumers' Association, published monthly. Each number covers about five items, and gives results of exhaustive tests and compares the goods offered by different makers as to quality and price. Nearly all public libraries keep back numbers in folders or books, fully indexed, either for reference or in the section 659.1.

The Hidden Persuaders by VANCE PACKARD (Longmans; Penguin) (659.1) This account of the techniques of American "mental-depth" advertisers is both alarming and entertaining. It is interesting, informative, and easy to read; it will cause you to look at advertisements more closely, and with more understanding and concern than before. Vance Packard's other books include:

246

The Status Seekers (301.4), in which he examines classes in American society, and how they behave and spend in order to maintain or improve their status; and *The Waste Makers* (339.4) in which the creation of artificial "needs" in order to justify massive over-production is carefully examined. (Both published: Longmans; Penguin).

Confessions of an Advertising Man by DAVID OGILVY (Longmans; Mayflower) (659.1)

The author is one of the most successful advertising agents in Britain, one of the few who can be said to equal the Americans in this field. His is a remarkably frank book when discussing the skills of his profession, and he is quite willing to justify his work in the face of critics of modern advertising.

CHAPTER SIXTEEN

The World of Work

In " The Grapes of Wrath", chapters of general comment are interleaved with the moving story of one small, dispossessed community in Oklahoma, driven from the cotton lands they once owned by the big corporations who were mechanising agriculture. Here the commentary poses the human problems of this economic change.

Some of the owner men were kind because they hated what they had to do, and some of them were angry because they hated to be cruel, and some of them were cold because they had long ago found that one could not be an owner unless one were cold. And all of them were caught in something larger than themselves. Some of them hated the mathematics that drove them, and some were afraid, and some worshipped the mathematics because it provided a refuge from thought and from feeling. If a bank or a finance company owned the land, the owner man said: The Bank—or the Company—needs—wants—insists—must have—as though the Bank or the Company were a monster, with thought and feeling, which had ensnared them. These last would take no responsibility for the banks or the companies because they were men and slaves, while the banks were machines and masters all at the same time. Some of the owner men were a little proud to be slaves to such cold and powerful masters. The owner men sat in the cars and explained. You know the land is poor. You've scrabbed at it long enough, God knows.

The squatting tenant men nodded and wondered and drew figures in the dust, and yes, they knew, God knows. If the dust only wouldn't fly. If the top would only stay on the soil, it might not be so bad.

The owner men went on leading to their point: You know the land's getting poorer. You know what cotton does to the land: robs it, sucks all the blood out of it.

The squatters nodded—they knew, God knew. If they could only rotate the crops they might pump blood back into the land.

Well, it's too late. And the owner men explained the workings and the thinkings of the monster that was stronger than they were. A man can hold land if he can just eat and pay taxes: he can do that.

Yes, he can do that until his crops fail one day and he has to borrow money from the bank.

But—you see, a bank or a company can't do that, because those creatures don't breathe air, don't eat side-meat. They breathe profits; they eat the interest on money. If they don't get it, they die the way you die without air, without side-meat. It is a sad thing, but it is so. It is just so. . . .

The squatting men looked down again. What do you want us to do? We can't take less share of the crop—we're half-starved now. The kids are hungry all the time. We got no clothes, torn an' ragged. If all the neighbours weren't the same, we'd be ashamed to go to meeting.

And at last the owner men came to the point. The tenant system won't work any more. One man on a tractor can take the place of twelve or fourteen families. Pay him a wage and take all the crop. We have to do it. We don't like to do it. But the monster's sick. Something's happened to the monster.

But you'll kill the land with cotton.

We know. We've got to take cotton quick before the land dies. Then we'll sell the land. Lots of families in the East would like to own a piece of land.

The tenant men looked up alarmed. But what'll happen to us? How'll we eat?

You'll have to get off the land. The ploughs'll go through the door-yard.

And now the squatting men stood up angrily. Grampa took up the land, and he had to kill the Indians and drive them away. And Pa was born here, and he killed weeds and snakes. Then a bad year came and he had to borrow a little money. An' we was born here. There in the door – our children born here. And Pa had to borrow money. The bank owned the land then, but we stayed and we got a little bit of what we raised.

We know that—all that. It's not us, it's the bank. A bank isn't like a man. Or an owner with fifty thousand acres, he isn't like a man either. That's the monster. . . .

The tractors came over the roads and into the fields, great crawlers moving like insects, having the incredible strength of insects. They crawled over the ground, laying the track and rolling on it and picking it up. Diesel tractors, puttering while they stood idle; they thundered when they moved, and then settled down to a droning roar. Snub-nosed monsters, raising the dust and sticking their snouts into it, straight down the country, across the country, through fences, through door-yards, in and out of gullies in straight lines. They did not run on the ground, but on their own roadbeds. They ignored hills and gulches, water-courses, fences, houses.

The man sitting in the iron seat did not look like a man: gloved, goggled, rubber dust-mask over nose and mouth, he was a part of the monster, a robot in the seat. The thunder of the cylinders sounded through the country, became one with the air and the earth, so that earth and air muttered in sympathetic vibration. The driver could not control it—straight across country it went, cutting through a dozen farms and straight back. A twitch at the controls could swerve the cat', but the driver's hands could not twitch because the monster that built the tractor, the monster that sent the tractor out, had somehow got into the driver's hands, into his brain and muscle, had goggled him and muzzled him—goggled his mind, muzzled his speech, goggled his perception, muzzled his protest. . . .

At noon the tractor driver stopped sometimes near a tenant house and opened his lunch; sandwiches wrapped in waxed paper, white bread, pickle, cheese, Spam, a piece of pie branded like an engine part. He ate without relish. And tenants not yet moved away came out to see him, looked curiously while the goggles were taken off, and the rubber dust-mask, leaving white circles around the eyes and a large white circle around nose and mouth. . . .

"Why, you're Joe Davis's boy!"

"Sure," the driver said.

"Well, what you doing this kind of work for—against your own people?"

"Three dollars a day. I got damn sick of creeping for my dinner —and not getting it. I got a wife and kids. We got to eat. Three dollars a day, and it comes every day."

"That's right," the tenant said. "But for your three dollars a day fifteen or twenty families can't eat at all. Nearly a hundred people have to go out and wander on the roads for your three dollars a day. Is that right?"

And the driver said: "Can't think of that. Got to think of my own kids. Three dollars a day, and it comes every day. Times are changing, mister, don't you know? Can't make a living on the land unless you've got two, five, ten thousand acres and a tractor. Crop land isn't for little guys like us any more. You don't kick up a howl because you can't make Fords, or because you're not the telephone company. Well, crops are like that now. Nothing to do about it. You try to get three dollars a day some place. That's the only way."

The tenant pondered. "Funny thing how it is. If a man owns a little property, that property is him, it's part of him, and it's like him. If he owns property only so he can walk on it and handle it and be sad when it isn't doing well, and feel fine when the rain falls on it, that property is him, and some way he's bigger because he owns it. Even if he isn't successful he's big with his property. That is so."

And the tenant pondered more. "But let a man get property he doesn't see, or can't take time to get his fingers in, or can't be there to walk on it—why, then the property is the man. He can't do what he wants, he can't think what he wants. The property is the man, stronger than he is. And he is small, not big. Only his possessions are big—and he's the servant of his property. That is so, too."

(from *The Grapes of Wrath* by John Steinbeck)

1. Trace how the land had come to be owned by land companies and banks. If you can, explain the system of "share-cropping".

2. How far do these tenants admit they have mismanaged their farms or used the wrong methods of farming?

3. How were the big land-owning companies going to farm the land? Give reasons why you think their treatment would, or would not, be better for the land.

4. List the different kinds of "owner men" that the author mentions. Did they act differently towards the tenants?

5. What is "the monster" behind the owner men and their tractors?

6. Why does the author describe the tractors as "having the incredible strength of insects"? Why is it important that they do "not run on the ground, but on their own road-beds"?

7. Why didn't the tractor driver guide his tractor to avoid the farms and other obstacles?

8. Why did the driver wear gloves, goggles and mask? Explain why he appeared to have white circles on his face when he removed them.

9. Why did the driver do this work? What does Steinbeck imply by calling him "goggled" and "muzzled"?

10. Who "owned" the lands before the first farmers arrived? Can one *blame* the settlers, or the owners, or the men who worked for them (like this tractor driver)? Were they responsible, or were they victims of the situation?

11. This was a clear case of "redundancy" – one man and a machine doing the work of twenty farmers. Is the situation described here an inevitable result, whenever there is progress in mechanisation? Could change have come to Oklahoma without this misery and disruption?

12. What was the tenant arguing against at the end of the passage, when he "pondered" in the last two paragraphs?

13. Do you agree with the picture here of big business as a "monster", living on profits and utterly impersonal? Do owners become slaves of their property as soon as it becomes at all large?

Au Jardin des Plantes

The gorilla lay on his back,
One hand cupped under his head,
Like a man.

Like a labouring man tired with work,
A strong man with his strength burnt away
In the toil of earning a living.

Only of course he was not tired out with work,
Merely with boredom; his terrible strength
All burnt away by prodigal idleness.

A thousand days, and then a thousand days,
Idleness licked away his beautiful strength
He having no need to earn a living.

It was all laid on, free of charge.
We maintained him, not for doing anything,
But for being what he was.

And so that Sunday morning he lay on his back,
Like a man, like a worn-out man,
One hand cupped under his terrible hard head.

Like a man, like a man,
One of those we maintain, not for doing anything,
But for being what they are.

A thousand days, and then a thousand days,
With everything laid on, free of charge,
They cup their heads in prodigal idleness.

JOHN WAIN

Discussing the Poem

1. What kind of place do you imagine *Le Jardin des Plantes* to be? Why, and under what conditions, was the gorilla kept there?
2. Is this poem a comment on human reasons for keeping animals in captivity? Is it also a comment on man's need to work, and the effect of "prodigal idleness"?
3. Although divided into three-line verses, the poem has no regular pattern of rhyme or even rhythm. But some interesting repetition does hold the poem together. Notice how and where phrases like "like a man", "burnt away", "tired with work", "not for doing anything" are repeated, sometimes with variations. Does this perhaps suggest the tedium of his unnatural existence?

Techniques

Exercise 1. Faced with the difficult task of telling the tenant farmers to leave, "some of the owner men were kind", and they searched for words with which to soften the blow, or to explain away the hard facts that the land did not pay and the tenants were to be evicted. Soft or evasive words that disguise harsh or unpleasant facts are called EUPHEMISMS. *Euphemism* is obviously related to *circumlocution* and other forms of *verbosity* that we have discussed before. Consider all the words and phrases that people use to soften the bare and bitter fact that a person is dead:

> He is no longer with us, sleeping his last sleep; he has crossed the bar, passed away, been taken, ended his days, departed this life, given up the struggle, paid his debt to nature, gone the way of all flesh, gone to a better place, breathed his last, given up the ghost, shuffled off this mortal coil, popped off, pegged out, kicked the bucket, gone West; or it was his last adventure or a happy release; etc.

Try to think of all the polite euphemisms people use for "lavatory" (which is itself a euphemism, meaning "wash-place").

Politicians are masters of euphemism, especially when there is an element of *litotes* or understatement. "High taxation" may be called "redistribution of wealth" and when prices go up it is called an "inflationary tendency".

(a) Below are ten euphemisms. Express each one in blunt, straightforward language.

e.g. a modest income = low wages.

hard of hearing	a gentle aid to regularity
a slight figure (of a woman)	the portly gentleman
speech impediment	skin blemishes
difference of opinion	alopecia
one of Her Majesty's guests	a drop too much

(b) Below are ten blunt words or phrases. Make up a euphemism to fit each one.

e.g. miserly stinginess = prudent thrift.

out of work	a mad murderer
bankrupt	to run away
a dustman	stealing
a farm labourer	crippled
a criminal	obstinacy

(c) Advertisers are particularly fond of euphemisms: they do not try to sell clothes to "fat women" or "big women", but to "well-built ladies with fuller figures". Plain girls are "unsophisticated"; people are "off colour" rather than ill. Collect at least ten good examples of euphemism in advertisements.

Exercise 2. The style of the passage includes a curious mixture of *direct* and *reported speech,* without any inverted commas. Find examples in the opening paragraph of direct speech without inverted commas. Is there some particular justification for this stylistic device in this case? Where in the second paragraph does the author change almost imperceptibly from direct to reported speech, and back? Notice, too, that the intermingling of direct and reported speech gives way to normal, formal direct speech punctuation as soon as the tenants are talking to a specific person, Joe Davis's boy, the tractor driver.

Turning the direct speech here into formal reported speech will involve applying most of the "rules" dealt with in Book Three, and also the advice to "improve" the style by using

Standard English equivalents for any colloquial language used in the conversation. The following is a reported version of the 6th, 7th and 8th paragraphs of the passage (page 249):

From: Yes, he can do that until his crops fail . . .
to: . . . we'd be ashamed to go to meeting.

The tenants agreed that a man could do that until his crops failed one day and he had to borrow money from the bank.

But the owners pointed out that a bank or company could not do that because those creatures did not breathe air nor did they eat side-meat. They breathed profits; they ate the interest on money. If they did not get it, they died in the same way as the tenants died without air or without side-meat, it was a sad thing, but it was so. It was just so. . . .

The squatting men looked down again and asked the owners what they wanted them to do. They could not take less share of the crop – they were half-starved then. The children were hungry all the time. They had no clothes, or only torn and ragged ones. If all the neighbours were not the same, they would be ashamed to go to meeting.

After studying this alongside the original direct speech, rewrite part of the final conversation in the passage as reported speech. Begin from: "Why, you're Joe Davis's boy!" and go on to ". . . That's the only way." (Six paragraphs).

Begin your answer like this:

The tenants called out in surprise to the driver when they saw who he was, and he acknowledged that he was Joe Davis's boy. Then one of them . . .

Exercise 3. Most précis or summaries are reports of what some one else has said or written, and it used to be conventional to put *all* summaries into formal reported speech. This is not now considered necessary, unless you are summarising a piece of personal opinion that is expressed in the *first person* (using "I me, we," etc.). The following passage is an example that should be summarised in reported speech. Your summary should contain between 110 and 130 words (the full passage has about 310). You should start with some clause like "The writer considered . . .", but do not waste words by repeating "he said" or "he thought" more than is absolutely necessary. State at the end the number of words you use.

I thought the Cotswold Hills were rather bleak: the landscape and the weather seemed to me as cold and hard and inhospitable as the wet, grey, stone walls and the damp-looking cottages. I was relieved to descend into the broad valley of the Severn, where the river winds its slow way into the Bristol Channel. The plain here seemed warm and soft and calm, and in the evening light even the Cotswolds in the distance were softened, so that they formed a perfect backcloth to the landscape by the river. This, I felt, was a peaceful and ordered scene – miles of green meadow were divided by hedges and dotted with trees, some grouped into little copses beside small, reedy ponds. This kind of scene has changed little for two hundred years, and is the kind of truly English scenery that our eighteenth century English landlords strove to create, quite different from the French land-scapes of that same period. In the eighteenth century the French laid out their vistas, walks and woods with mathematical precision; their trees and hedges were like troops on parade, uniform, stiffly to atten-tion, each one in his place. A French garden, like that at Versailles, looks as if a giant hand has placed ruler and compasses across the landscape, with infallible accuracy. But here in the Severn Valley, the English landlords placed every tree perfectly to show its own full glory, so that it was free to flourish in its natural form, and so that the wide view was rich in a diversity of shapes and variety of colour. Where else in the world, I thought, would one see so many subtly different shades of green? Yet this is certainly no wilderness; it is not Nature let loose, as in a jungle, where plants suffocate one another. It is an ordered English landscape, created by men for their own pleasure and convenience.

Précis Rule 8. REPORTED SPEECH :
It is not essential to use past tense and third person for *all* précis, but where the original passage is written in the first person, the summary must make it clear that you are reporting someone else's views.

Topics for Written Work

1. When driven off their lands, the tenant farmers in *Grapes of Wrath* began trekking westward towards California, which for them was a land of prosperity and promise where they expected to find work and wealth. On the road with their moveable possessions piled high on old lorries and cars, they were very like other refugees through the ages, fleeing from war, persecution or poverty towards some haven of refuge. The twentieth century has seen many such treks, as each of the political revolutions, minor wars, or the local campaigns of the two world wars has rendered new groups of people homeless. At this moment there are refugee families all over the world

living in very poor conditions or constant fear. Try to imagine what it must be like to leave home and possessions, fleeing from persecution or certain death, and struggle through to some strange country, hoping for a chance to start a new life.

Oxfam, U.N.I.C.E.F., War on Want, The Christian Aid Department, and similar organisations will probably be able to supply pictures, facts and figures to help stimulate your imagination. Write a description or a poem on the theme of refugees and the starving, homeless families of the world. Here is an example in the form of a free verse poem:

> I am looking at a picture of Tibetans
> Fleeing not only from the Chinese,
> But from cold and hunger,
> Shivering and starving in cold winter weather.
> Their skins are spotted and bulged,
> Through diseases like Trachoma and Tuberculosis;
> In my comfortable country,
> I have been asked to help them,
> While they beg for food in a slum land.
> They have no clothes
> Except for a few old rags.
> They are hopeless in a wild wilderness,
> They cannot help themselves,
> They cannot even hope for themselves.
> Unsturdy, walking with bones sticking out,
> Dying young without a hope.
> While everybody in this country is so comfortable
> And pleased with themselves,
> It's an effort to put a penny in a box.
>
> MICHAEL

2. Employers with vacancies to fill always hope to have more applicants than they have posts; the more worth-while the job, the more likely is it that there will be competition for it. In such circumstances, employers usually make a short-list of applicants who will be interviewed, and they must select these on the basis of their qualifications, experience, and letters of application alone. Much may therefore depend on this letter, and it should give an immediate good impression, together with any information about the applicant that may help persuade the employer to select him for interview.

As practice in writing letters of application, imagine that you very much want to be selected for one of the following

vacation jobs. Write a business letter, giving special attention to neat and correct setting out and style, in your own hand-writing. Think out carefully what information you should give without seeming conceited, and trying to keep the letter clear, brief and polite.

(a) Activity Leaders required at Buttons Holiday Camps. Boys and girls fifteen or over, good education, life-saving and interest in games or children added recommendations. Four-week con-tracts July–September. Full board, one free day in six, generous pocket-money. Apply Personnel Manager, Buttons Camps Ltd., 20 Lost Row, N.C.2.

(b) Students of fifteen plus wanted as relief shop assistants for West End stores. Applicants should be intelligent, interested in people, well-spoken, good at figures, available for at least six weeks. Excellent pay and conditions. Apply Manageress, John Peters, High Road, Kingsenton, W.30.

(c) WANTED: Ice-cream salesmen for cross-Channel hover-ferries. Basic French essential. Generous commission for young people willing to work hard through summer holiday. Write: Hover-sport Ltd., Highcliffe, Folkstown, Kent.

(d) Edinburgh Festival: sympathetic girls wanted for Festival crèche and baby-sitting service. Previous experience with young children preferred. Generous free time, full board, spending money and fares from any part of G.B. Apply: Altourist Services, Princesses Street, Edinburgh, 40.

(e) Scholarly young man wanted to assist with cataloguing historical papers during summer vacation. No previous training required. Board and lodging in quiet village. Pocket money. Apply Professor Brainsworth, The Rectory, Castle Ancient, Sussex.

Oral Work

1. Following on from your application for vacation work in Topics for Written Work, 2, hold imaginary interviews for these or similar jobs. Both the interviewer and the applicant should give some thought to the kind of questions and answers that would best help select the appropriate candidate. If a number of applicants are interviewed in front of an audience, then the listeners should be prepared to comment, and criticise the conduct of the interviews, and to vote on which applicant most deserved the job.

Remember that the basic aim of such an interview is to set the candidate talking about himself in a way that will reveal the kind of person he is and something of his interests and back ground. Candidates should always try to answer more fully than with a simple "yes" or "no", and be prepared to follow up with examples or comment whenever there is an opportunity. They should obviously speak up and talk as clearly and correctly as they can, without sounding forced or unnatural.

2. Members of the class who have had part-time or holiday jobs should each prepare a short talk for the class. State clearly what the work consists of, what skill or training is required, the hours, the wages and the conditions. Describe the people you work with and the routines involved, and generally try to sum up what is attractive or satisfying about the work and what kind of people you could recommend it to.

Activities and Research

1. Find out what the following people do for a living:

solicitor, barrister, accountant, actuary, auctioneer, broker, jobber; librarian, archivist, curator, copywriter, compositor, stereotyper, proof-reader;
chiropodist, opthalmic optician, orthoptist, dietitian, pharmacist, veterinary officer, occupational therapist;
cooper, card tenter, loomer and twister, patternmaker, fitter, turner, welder;
quantity surveyor, site surveyor, glazier, tiler, milliner, gown hand, cutter;
probation officer, children's officer, health visitor, educational psychologist, personnel officer, inspector of factories, inspector of taxes;
metallurgist, mining engineer, production engineer, chemical engineer, statistician, food technologist, public analyst.

2. Choose a particular group of careers and make a study of the opportunities in that field, the qualifications required at different levels of entry, the prospects for promotion, salaries and working conditions, and generally what the careers have to offer. All public libraries have books and guides giving information on careers, often in the form of pamphlets and booklets. Your school probably has its own arrangements for giving information about careers and choosing suitable courses of training. Pick a field in which you are already interested; e.g.:

branches of engineering	mathematics	nursing
printing	forestry	insurance
merchant navy	law	

Most careers guides will give a full list.

3. Make a study of the refugee problems in the world today, obtaining up-to-date information from the various relief organisations, especially those mentioned on page 258.

Further Reading

The Grapes of Wrath by JOHN STEINBECK (Heinemann; Pan)
This novel, first published in 1939, has become a classic of American literature. The story is centred on the Joad family, including young Tom who returns from serving a prison sentence only to find his father's farm destroyed and ploughed up and the family all ready to move West to find new work. California, when they reach it after much hardship, offers little work, poverty in the labour camps, and more violence. Their story is a sombre one, but the family never completely lose their faith in life.
Steinbeck's long short stories:
Of Mice and Men and *The Pearl* (Heinemann; Pan)
Both deal with people who find themselves outcasts from society. The first is the story of the odd but completely genuine friendship between Lennie, who is very slow-witted but enormously powerful and a tremendous worker, and George, who uses his intelligence to protect Lennie and tries vainly to see that he does not abuse his terrible strength. The second concerns a family of Mexican peasants who find "the pearl of all the world", but discover that this fabulous wealth brings not happiness or security, but violence and terror.
The Kitchen by ARNOLD WESKER (Cape) (822.91)
This play is set in the kitchen of a large restaurant (the author had worked as a pastrycook in similar places). In the rush of work in this hot and crowded place, cooks and waitresses have little time to understand one another; they get in one another's way, sometimes hit out, easily despair. The play has interesting variety of pace and a powerful climax.

CHAPTER SEVENTEEN

In Love

Jane came to Thornfield Hall as a governess to Mr. Rochester's ward, and soon became attached to her rather melancholy but strong-minded employer. When he declared his love and asked her to marry him, her happiness seemed at last assured.

"Jane!" called a voice, and I hastened down. I was received at the foot of the stairs by Mr. Rochester.

"Lingerer," he said, "my brain is on fire with impatience; and you tarry so long!". . . .

There were no groomsmen, no bridesmaids, no relatives to wait for or marshal: none but Mr. Rochester and I. Mrs. Fairfax stood in the hall as we passed. I would fain have spoken to her, but my hand was held by a grasp of iron: I was hurried along by a stride I could hardly follow; and to look at Mr. Rochester's face was to feel that not a second of delay would be tolerated for any purpose. I wonder what other bridegroom ever looked as he did—so bent up to a purpose, so grimly resolute; or who, under such steadfast brows, ever revealed such flaming and flashing eyes?

I know not whether the day was fair or foul: in descending the drive I gazed neither on sky nor earth: my heart was with my eyes; and both seemed migrated into Mr. Rochester's frame. I wanted to see the invisible thing on which, as we went along, he appeared to fasten a glance fierce and fell. I wanted to feel the thoughts whose force he seemed breasting and resisting.

At the churchyard wicket he stopped: he discovered I was quite out of breath. "Am I cruel in my love?" he said. "Delay an instant: lean on me, Jane."

And now I can recall the picture of the grey old house of God rising calm before me, of a rook wheeling round the steeple, of a ruddy morning sky beyond. I remember something, too, of the green grave-mounds; and I have not forgotten, either, two figures of strangers, straying amongst the low hillocks, and reading the mementoes graven on the few mossy headstones. I noticed them, because, as they saw us, they passed round to the back of the church; and I doubted not they were going to enter by the side-aisle door, and witness the ceremony. By Mr. Rochester they were not observed; he was earnestly looking at my face, from which the blood had, I dare say, momentarily fled: for I felt my forehead dewy, and my cheeks and lips cold. When I rallied, which I soon did, he walked gently with me up the path to the porch.

We entered the quiet and humble temple; the priest waited in his white surplice at the lowly altar, the clerk beside him. All was still: two shadows only moved in a remote corner. My conjecture had been correct: the strangers had slipped in before us, and they now stood by the vault of the Rochesters, their backs towards us, viewing through the rails the old time-stained marble tomb, where a kneeling angel guarded the remains of Damer de Rochester, slain at Marston Moor in the time of the civil wars; and of Elizabeth, his wife.

Our place was taken at the Communion rails. Hearing a cautious step behind me, I glanced over my shoulder: one of the strangers—a gentleman, evidently—was advancing up the chancel. The service began. The explanation of the intent of matrimony was gone through; and then the clergyman came a step further forward, and, bending slightly towards Mr. Rochester, went on:

"I require and charge you both (as ye will answer at the dreadful day of Judgment, when the secrets of all hearts shall be disclosed), that if either of you know any impediment why ye may not lawfully be joined together in matrimony ye do now confess it; for be ye well assured that so many as are coupled together otherwise than God's Word doth allow, are not joined together by God, neither is their matrimony lawful."

He paused as the custom is. When is the pause after that sentence ever broken by reply? Not, perhaps, once in a hundred years. And the clergyman, who had not lifted his eyes from his book, and had held his breath for a moment, was proceeding: his hand was already stretched towards Mr. Rochester, as his lips unclosed to ask, "Wilt thou have this woman for thy wedded wife?"— when a distinct and near voice said:—

"The marriage cannot go on: I declare the existence of an impediment."

The clergyman looked up at the speaker, and stood mute: the clerk did the same: Mr. Rochester moved slightly, as if an earthquake had rolled under his feet: taking a firmer footing,

and not turning his head or eyes, he said, "Proceed."

Profound silence fell when he had uttered that word, with deep but low intonation. Presently Mr. Wood said:–

"I cannot proceed without some investigation into what has been asserted, and evidence of its truth or falsehood."

"The ceremony is quite broken off," subjoined the voice behind us. "I am in a condition to prove my allegation: an insuperable impediment to this marriage exists.'

Mr. Rochester heard, but heeded not; he stood stubborn and rigid: making no movement but to possess himself of my hand. What a hot and strong grasp he had!—and how like quarried marble was his pale, firm massive front at this moment! How his eye shone, still, watchful, and yet wild beneath.

Mr. Wood seemed at a loss. "What is the nature of the impediment?" he asked. "Perhaps it may be got over—explained away?"

"Hardly," was the answer; "I have called it insuperable, and I speak advisedly."

The speaker came forward, and leaned on the rails. He continued, uttering each word distinctly, calmly, steadily, but not loudly—

"It simply consists in the existence of a previous marriage. Mr. Rochester has a wife now living."

My nerves vibrated to those low-spoken words as they had never vibrated to thunder—my blood felt their subtle violence as it had never felt frost or fire: but I was collected, and in no danger of swooning. I looked at Mr. Rochester: I made him look at me. His whole face was colourless rock: his eye was both spark and flint. He disavowed nothing: he seemed as if he would defy all things. Without speaking; without smiling; without seeming to recognise in me a human being, he only twined my waist with his arm, and riveted me to his side. "Who are you?" he asked of the intruder.

"My name is Briggs, a solicitor, of — Street, London."

"And you would thrust on me a wife?"

"I would remind you of your lady's existence, sir; which the law recognizes, if you do not.". . .

"How do you know?"

"I have a witness to the fact; whose testimony even you, sir, will scarcely controvert."

"Produce him—or go to hell."

"I will produce him first—he is on the spot: Mr. Mason,

have the goodness to step forward."

Mr. Rochester, on hearing the name, set his teeth, he experienced, too, a sort of convulsive quiver; near to him as I was, I felt the spasmodic movement of fury or despair run through his frame. The second stranger, who had hitherto lingered in the background, now drew near; a pale face looked over the solicitor's shoulder—yea, it was Mason himself. Mr. Rochester turned and glared at him. His eye, as I have often said, was a black eye: it had now a tawny, nay, a bloody light in its gloom; and his face flushed—olive cheek and hueless forehead received a glow, as from spreading, ascending heartfire: and he stirred, lifted his strong arm—he could have struck Mason—dashed him on the church floor—shocked by ruthless blow the breath from his body—but Mason shrank away, and cried faintly, "Good God!". . .

"Courage," urged the lawyer—"speak out."

"She is now living at Thornfield Hall," said Mason, in more articulate tones; "I saw her there last April. I am her brother."

(from *Jane Eyre* by Charlotte Brontë)

Appreciation and Discussion

1. Does Mr. Rochester show any feeling or consideration for Jane?

2. Why didn't Mr. Rochester notice the strangers, either in the churchyard or before the ceremony began?

3. What gives the impression that Mr. Rochester half expected to hear objections to his second marriage?

4. What impression do you form of Briggs from the way he speaks and acts in this scene? Is he contrasted with Mr. Rochester and with Mason?

5. What does the incident here imply about the feelings between Mr. Rochester and his brother-in-law, Mason?

6. Why did Mr. Rochester want such a quiet wedding? How is the quietness and solemnity of the occasion emphasised in this description?

7. What, judging from this extract, do you think Jane found attractive about Mr. Rochester?

8. In what ways did Mr. Rochester show his strong-mindedness and impatience? Does it seem that he is

particularly determined to see this ceremony performed; and if so, why?

9. Why is there such a difference in the reactions of Mr. Rochester and of Jane to the announcement of Briggs? Explain the meaning of: "He disavowed nothing: he seemed as if he would defy all things."

10. What (in the Church of England) is the normal procedure for ensuring that there is no "just cause or impediment" why a couple should not be married? Was it really necessary for Briggs and Mason to make their declaration so dramatically, and at the "eleventh hour"?

11. Mr. Rochester's first wife was in fact incurably insane: does this add meaning to the words ". . . your lady's existence, sir, which the law recognises, if you do not"? What would the legal position be today?

12. Explain or comment on the following words or phrases: I would fain have spoken; both seemed migrated into Mr. Rochester's frame; fierce and fell; the mementoes graven; I rallied; my conjecture; the intent of matrimony; stood mute; with deep but low intonation; subjoined; an insuperable impediment; testimony; contravert; convulsive quiver; tawny; more articulate tones.

13. What is the quietest or simplest kind of wedding ceremony available in this country today? What is there to be said for, and against, gay and elaborate weddings with large numbers of guests and all the expensive ceremony and entertainment?

Discussing the Poem

1. How does the poem suggest that the two lovers are alone in a rather hostile world, *before* the last verse?

2. Discuss the choice of words and comparisons, especially: "the black leather strap", "a white ribbon", "two heavy fruits on the plaited basket", "slides into light".

3. How does the poem appear as tightly constructed in regular verses when it has in fact no rhyme scheme? Does *alliteration* contribute to this effect? Why are "linkt" and "interlockt" spelt in this unusual way?

Night Ride

Along the black
leather strap
of the night
deserted road

swiftly rolls
the freighted bus.
Huddled together
two lovers doze

their hands linkt
across their laps
their bodies loosely
interlockt

their heads resting
two heavy fruits
on the plaited
basket of their limbs.

Slowly the bus
slides into light.
Here are hills
detach'd from dark

the road, uncoils
a white ribbon
the lovers with
the hills unfold

wake cold
to face the fate
of those who love
despite the world.

HERBERT READ

Exercise 1. Following the older conventions, the extract from *Jane Eyre* uses the colon as a slightly less definite stop than the full-stop, and the semi-colon as a less marked pause than the colon. This is particularly clear in the paragraph beginning:
"My nerves vibrated to those low-spoken words . . .

Modern conventions reserve the colon for an introductory use: it will be followed by a list, an explanation, a quotation in direct speech, or occasionally an afterthought. Discuss the six colons that the author uses in the first five paragraphs of the passage—which ones would be justified in modern usage?

The most common mistake in students' writing today is to use too many commas and too few semi-colons. In the following passage, describing correct procedure at a formal church wedding, there are twenty-five commas, many of which should be semi-colons (a few might be colons). Rewrite the passage changing commas to semi-colons (or colons) where necessary, and making no other changes.

The ushers arrive at the church first, it is their duty to show guests to their places, these are fixed by tradition, guests of the bride go to the left of the aisle, guests of the groom go to the right side, close relatives or guests of honour take front pews on the appropriate side, the first on the right being reserved for the groom and best man, with his parents immediately behind him. The bride is the last to arrive, she is accompanied by her father and immediately preceded by her bridesmaids, they wait for her in the porch.

When the bride and her attendants are ready, she walks down the aisle, taking her father's right arm. All guests should stand during this march, the groom and best man also move forward to the foot of the chancel steps, there the bride will join him, the father and best man stand a little behind the couple, at the sides, during the actual ceremony.

Immediately after the service, the clergyman leads bride and groom into the vestry, the best man escorts the bridesmaids, the parents of bride and groom also follow. The rest of the guests remain seated while the register is signed. From there the bride leads a procession back up the aisle, she takes her husband's left arm. In this procession, it is usual for her mother to take the groom's father's arm, the groom's mother accompanies the bride's father, then follow the best man and chief bridesmaid, finally the other bridesmaids and close relatives join the procession. Other guests should remain in church, until the procession has reached the porch.

Exercise 2. Look up the form of "Solemnization of Matrimony" in the Church of England *Book of Common Prayer* (the standard 1571 version). You will find the words that Charlotte Brontë has quoted almost exactly the same. Suppose you had to translate or PARAPHRASE them in modern English? Would the following be an accurate equivalent?

I solemnly ask you to declare openly now any obstacle that either of you knows of that would prevent your being legally united in marriage. Speak as truthfully as you will at the terrible day of judgement, when everyone's secrets will be known. For you must realise that anyone marrying contrary to the laws of *The Bible* is not married in God's sight, and the marriage is not legal.

Notice that a *paraphrase* (unlike a précis) is often longer than the original, and must provide a translation of all difficult words, and simplify any complicated sentence construction. In style, it is often less subtle or less beautiful.

(a) Look through the rest of the marriage service, discussing any difficult language. Then attempt written paraphrases of the central question and answer passages in the ceremony:

Wilt thou have this Woman to thy wedded wife, to live together after God's ordinance in the holy estate of Matrimony? Wilt thou love her, comfort her, honour, and keep her in sickness and in health; and, for- saking all other, keep thee only unto her, so long as ye both shall live?

I —— take thee —— to my wedded wife, to have and to hold from this day forward, for better for worse, for richer for poorer, in sickness and in health, to love and to cherish, till death us do part, according to God's holy ordinance; and thereto I plight thee my troth.

(b) Paraphrase the following comment on the new fashion of using forks at meals in Italy—it is from Thomas Coryat's book *Crudities,* published in 1611.

The Italians, and also most strangers that are commorant in Italy, do always at their meals use a little fork when they cut their meat. For while with their knife, which they hold in one hand, they cut the meat out of the dish, they fasten their fork which they hold in their other hand upon the same dish, so that whatsoever he be that, sitting in the company of any others at meal, should unadvisedly touch the dish of meat with his fingers from which all at the table do cut, he will give occasion of offence unto the company, as having transgressed the laws of good manners, in so much that for his error he shall be at least brow beaten if not reprehended in words.

Note that "commorant" means "resident", and "browbeaten" probably means "criticised by stern looks", in this context.

Exercise 3. (a) We discussed in Chapter Fifteen (on page 240) how we *stress* particular syllables of words more than others, and how a change of stress can indicate a shift of meaning (or function) in some cases. All words have a natural pattern of stresses, and most dictionaries indicate how to pronounce those words that might seem unfamiliar or puzzling in this respect, usually with an accent mark like this. Pronounce the following words according to the stresses marked, and discuss the difference in meaning:

éntrance—entránce; fórearm—foreárm; súrvey—survéy; ínsult—insúlt; contráry—cóntrary; énvelope—envélop.

Most words in English carry one main stress, and as the word is altered by adding suffixes, so the stress may alter:

démonstrate—demónstrative—demonstrátion.

Faced with an unfamiliar word, one may in fact be able to decide on the pronunciation only by consulting a dictionary: ruridecanal; panacea; mandatory.

Rewrite all the following words so as to show the correct stress by an accent mark:

anticipation	intake	linoleum	resonance
diameter	inroad	linotype	surpass
diametrical	insane	mausoleum	surplus
diamond	insect	resolute	ultimate
intact	inscribe	resolution	ultimatum

Finally, discuss the current uncertainty about the correct pronunciation of:— controversy; surmise; umbilical.

(b) The same accent marks can be used to show the rhythm, or stress pattern, of a poem. For instance, *Night Ride* has two stresses in each line:

Alóng the bláck
léather stráp
óf the níght
desérted róad

swíftly rólls
the fréighted bús.
Húddled togéther
two lóvers dóze

Write out the next two verses showing the rhythm in this way, and discuss whether the last line of the fourth verse should be considered irregular.

Now turn back to page 182. The poem *This Excellent Machine* has a regular rhythm pattern of five stresses to a line, starting like this:

This éxcellént machíne is néatly plánned,
A chíld, a hálf-wit woúld not feél perpléxed:
No chánce to érr, you símply préss the bútton –
At ónce each cóg in mótion móves the néxt, . . .

Rewrite the remainder of the first verse to show its rhythm pattern in this way.

(c) *Alliteration* (the repetition of consonant sounds, especially at the beginning of words) is usually associated with stressed syllables. Thus in the passage from *Jane Eyre,* we find:

who . . . ever revealed such <u>fl</u>aming and <u>fl</u>ashing eyes?
I know not whether the day was <u>f</u>air or <u>f</u>oul.

Rewrite the following excerpts from the passage, underlining the alliteration in a similar way.

(i) . . . on which, as we went along, he appeared to fasten a glance fierce and fell.

- (ii) Wilt thou have this woman for thy wedded wife?
- (iii) Mr. Rochester heard, but heeded not.
- (iv) How his eye shone, still, watchful, and yet wild beneath!
- (v) . . . my blood felt their subtle violence as it had never felt frost or fire.
- (vi) He could have struck Mason—dashed him on the church floor—shocked by ruthless blow the breath from his body—but Mason shrank away.

Discuss the use of alliteration in the poems *A New Song of New Similes* on page 85, *Headline History* on page 113, and *Night Ride* on page 269.

Topics for Written Work

1. Write a personal account of any ceremony or solemn occasion you have been present at, or possibly one you have followed closely on film or television. You have a complete range of choice from the most dignified state occasions, through the family celebrations of marriage or christening, or even a funeral service, down to any special church service or similar local festival. Do not try to imagine yourself as the bride or the guest of honour, nor to tell a dramatic story of the kind Jane Eyre had to record. Simply try to describe the excitement and other emotions you felt as one of the people involved, the tension of the time of preparation and waiting beforehand, and the beauty and dignity of the ceremony itself and the reactions of the people involved as far as you could appreciate them. Personally selected detail and honesty about your own feelings will help make this an interesting description.

2. If possible, take the same occasion as you described in 1, above, and *report* it in a style suitable for a serious newspaper or magazine. Think about the changes of emphasis that will be necessary if this is to be a piece of news reporting, and appeal to a wide range of newspaper readers. Probably your report will be shorter, and it should have a suitable "headline", and all the basic information about place, time and people involved.

Oral Work

1. Discuss the two related subjects of etiquette and traditional ceremony.

Would you make a distinction between "good manners" and "etiquette"? How far are manners a matter of "snobbery"? Can you give several examples of utterly different, or opposite, codes of behaviour to be found in different societies round the world? Try to agree on one list of rules of conduct (in the company of other people) that seem to be sensible and considerate, and on another list of conventions that no longer have any real meaning. Which list would you put the following into, for instance?

Gentlemen raising their hats to ladies;
saying "How do you do?" when you are introduced to someone;
the rule that you should never cut a bread roll with a knife at a formal dinner;
saying "please" and "thank you";
seeing that other people are served before you help yourself to something;
not combing your hair or cleaning your nails at the meal-table;
writing letters of thanks;
asking the company present if one may smoke;
men walking on the side nearest the road when accompanying women along the pavement.

If some codes of behaviour show a sensible consideration for other people, then what justification is there for more elaborate ceremonies and traditions? Why do people enjoy formal weddings, royal occasions, military pageantry, elaborate church services, even solemn funerals? Is there a reason why people organise formal dinners and dances or keep up ancient traditions in dress or procedure?

Given a free choice, would you want for yourself an elaborate and expensive wedding, or a plain and simple one? Would *you* enjoy formal dinners and dances, in full evening dress, or prefer an informal and relaxed party? Is there a danger that solemn traditions will become empty and meaningless, and be kept up out of mere "snobbery", rather than any sincere respect for their history or significance?

2. Formal occasions and ceremonies—real or imaginary—

lend themselves well to the recorded running commentary. Attempt to make such a recording, possibly with appropriate sound-effects as well.

The incident from *Jane Eyre* might be treated in this way, with recorded voices of the characters taking part; or it might be acted "live" as a short class-room play.

Activities and Research

1. Study a number of books of etiquette, past and present. They are usually classified at 395 on the Dewey system. Different groups could approach them in different ways. Some might extract information on the correct procedure for certain occasions—weddings, christenings, cocktail parties, dining out, dinner parties at home, dances, etc. Others might compare manners of the past with those of today. Others might make a more critical study of the advice offered.

2. Make a survey of the basic etiquette of letter writing. Include examples of correct setting out, address and conclusion. Cover invitations and the answers to them, business letters, letters of thanks and other "duty" letters. Finally, include advice on correct modes of address (e.g. how to address an archbishop or a duke), and the correct setting out of titles, decorations and qualifications when writing the envelope.

3. Pair off the following lovers from legend, fiction or history correctly, e.g. Venus and Adonis:

Abelard	Beatrice	Orpheus	Heloise
Adonis	Cleopatra	Paris	Hero
Aeneas	Cressida	Pyramus	Hippolyte
Antony	Dido	Romeo	Iseult
Dante	Eurydice	Theseus	Juliet
Launcelot	Guinevere	Tristram	Penelope
Leander	Lady Hamilton	Troilus	Thisbe
Nelson	Helen	Ulysses	Venus

Find out their story in each case and write a brief summary of it.

Further Reading

Jane Eyre by CHARLOTTE BRONTË (Various publishers)
Jane is an orphan. After a few miserable years as pupil and teacher at Lowood school, she finds some happiness in the company of the sardonic Mr. Rochester, to whose daughter she is governess But his plans to marry are temporarily thwarted by the revelation of his previous marriage, to a woman still living, but incurably insane. Jane leaves Thornfield in despair, but is eventually reunited with Mr. Rochester. If you enjoy this classic love story, you may also like *Wuthering Heights* by EMILY BRONTË, which is an even more wild and romantic story centred around the love of Heathcliff, a gypsy orphan adopted by Mr. Earnshaw but resented and humiliated by Earnshaw's own son Hindley. The story spans three generations, set against the bleak background of the Yorkshire moors.

A Farewell to Arms by ERNEST HEMINGWAY (Heinemann; Penguin)
This love story is one of the greatest novels of the First World War. The hero is an American ambulance officer, serving in Italy, and his disillusionment with the war is contrasted with his passion for the Scottish nurse whom he meets again when wounded in hospital. They fall in love, and try to find peace in Switzerland, where Catherine is to give birth to their child.

The Taste of Too Much by CLIFFORD HANLEY (Blackie)
This is a modern story of growing up and first love, set against a realistic Glasgow background, with some vivid characterisation and considerable understanding of the feeling of young people towards each other.

The Summer After the Funeral by JANE GARDAM (Hamish Hamilton; Penguin)
Athene Price is a beautiful girl who feels herself to be a reincarnation of Emily Brontë, and this story of her disorganised seventeenth year is both funny and sad.

The L-Shaped Room by LYNNE REID BANKS (Longman; Penguin)
This story of a girl and her pregnancy remains topical, compelling, convincing and very popular with readers of 14 and over.

Supplementary Exercises

(a) Rephrase each of the following so as to use an apostrophe to form the possessive;
> e.g. Wings belonging to butterflies—butterflies' wings.
> employees of Messrs. Smith and Simpson
> employees of Simpson Brothers
> for the sake of goodness
> the invitation sent by Peter
> the invitation sent to Peter
> the birthdays of their aunts Matilda and Grace
> the church of St. Mark and St. John
> the dance named after St. Vitus
> the mount named after St. Michael
> the rod of Moses
> the powers of the magistrates
> the powers of a J.P.

(b) Rewrite the following so that each sentence is turned *completely* into the *plural*:

1. His son's bicycle wasn't padlocked and it's been stolen.
2. An M.P. had been asking an awkward parliamentary question about the duchess's pearl and the detective's search for it.
3. A man's club is not a place for a young lady's conference.
4. The widow's home was built by the Citizen's Aid Fund after a year's intensive fund raising.
5. He very much coveted the King's cousin's reindeer, but then he was always envying another's possession.

Revision Exercise 7

(a) Rewrite the following, inserting all the capital letters, punctuation and paragraphing necessary to set it out correctly. It is mainly conversation:

> mrs jones did not seem to notice anything well i shall hope to see you tomorrow joan she said and turned to her son what would you like to do tomorrow shall we all go for a picnic george winked at joan and said i think joan wants to try water-skiing she has been looking on enviously down by the boat-house all day you cant expect me to join you at that you know replied his mother

278

although i might come and spend the afternoon down by the lake oh please do exclaimed joan obviously excited i should so love to try water-skiing with george youre bound to go under at first george warned her but i think i shall enjoy coming to your rescue we can hire one of the clubs boats and all the other equipment in the morning

(b) Take the same passage, and rewrite it as *reported speech.*

Revision Exercise 8

(a) The following six words are *synonyms,* yet there is a difference in meaning between them. Explain the six distinct shades of meaning:
   expedition, excursion, outing, hike, trek, pilgrimage.
   Similarly the words in the following pairs are in each case roughly synonymous, but have distinct shades of meaning. Make up a sentence for each word to illustrate its meaning as distinct from the other in the pair.

accurate	ambiguity	audience	belief
correct	doubt	congregation	dogma
canal	collision	dip	velocity
aqueduct	clash	dive	acceleration
vibrate		stray	
pulsate		digress	

(b) What difference in meaning is made by the change of *preposition* in the following? Again, illustrate by using each in a sentence so as to distinguish it from the other in the pair:

concerned about	disagree with	disappointed at
concerned with	disagree about	disappointed with
exported from	laugh with	made with
exported by	laugh at	made of
responsible for		think about
responsible to		think of

Revision Exercise 9

(a) The following are words commonly misspelled by fourth formers, given in the form of ANAGRAMS, i.e. with their letters re-arranged. Thus "opinion" (which is often wrongly given a double –pp–) is the answer to this one:
   poinoin — o_____ (noun)
You will see that the correct initial letter and the part of speech are given as an additional help. Identify the following:
1. failutube   b_____ (adj.)   2. sunibess   b_____ (noun)
3. fidineet   d_____ (adj.)   4. predaspia   d_____ (verb)

5. gagetearex   e_____ (verb)   6. cignexit   e_____ (adj.)
7. scenasery   n_____ (adj.)   8. pottoupriny o_____ (noun)
9. eviceer   r_____ (verb)   10. yencres   s_____ (noun)

Now exchange books or folders of recent written work, so that each member of the class can pick out some spelling mistakes from his neighbour's work. Then rearrange these as anagrams, so making up short tests for one another, on the lines of the list above.

(b) Correct what is incorrect or unfortunate about each of the following sentences. Be prepared to justify the changes you make. In many sentences, there is more than one mistake (of grammar, vocabulary or style).

1. He was very nearly driven to commit suicide several times.

2. Walking down Oxford Street, all the buses and cars there struck him immediately.

3. He keeps an attic full of boxes containing books and stationary into which he disappears when he is tired of you and I.

4. I don't disapprove of cursing with hounds; I have often felt like trying to hunt myself.

5. Singapore is a port at the bottom of the Straits of Malacca and the urbane population there is very thick.

6. He was able to save his friend alone without his dog.

7. The director of the firm only has the authority to undo the safe, not the caretaker.

8. A stool is a seat you can sit on without arms or a back.

9. Him complaining was not only irritating but also he was wasting energy.

10. Each customer has a close shave with their haircut in our barber's shop, and they get there money back if not satisfied with it.

Précis Exercise 4

Deduce from the details in each of the sentences in the following passage exactly what are the main features of school life that John dislikes, and re-write your summary in between 45 and 65 words. The passage contains about 210 words; remember to state the exact number of words you use. *(For Précis Rule 5, see page 158.)*

John disliked school for various reasons. He disliked getting up in the morning even in the holidays, and when the alarm went and he peeped from under the bed-clothes on a raw autumn morning, he hated the whole idea of an early start. He hated too putting on that dowdy uniform, with that absurd little cap perched on his fine, long hair. When he had entered the grim, iron

280

gates, he revolted against being told not to play football in the quadrangle, not to drop litter, not to chew, not to smoke. In the school assembly, he hated listening for hours to the headmaster's sermons and announcements, and to the exhortations to work harder or behave politely on the buses, or get his hair cut. He hated being bored by academic subjects like history or German, being forced to listen for long double periods to dull lessons, and then punished for yawning or for carving his name on the desk. On the rugby field he felt cold and confused, and he could not see why he should be forced to join in a game that he found brutal and dirty. Finally, he hated prefects who ordered him about, and put him in detention or gave him lines, and turned him out of the building during the lunch-hours.

Précis Exercise 5

In the following passage there are three main points (two of them could be subdivided) and then a conclusion. First, *write these points* out in note form. Then write a summary, using these notes, in between 80 and 100 words. The passage has about 300 words; state the number you use. *(For Précis Rule 6, see page 186.)*

Smoke is one of the problems of our urban and industrial society, for it has been proved that smoky and sulphurous air affects our general health. Not only is there more bronchitis and chest illness among town-dwellers than in the country, but there is no doubt that the fresher air and clearer sunlight in the countryside give the countryman a greater resistance to many other illnesses than his town cousin has. In periods of foggy weather, this problem of smoke and health becomes far more acute, and the figures show dramatically how serious a menace smoke is. In the great "smog" of 1952, for instance, 4,000 Londoners with weak chests died as a result of atmospheric conditions. Then, of course, smoke and soot cause dirt, and fumes speed up corrosion. Woodwork needs more frequent painting, curtains and soft furnishings need more washing. Stone, brick and metal all need to be protected against the attack of sulphurous fumes. The cost of all this washing, cleaning, painting and renovating in areas polluted by smoke is noticeably higher than in those areas where smoke is controlled; and the cost to the whole nation of the dirt and corrosion for which smoke is responsible has been estimated at £250 million a year. Moreover, burning fuel in such a way as to make smoke is in fact inefficient and costly. The slow-burning grate and the slow-combustion stove, using smokeless fuels, extract more heat from less fuel, and convect warm air round a wider area. Thus, although smokeless fuels are more costly than ordinary coal per ton, in the long run fuel bills are also cheaper. These arguments for establishing more "smokeless zones" throughout the country are overwhelming; we should aim at nothing less than making the whole of Great Britain into one "smoke control area".

Précis Exercise 6

Remembering Précis Rules 1 to 7, summarize the following passage in your own words, reducing it from about 300 words to between 110 and 130 words. *(For Précis Rule 7, see page 221.)*

A few years ago the Russian newspapers *Komsomolskaya Pravda* and *Literaturnaya Gazeta* were demanding an end to a new kind of piracy on the River Volga, reminiscent of the conditions in the seventeenth and eighteenth centuries, when Stenka Razin and the Tartar brigands terrorised that part of Russia. These modern buccaneers were combining poaching with piracy and their target was the sturgeon for the lucrative caviarre racket. In some places river police and fishing officials were reported to be co-operating in or conniving at these practices, but in other cases launches had been engaged in armed attacks on river police. Once a launch rammed a patrol boat and bandits then attempted to kill the crew. These river pirates used the most modern weapons and methods. They even used high voltage electricity to kill hundreds of sturgeon at once by shock. They then removed the caviarre from the fish, throwing the remains back, and sold the produce illegally on the "black market", where they could make several thousand roubles from one night's haul. They had also been catching the sturgeon as they moved up river to their spawning grounds, often just after the authorities had deliberately transferred hundreds of the fish to higher parts of the river, since the new dams on the Volga would otherwise have prevented them from migrating and breeding. At least one thousand poaching operations of various kinds were reported in two years, and there had been some fifty armed attacks and twelve attempted assassinations of river policemen. The Russian press was naturally raising a hue and cry against these practices, and especially about the charges that the police had been bribed or threatened into taking no action in many cases. The fishing authorities, too, were most concerned at this further threat to their valuable sturgeon, which were already declining in numbers.

From Study of Chapters Eight and Ten, you will see that noun clauses can be introduced by "that", "what", "how", "if", "whether", "where", "when", "who", "whom", "which", "whatever", etc. and also by no introductory word (or the word "that" *understood*).

For example, the sentence:

How he managed to do it was *what* we all wanted to know.

would be analysed in columns like this:

	CLAUSE	KIND	FUNCTION	RELATIONSHIP
I.A	. . . was . . .	Main clause		
a¹	how he managed to do it	Subordinate clause	Noun	Subject of verb "was" in main clause "A"
a²	what we all wanted to know	Subordinate clause	Noun	Complement of verb "was" in main clause "A"

Analyse the following sentences; those marked (2) contain two subordinate clauses.

1. He said that he had been practising.
2. What he had been practising he did not clearly say.
3. We therefore didn't believe he had been practising at all.
4. Whom we should send was the difficult question.
5. He told how he had climbed to the top.
6. We, however, doubted if he had ever reached it.
7. He also explained where he had been training.
8. Which equipment he had used puzzled us until he showed us. (2)
9. He could say whatever he liked.
10. If he did not prove it, we would not believe what he asserted. (2)
11. He told us when we should come and where we should go.
12. We knew he was lying all the time.

"When" and "where" clauses can be adverb, adjective or noun clauses; "who" and "which" clauses can be adjective or noun clauses; "that" clauses and those without introductory words can be noun or adjective clauses; one should therefore think carefully about the function of such clauses when analysing sentences. Here are two examples:

(i) When the crowd came down the street, I asked someone who was coming.

(ii) Someone who was coming down the street said they were protesting about higher taxes.

	CLAUSE	KIND	FUNCTION	RELATIONSHIP
1.A	I asked someone	Main clause		
a^1	when the crowd came down the street	Subordinate clause	Adverb of time	Modifies verb "asked" in main clause "A"
a^2	who was coming	Subordinate clause	Noun	Object of verb "asked" in main clause "A"
2.A	someone . . . said	Main clause		
a^1	who was coming down the street	Subordinate clause	Adjec-tive	Qualifies pronoun "someone" in main clause "A"
a^2	(that) they were protesting about higher taxes	Subordinate clause	Noun	Object of verb "said" in main clause "A"

Analyse the following sentence in columns. Three of them contain two subordinate clauses.
1. I go to a school where they teach a lot of science.
2. I first went to this school when my parents moved here.
3. The headmaster told us when the prize-giving would be.
4. He also told us who would distribute the prizes.
5. The man who distributed the prizes was an eminent professor of atomic physics.
6. He talked about an experience that he had during the war.
7. At the time when they first developed the atomic bomb, he was a junior member of the research team.
8. He told us we ought to consider the consequences of anything we decided to do.
9. Atomic power was something that men could use for good or that they could use for evil.
10. Men did not always know which course they should choose.
11. When the politicians chose the wrong course, the scientists blamed themselves, because they should advise the politicians.
12. After he had talked so seriously, he told some funny stories.

So far we have seen that "as" can introduce the following kinds of subordinate clause:

(i) *adverb of manner:* Hold your knife and fork *as I showed you.*

(ii) *adverb of cause: As you arrived late,* you have missed the soup.

(iii) *adverb of time: As the waiter bent over me,* he spilt soup on my jacket.

It also introduces adjective clauses in the constructions "such . . . as", "same . . . as".

(iv) *adjective:* He had such manners *as you might expect of a pig.*

And it appears in "as if" and "as though".

(v) He acted *as (he would)* if he did not want to be asked again.

(vi) He acted *as though he did not care.*

In these cases the "as" clause is again *adverb of manner* (see Chapter II, page 172).

The following sentences include similar "as" constructions, together with some general revision of the analysis work in this book.

1. As Bob wanted to be asked again, he tried to behave perfectly.
2. As he entered the room, he saw Jennifer's grandmother rising to meet him.
3. He behaved as a polite young man should.
4. Indeed he acted as if his future depended upon his making a good impression.
5. As he sat stiffly in his chair and made polite conversation, Jennifer could hardly stop giggling.
6. She knew her grandmother was not at all the same kind of person as she was pretending to be.
7. Indeed her grandmother was so nervous herself that she was being extra formal.
8. She treated Bob as if he were a young prince.
9. If Jennifer had only made less fuss about Bob, her grandmother would not have worried about having him to tea.
10. Now Bob was feeling awkward and Jennifer's grandmother went on as though she were entertaining royalty.

Books Recommended

An alphabetical author index of the books recommended in the
Further Reading sections of this volume.

HANLEY, CLIFFORD	*The Taste of Too Much* ..	Blackie
HEMINGWAY, ERNEST	*A Farewell to Arms*	Heinemann; Penguin
LAWRENCE, D. H.	*Selected Tales* (ed. Serraillier)	Heinemann
	Sons and Lovers and *The White Peacock*	Heinemann; Penguin
LEE, LAURIE	*Cider with Rosie*	Hogarth; Chatto & Windus; Penguin
MACDONALD, BETTY	*The Egg and I*	Mayflower
OGILVY, DAVID	*Confessions of an Advertising Man*	Longman; Mayflower
ORWELL, GEORGE	*Animal Farm* and *Nineteen Eighty-Four*..	Secker & Warburg; Penguin
	Collected Essays, Down and Out in Paris and London and *The Road to Wigan Pier*..	Secker & Warburg; Penguin
PACKARD, VANCE	*The Hidden Persuaders, The Status Seekers* and *The Waste Makers*	Longman; Penguin
PARKER, TONY (ed.)	*The Man Inside*	Joseph
PARKER, TONY and ALLERTON, ROBERT	*The Courage of His Convictions*	Arrow
PINTER, HAROLD	*The Dumb Waiter, The Room* and *A Slight Ache* ..	Methuen
SALINGER, J. D.	*The Catcher in the Rye* ..	Hamish Hamilton; Penguin
SANSOM, WILLIAM	*Fireman Flower*	Hogarth; Chatto & Windus
	The Last Hours of Sandra Lee and *The Stories of William Sansom*	Hogarth
SHERRIFF, R. C.	*Journey's End*	Heinemann
SHUTE, NEVIL	*A Town Like Alice*	Heinemann; Pan
SILLITOE, ALAN	*The Loneliness of the Long Distance Runner* and *Saturday Night and Sunday Morning*	W. H. Allen; Longman
SIMPSON, N. F.	*The Hole—Plays and Sketches*	French
SMITH, DODIE	*I Capture the Castle*	Heinemann; Penguin
SOLZHENITSYN, ALEXANDER	*One Day in the Life of Ivan Denisovitch*	Gollancz; Penguin
STEINBECK, JOHN	*The Grapes of Wrath, Of Mice and Men* and *The Pearl*	Heinemann; Pan

THOMAS, DYLAN	*Portrait of the Artist as a Young Dog, A Prospect of the Sea, Quite Early One Morning and Under Milk Wood* ..	Dent
THURBER, JAMES	*Further Fables for Our Time, The Thurber Carnival* and *The White Deer*	Hamish Hamilton; Penguin
WATERHOUSE, KEITH	*Billy Liar, There is a Happy Land*	Joseph; Penguin
WAUGH, EVELYN	*Scoop*	Penguin
WELLS, H. G.	*Selected Short Stories*	Penguin
	The History of Mr Polly, Kipps and *Tono Bungay* ..	Collins; Longman; Pan
WESKER, ARNOLD	*The Kitchen*	Cape
WYNDHAM, JOHN	*The Day of the Triffids* ..	Hutchinson; Joseph; Penguin
	The Kraken Wakes	Longman; Joseph; Penguin
	The Midwich Cuckoos and *The Chrysalids*	Joseph; Penguin

Index

An alphabetical list of the main comprehension, techniques and composition work in Book Four. References are to page numbers.